HUGO A. KEESING

THE
JESUS
PEOPLE

Ronald M. Enroth

Edward E. Ericson, Jr.

C. Breckinridge Peters

THE

JESUS
PEOPLE

Old-Time
Religion
in the
Age of Aquarius

WILLIAM B. EERDMANS PUBLISHING COMPANY
Grand Rapids, Michigan

First printing, February 1972
Second printing, May 1972

Grateful acknowledgment is made to the following individuals and news media for the photographs used in this book. Specifically, the sources are as follows: *KQED-TV, San Francisco* — pages 2, 3, 9, 84, 87, 89, 92, 144, 155, 163, 194, 229; *Carl Parks* — pages 19, 67, 127, 136, 161, 187, 207; *Robert J. Shiflet, Mineral Wells, Texas* — pages 21, 115, 210; *The Shreveport Journal* — pages 26, 37, 46; *The Los Angeles Times* — page 33; *Steve Sparks* — pages 72, 81, 102, 105, 159, 221; *Christian World Liberation Front* — pages 112, 140, 244; *Marker Karahadian, Santa Rosa, California* — page 223.

CONTENTS

FOREWORD

One of the problems always confronting chronicles of contemporary events is that of datedness. By the time the research is published, some of it is obsolete. The risk is minimized if the authors resort to generalized description rather than highly specific chronicling. But along with the risk disappears the spice of detail. We have chosen to take our chances that some of the facts in the book will be obsolete upon publication, since we feel keenly both the need to offer supporting evidence for our evaluative reflections and the intrinsic interest of the facts themselves. As far as the facts are concerned, this book is a description of the state of the Jesus Movement as of the fall of 1971.

Writing this book has been for us the occasion for a reexamination of our Christian faith, and we trust that our readers will have a similar experience as they read this story of the Jesus People.

Our indebtedness is great to many persons who have helped us in the preparation of this book. Our greatest debt is to Laura Weiss, our devoted secretary in this endeavor. Also, Janice Ericson deserves special thanks for typing the manuscript. Many students, alumni, and faculty colleagues at Westmont College have helped in our research efforts, most notably Rick Josiassen, Arvin Engelson, Dana Alexander, Charlene Herrick, Sharon Gallagher, Brendan F. J. Furnish, and Gerald Jamison. More Westmonters than we could hope to name have given us invaluable leads in our research efforts. Other friends whose cooperation has greatly aided our research are Dean Ebner, Richard Eley, Ted Wise, Marianne Creveling,

7

Vicar Jim McEachern, and Emiko Omori of KQED-TV in San Francisco. To all these friends we express our heartfelt gratitude. We hope that they will feel that the end result to which they have contributed is one worthy of their efforts. The views expressed in this book are our own and do not necessarily reflect the outlooks of those who have so graciously helped us.

Ronald M. Enroth
Edward E. Ericson, Jr.
C. Breckinridge Peters

one

INTRODUCTION

Something's Happening Here but It Just Ain't Exactly Clear

SOMETHING NEW AND STRANGE HAS HIT THE CURRENT RELIGIOUS scene in America, and most observers are baffled by it. Hippies and drug addicts are becoming Christians in significant numbers. Both secular and Christian press have devoted considerable space to describing and interpreting this phenomenon.

The new Christians are known variously as Jesus Freaks, Jesus People, Street Christians; there is talk of a Jesus Movement, or a Jesus Revolution. The terms "Jesus Freaks" and "Street Christians" derive from the fact that many of those involved in this new movement were formerly on drugs (drug freaks) or had adopted the transient life style of dropouts from straight society. "Freak" does not have bad connotations in the counter-culture, however jarring it may sound to straights. We have chosen the blander term *The Jesus People* for our title, because not all of the new converts have used drugs or rejected straight society, though the majority — and certainly the pacesetters among them — have. "Jesus People" is a more inclusive term, not a more humane one.

Our research has uncovered numerous errors in published accounts of the Jesus People. In general, more accurate descriptive information is provided by the secular sources than by the Christian ones. Most of the Christian writers seem so

9

eager to offer their interpretations that they have done a shoddy job of research. They either prejudge the situation or generalize from a small amount of data and presuppose that the whole phenomenon is like one or another local manifestation of it. On the other hand, most accounts in the secular press lack a solid understanding of Christian doctrine and a personal experience of the life-transforming power of redemption in Christ.

A survey of some of these articles is revealing. By far the best descriptive treatment to date is the cover story on "The Jesus Revolution" in *Time* magazine, June 21, 1971. However, it casts its net so wide as to include Catholic Pentecostals, commercial musicals such as *Jesus Christ Superstar* and *Godspell,* and the conversions of such singing stars as Johnny Cash and Paul Stookey. *Look* carried a brief, impressionistic article in its February 9, 1971, issue. It is sympathetic in tone; and its descriptions, mainly of two churches and a hot-line service in Southern California, are accurate as far as they go. In the May 14, 1971, issue of *Life* there was a story entitled "The Groovy Christians of Rye, N. Y.," dealing only with The Way and its local director in Rye, Steve Heefner. *Ramparts,* viewing everything through political eyes, commissioned James Nolan to find, if possible, a link between right-wing political groups and the Jesus People. He did not even discover the very few pieces of evidence that we have found, which assuredly are totally inadequate to substantiate any connection between the two. Nolan's "Jesus Now: Hogwash and Holy Water" in the August 1971 issue, with its self-admitted anti-Christian bias clearly showing, panned the whole movement, but it did include several legitimate criticisms. A series of front-page articles in the Chicago *Tribune* had difficulty even seeing the difference between the Jesus People and a Satanist cult, The Process Church of the Final Judgment.

Articles in religious periodicals express widely divergent opinions of the Jesus People. *Christianity Today* has provided extensive news coverage of the movement, most of it by Edward E. Plowman, who strongly hopes for the success of the movement and sees it through rose-colored glasses. Plowman's romanticizing of the movement is illustrated by his repeated use of the term "Street Christians." As Larry Norman, a leading figure in the movement, told us, there is no such thing. When street people become Christians, they stop being street people.

At the opposite extreme is a story by Garner Ted Armstrong in *The Plain Truth,* March 1971, entitled "The Jesus Trip." Armstrong assumes that Jesus People are just hippies who still take drugs and engage in free sex. Had he done the least bit of investigating, he would have learned of the Jesus People's critique of illicit drugs and sex as "bad scenes" and, indeed, sins. Long hair on a male seems enough to prove to Armstrong that he could not possibly be a Christian.

Considerably more factual but only slightly less hostile is Gary North's "The Jesus Freaks and Their Groovy God," carried in *The Christian News,* June 21, 1971. While North, too, is bothered by male long hair, his criticism essentially focuses from the perspective of rigidly Reformational thought, on fundamentalism's over-emphasis of experience. Also from a Reformed viewpoint, albeit a broader and more human one, is Marlin Van Elderen's "The 'Jesus Freaks': Some Thoughts on a Religious Phenomenon" in *The Reformed Journal* of May-June 1971. It contains some incisive criticisms, but because it is almost wholly devoted to a critique of Arthur Blessitt's book, *Turned On to Jesus,* it makes the mistake of generalizing from Blessitt to the whole Jesus Movement. Not all the Jesus People are as egotistical as Blessitt. Still another Reformed perspective is seen in Jon Reid Kennedy's "Dropping Out Into Jesus" in *Vanguard,* March 1971. Since Kennedy generalizes from the much more palatable Christian World Liberation Front, his treatment is favorable. Kennedy is attracted by the externals of the hip life style, and he seems to feel that the Jesus People would be fine if only they would share his enthusiasm for Francis Schaeffer and other elements of the Reformational line that *Vanguard* espouses.

Most treatments currently in print assume, mistakenly, that the Jesus People present a unified front, so that one may generalize from a part of the movement to the whole. Actually, there is so much diversity within the movement that some elements of it consider others non-Christian, even demonic. Also, there is a surprising isolation of groups, so that one group usually knows little about others, especially those separated geographically. Many of our acquaintances, learning of our research for this book, have asked us whether the Jesus People are good or bad. It is precisely this kind of monolithic judgment that we find ourselves unable to pass. We are basically favorable toward some groups and individuals, basically unfavorable toward others. In all cases, we find some things to praise and some to criticize, but the balance shifts, sometimes drastically, from element to element within the movement. Nevertheless, there are some unifying threads that run through all the segments and make it proper to consider the Jesus People as one movement. Thus, some general judgments, both favorable and unfavorable, apply in varying degrees to all of the subgroups.

* * *

It is difficult to trace the origins and history of the Jesus Movement, because it does not have a clear beginning in time with one person or group. Its self-consciousness as a movement emerged only gradually. Furthermore, there are several who claim to have begun the revolution. In one sense, none of the claims is wrong. There are several ministries that began independently in 1967 and early 1968 which lie behind the Jesus Movement of today. Lonnie Frisbee, a leading Jesus Freak, has a fascinating explanation for the rise and success of such ministries at that period. He suggests that the Six-Day War of June 1967 between Israel and the surrounding Arab nations set the stage for the last days before Christ's second coming. When Israel regained her long-lost territory, a prophecy was fulfilled that signaled the beginning of the end times. The Book of Joel had prophesied that the earthly return of Christ would be preceded by a great outpouring of the Holy Spirit, which would take the form of much witnessing and a highly intensified devotion on the part of believers in Christ. Joel's prophecy placed youth in the vanguard of the spiritual revolution, which, Lonnie Frisbee contends, is being fulfilled now by the Jesus People.

There was, however, also a movement of the Spirit that arose from within the Haight-Ashbury district of San Francisco during the golden days when it was the mecca of the counterculture. Though we found no direct connection between this

12

Bay Area group of hippies-become-Christians and the various other ministries that started during roughly the same period, these youthful converts have dispersed to different localities and exercised a wide impact on the shape of the Jesus Movement as a whole.

The central figure in this group was Ted Wise. Deeply involved in drug use, Wise became a Christian in late 1966 while working as a sailmaker in Sausalito, California. He and his wife Elizabeth began talking to people on the streets of Haight-Ashbury about Jesus Christ. He was still smoking marijuana, and this brought him into contact with Steve Heefner, a disc jockey, and Jim Doop, a cigarette salesman, boyhood friends from Des Moines who had come to San Francisco to make the scene and to experiment with drugs. Wise found them naive and began talking to them about Christ. Doop and Heefner became Christians. Soon Danny Sands, an old friend of the Wises, did also. Impressed by the biblical story of the rich young ruler, Sands sold everything he owned; and he and his wife and two children drove up and down California in an old, beat-up station wagon for a month or two. Then they returned to the Bay Area and, not having a place to live, moved in with the Wises in Sausalito. Soon the house became home for other friends who had become Christians.

In late 1967 this group of people began a coffee house ministry in Haight-Ashbury. They rented a storefront for a remarkably small amount of money and used it simply for rapping with street people about Jesus and the Bible. They called it The Living Room. For this ministry they were able to secure backing from some local pastors, including Edward Plowman of *Christianity Today*. The coffee house lasted for two years, during which time contact was made with thirty to fifty thousand young people.

Meanwhile, their living conditions were becoming more and more crowded. They rented an old two-story farmhouse in the middle of a tract of small homes in Novato, California. About a month later they met a young man on the street who was freaked out on LSD and was talking incoherently about Jesus Christ and flying saucers. His name was Lonnie Frisbee, and he was a student at San Francisco Academy of Art. He moved in with them and quit school. Later, he was married in Novato. Thus the house sheltered five couples: the Wises, the Sands, the Heefners, the Doops, and the Frisbees. In addition, single youths, especially Novato teen-agers, moved in and out.

A neighbor-friend suggested that the commune be called The House of Acts. Frisbee liked the idea, and he painted a sign and posted it, but Sands tore down the sign, partly because he disliked the idea of having one and partly because it would require them to bring the house in line with a stiffer building code. Nevertheless, The House of Acts was important, because it brought the idea of a Jesus commune to the level of consciousness.

After a while, Frisbee felt that the Lord was calling him to Southern California to start a similar ministry there. He and his wife hitchhiked down and almost immediately met a fellow named John Higgins, who wanted to do the same kind of thing as Frisbee. The two rented a small house in Costa Mesa, and their experience repeated that of The House of Acts. Hundreds of young people came by and professed salvation. Soon they moved to nearby Santa Ana and opened a similar ministry, which they christened The House of Miracles.

Frisbee's departure signaled the beginning of the dispersion of The Living Room set. Heefner and Doop were recruited by Victor Wierwille of The Way, an ultra-dispensationalist ministry headquartered in New Knoxville, Ohio. Heefner became the director of The Way East in Rye, New York; Doop the director of The Way West in Mill Valley, California. Wise now runs a drug prevention center in Menlo Park, south of San Francisco, and is active in the Peninsula Bible Church of Palo Alto. Frisbee has since served as youth minister at Calvary Chapel of Costa Mesa (see chapter four). Higgins went to Eugene, Oregon, and established a commune named Shiloh Ranch. The Shiloh communes have multiplied until this ministry encompasses, at last count, thirty-seven houses scattered across the nation.

Although this group of Christian workers did not initiate anything like a majority of the separate works loosely collected under the label of Jesus People, they continue to have strong influence within the movement. And they seem to be as close as one can come to locating the first stirrings of the spiritual revolution within the counter-culture. The Jesus Revolution has so many facets that it would be incorrect to impose any unifying pattern upon it. But The Living Room and The House of Acts provide models whose outlines may be observed in varying degrees in a number of subsequent Jesus People ministries.

* * *

The Jesus People consider themselves participants in a genuine movement of the Holy Spirit. They like to compare themselves to the Great Awakening of the eighteenth century, about which most of them know very little other than the name itself. It is unarguable that many manifestations in the movement are faddish. Is this all just so much sound and fury, another passing fad, or is it a revival that will have a lasting impact? It is our hope that the evidence presented in this book will go a long way toward helping interested observers and participants make a reasoned judgment of the matter.

The Jesus People got their start in California, that hothouse for eccentric religious cults and movements, and they are still strongest there. There is also a substantial contingent in the Pacific Northwest. However, the movement's influence is now being felt nationwide and even in a few foreign countries. There is some doubt in our minds whether the phenomenon is as large in numbers as most accounts of it would lead one to believe. The communications media seem mesmerized by the youth culture, and they have appropriated the Jesus Freaks as colorful successors to the equally colorful hippies and psychedelic drugsters. David Wilkerson's figure of 300,000 Jesus People seems exaggerated, as do the figures that are generally given for individual ministries. But this does not minimize its importance for the current religious scene in America. Just as the true beatniks were a relatively small group who had an influence far exceeding their numbers, so the Jesus People are having and will have an impact far exceeding their numbers. It is this which gives urgency to our attempt to come to terms with the movement.

In ideology, the Jesus People cover a surprisingly wide range. There are the very bluntly anti-establishment and rigidly legalistic Children of God and their only slightly less blunt counterparts, the Christian Foundation of Tony and Susan Alamo. There are the free-lance evangelists like Arthur Blessitt and Duane Pederson, who have foresworn any affiliation with organized religion. There are the hip churches, whole congregations tuned in to the subculture of the new converts — for instance, Calvary Chapel of Costa Mesa and Bethel Tabernacle of Redondo Beach, California. There is the campus-oriented ministry in Berkeley known as the Christian World Liberation Front.

Christian communes play an important role in the movement. Coffee houses may be found in almost every major city and in many small towns across the nation. Also prominent are Jesus newspapers, the best known of which is the *Hollywood Free Paper*. Music in the youthful idiom, composed by new converts, is a staple of Jesus People evangelism. Perhaps the best of the Jesus rock musicians is Larry Norman. All of these individuals and ministries, along with many others, are discussed in chapters two to seven.

Chapters eight to eleven discuss the major tenets of the movement. The most important defining characteristic of the Jesus People is their fundamentalistic insistence on the simple gospel, an essentially anti-intellectual and anti-cultural view of the world as a wrecked and sinking ship from which as many as possible must be saved. Another defining characteristic is their strong apocalyptic belief that we are living in the last days and that they are the last youth generation that will live on the earth. A third trait is their espousal of the charismatic gifts, primarily speaking in tongues, but also physical healing and other manifestations generally associated with Pentecostalism. Almost all of the Jesus People are charismatic; an exception is the San Francisco Bay Area, where the influence of the non-charismatic Christian World Liberation Front and Peninsula Bible Church predominates. Finally, the Jesus People try to achieve a sense of community, often by establishing Christian communes. They believe that the institutional church has been woefully inadequate in providing this sense of community for all except those of the straight middle-class world.

Our aim is to present a more or less comprehensive overview of the movement that provides factual information with which readers can make their own independent evaluations.

16

Secularists are likely to see the movement in political terms and to view it as an escape from the harsh realities of a complex technological society. Liberal Christians, who thought that the disease of super-literal interpretation of the Bible was a thing of the past, will be nonplussed. Christians in the Reformed tradition will be generally disapproving of the Jesus People's lack of a sense of cultural mandate or covenant theology. Fundamentalists will be confused because the Jesus People say the right things in the wrong language. Besides, they are long-haired, hippie-looking, and alienated from the established churches. Theologically, the Jesus People are fundamentalists; sociologically, they are not.

We do not come to the study of the Jesus Movement as objective reporters, though we have tried to do justice to the various aspects of it that we have observed. As evangelical Protestants we accept the historic orthodox doctrines of the Christian church. We place much greater emphasis on a rational apologetic for the faith than do the Jesus People. We approve of their concern for the personal experience of the new birth, for finding meaning in life through the God of the Bible, and for joy and zeal in Christian service. We disapprove of their simplistic mentality, the excessive emphasis on experience and feeling, and their bias against intellectual pursuits, social involvement, and human culture in general. Since the movement is so variegated, we have evaluated each group or leading personality separately, for to cast one judgment (for or against) regarding the Jesus People would be to fall into their own error of oversimplification.

Part One

THE PEOPLE

two

THE DOOM-SAYING EXCLUSIVISTS

Hell! No, We Won't Go

ON HOLLYWOOD BOULEVARD LEGITIMATE AND ILLEGITIMATE
business mingle. Suits, ties, and the opulence that is Beverly
Hills mix with long hair, bell bottoms, and the relative poverty
of the street amid benign smiles of indulgent incredulity.
Since early in the Jesus Movement, the interested observer
has been most likely to see the Jesus People in action there,
witnessing on the streets. Once large numbers of them found
their way there; by summer 1971, only two groups were active
on the boulevard: the Children of God and the Christian
Foundation of Tony and Susan Alamo. These two groups,
strikingly similar to each other, are significantly different from
most other Jesus People.

Both groups emphasize the coming judgment of God on a
wicked world. Instead of opening with the patented "Jesus
Loves You" of most Jesus People, these groups open with,
"Repent! Jesus is Coming! The End is Near!" Both see themselves as the fulfilment of prophecy about the remnant that
will witness faithfully in the last days. Both are exclusivist:
they consider themselves virtually the only faithful followers
of God today and see other Christians as half-hearted, carnal,
and hypocritical. Both groups insist on the living arrangement
of communes, though neither likes that name because it suggests, to them at least, sexual immorality. The Children of

21

God call their communes colonies; the Alamos call theirs foundations. And both groups believe that the King James Version is the only inspired version of the Bible, that all other versions originate with Satan.

While some of the Jesus People outside these two groups consider them to be only tangentially related to the movement and not a major part of it, several facts belie this view. Their theological positions are more akin to those of other Jesus People than different; they are growing at a significant rate, especially the Children of God, who may be the fastest-growing segment of the Jesus Movement; and they have a stability of organization that far exceeds almost anything else in the Jesus Movement. Perhaps because they are the most bizarre of the subgroups, they are the most interesting and demand the lengthiest explication.

* * *

It was difficult for us to obtain information about the origin and history of the Children of God. Many of its members simply do not know. Those who know are not interested in talking about it, because their interest in talking to anyone is in trying to convert him and proselyte him into joining the Children. Published accounts contradict each other. After much effort, we have succeeded in tracing — for the first time in print — the main outlines of the history of the group.

The sect was founded by David Berg, an ordained denominational minister now in his fifties. Berg had pastored a church in Arizona that worked primarily among Indians. He claims to have constructed the building with his own hands. His separation from this church was accompanied by hard feelings. An acquaintance of his said that he was kicked out; his own explanation is that his salary was insufficient to support his family of six. It is probably from this occasion that his hostility to the institutional church stems.

The Berg family moved to Southern California, and Berg went to work for the Rev. Fred Jordan, a Pentecostal evangelist who in 1944 had established a ministry christened the American Soul Clinic. Berg's job was public relations and lining up new radio outlets for Jordan's radio program "Church in the Home" (since graduated to television). Relations between

22

Berg and Jordan were never good. Matters came to a head when Jordan demanded that the parents-in-law of one of Berg's sons get off his ranch in Texas, which at the time was being used as a training center and rest station for missionaries. Berg quit.

For a brief period he and his family and close friends hit the open road, soon settling at Huntington Beach, where Berg's mother, the radio evangelist Virginia Brandt Berg, was residing. Berg wrote an anonymous booklet depicting his mother's life: *The Hem of His Garment: The Life Story of Virginia Brandt Berg.* The pamphlet is still read by the Children of God, and it is the only book (to our knowledge) other than the Bible that the disciples are allowed to read. The Children know her enigmatically as Grandma Berg — enigmatically, since Berg now keeps his identity secret from his followers and only those who were with him from the beginning know who their leader is.

In late 1967 or early 1968 Berg took over the direction of a coffee house in Huntington Beach established by Teen Challenge and named The Light Club. Berg named his ministry Teens for Christ. Soon he had several young male converts sleeping on the premises and was conducting Bible studies during hours when the coffee house was not open.

From the earliest days of Teens for Christ, Berg sought to establish a communal pattern of living. He encouraged his followers to withdraw from their jobs and drop out of the system. A few held on to their jobs for a while and contributed substantially to the group's keep, but soon they either capitulated to Berg's dropout teaching or left the group.

Berg was a highly authoritarian boss with a dour personality, but he was able to instill a fanatic loyalty to him in his close-knit group of followers. The whole inner circle of the leadership of the Children of God is composed of the family members and their comrades from the earliest days in Huntington Beach. The four Berg children — all in their twenties and married — are mainstays in the ministry. The oldest, Linda, is married to John Treadwell, who also worked for Fred Jordan and quit at the same time Berg did. Daughter Faith is married to Arnold Dietrich, who is now the chief lieutenant of Berg, in charge of the whole operation of the

23

Children of God. Treadwell occupies almost as exalted a position. All the Berg children are active leaders who have inherited their father's charisma.

The Teens for Christ ministry lasted about a year and a half, until Berg received a prophecy ordering the work to be shut down, since California was doomed and would soon fall into the ocean during an earthquake. Berg sent his followers to Tucson and Palm Springs. In Tucson the group was given a church building to use, but soon was kicked out. Then the group began its nomadic wandering, which lasted for eight months.

When Berg received his vision of California dropping into the ocean and the command to leave Huntington Beach, the group had grown to more than fifty. After their eight months of wandering and witnessing, they had expanded to well over one hundred. During this nomadic period they began designating themselves the Children of God, and their already radical notions became more and more defiantly bizarre and cultic. Berg claims to be Jewish, and he and his family are proud of this ancestry. His son Paul used to read the newspapers avidly looking for stories about Israel and clipping them. Their imaginations were fired by the Israeli kibbutzim. They also delighted in finding parallels between themselves and Old Testament Israel: wandering in the wilderness, organizing by tribes, being God's chosen people, and others. Members of the group took on biblical, usually Old Testament, names.

One of the earliest corporate activities of the Children was to descend on a church service in progress, marching in fifty or sixty strong, finding seats in the very front (sometimes sitting on the floor in front of the first pew), and generally creating a disturbance. They came in barefooted and in full hippie regalia. Their unstated purpose was to satisfy their need for feeling persecuted and unwanted and to confirm their anti-church prejudice. These visitations were in no way intended to be constructive. Generally, the Children were spectacularly successful in achieving their goal, and on several occasions they were asked to leave. In one case, however, the preacher interrupted the course of the service to extend them a special welcome; they never returned to that church. These visits extended over a few months and occurred about twelve or fourteen times. Almost all of the incidents happened in Orange County, California. Newspapers carried stories of these happenings, and the Children of God got their first taste of publicity — a taste that has become insatiable.

After about eight months of wandering, during which time they occasionally had to resort to eating grass in order to survive (so they tell it), they were granted a reprieve by Berg's ex-employer, Fred Jordan. He allowed them to encamp at his Texas ranch, which was standing virtually empty, for a month or so. They fixed and cleaned it up, and he liked that. He let them stay on indefinitely. When they arrived at the ranch, they were from 100 to 150 strong.

It was apparently during this nomadic period that Berg began receding from the spotlight, turning it over to his children and their spouses. Ask a recent recruit if he knows David Berg, and you will draw a total blank. Most do not know who Joshua (Arnold Dietrich) and Jethro (John Treadwell) are. They know the elder of their own commune, but no others. The reason given to the disciples for keeping the identity of their leaders secret is that when the inevitable persecution of God's elect (their group) comes, Satan's henchmen will seek to destroy the elders. The fewer who know their identity and whereabouts, the better. Berg gives his lieutenants the additional explanation that he wants to devote himself to cultivating the most intimate possible relationship with God, so that his messages to the disciples will be pure and Spirit-directed. At latest report, Berg was in Israel (in the early days the family often talked about "returning" there) writing a book — a strange occupation for the leader of a cult devoted to reading no books but the Bible.

The early members of the group delight in edifying newer members and outsiders with the stories of the early nomadic days. They note proudly the parallels between themselves and Jesus: "The foxes have holes, and the birds of the air have nests; but the Son of man hath not where to lay his head." Repeating the oral traditions of their epic beginnings is necessary lest the younger brothers and sisters lose sight of the historic importance of those pioneer days. For the Children of God are no longer outcasts wandering in nomadic

25

Entrance to the Texas Soul Clinic

tribes. They now have more than forty colonies, and while some of these still provide little more than meager subsistence and the flimsiest of shelters, some of them offer a degree of comfort unknown to the founders.

In early 1970 Fred Jordan proffered them a degree of security previously unknown. Not only did he give them the run of his 400-acre ranch (the "Texas Soul Clinic") located near the ghost town of Thurber, Texas, seventy miles west of Fort Worth. He also allowed them to take over a near-defunct six-story rescue mission in the Skid Row of Los Angeles. The deal between Jordan and Berg's Children clearly benefited both parties. The Children got roofs over their heads and funds and supplies from Jordan. In exchange, Jordan was able to display the colorful Children on his weekly hour-long television show "Church in the Home."

Jordan describes himself as a representative of the establishment who felt a need to reach radical youth. Since he could not do this himself, he associated with the Children of God. On his television show Jordan often spoke as if the Children of God were his ministry, but this was not at all the case. He was the benefactor, not the administrator. His program distorted the Children of God by making them look more ordinary and unexceptional than they really are. He camouflaged those eccentric doctrines with which he did not agree. His appeal to businessmen for funds to support the Children of God was, "You'd better help us reach these tough kids, or they'll destroy your businesses. We're the only ones who can reach them." Jordan plays on the desire of right-wingers to keep America Christian and orderly, followed by an appeal for funds. But the Children are anything but right-wing. They prefer the image of revolutionary cadres and scoff at America and its "church addicts."

While the Children of God proclaim an uncompromising line to potential recruits, their liaison with Fred Jordan was a serious compromise. They knew that he was using them, picturing them as something other than what they are, but they were willing to make this concession in order to gain important bases of operation from which to recruit new members. Their rationalization was that "it's his show" and that they got out as much of the "truth" as they could. Liaison with Jordan was a case of using "the system" to promote the gospel, while staying out of the system. They were willing to say that Jordan was a good brother despite his carnality. One will never hear them say that about any other outsider. When pressed, however, they showed little respect for Jordan.

Jordan's climactic effort on behalf of the Children was to be the development of a 110-acre date and citrus ranch in Coachella, California, "The Children of God Ranch." This was to be another base like that in Texas, where new recruits could be secreted and propagandized ("brainwashed" is Fred's term: "We clean their brains"). He printed a full-color poster describing the opulent plant with its swimming pool, fountain, reflection pool, and fenced-in compound (to keep intruders out or recruits in?). He appealed for $544,720 for the project, $160,000 of which he claimed to have raised in two months.

In late September 1971, Jordan kicked the Children off the three properties — Los Angeles, Coachella, and Thurber — which he had let them occupy a year and a half earlier. The rupture was predictable to any student of the situation; only the timing was uncertain. He tried once too often to tell them how to run their affairs, and when they resisted his efforts at co-optation, his hand was forced.

The issue that brought matters to a head centered on the Coachella property. Several faithful supporters of Jordan had visited the ranch and were surprised to find that the Children of God occupied only a ten-acre parcel. They asked the elder there — Belteshazzar — why they were not using the 100-acre plot for which Jordan had appealed for funds in the name of the Children of God. Belteshazzar told them that he did not know, but would ask Jordan. When he confronted him about the matter, Jordan was incensed. Belteshazzar said that the donors gave their money to let the Children use the whole ranch; Jordan replied that the property was his, not theirs. Legally he was correct, for he kept all the real estate and equipment at all three sites in his name.

Jordan then asked other Children of God elders to replace Belteshazzar as the Coachella elder. When they refused, he tried to evict the elders and persuade the rank and file to stay with him in the secure and comfortable environs of his properties. He miscalculated badly; to a man, the rank and file moved out at once. Ruefully, Jordan asked for an opportunity to talk to the group, with the leaders to be barred from the meeting. The elders refused the request, though it seems highly unlikely that even the persuasive Jordan could have swayed any significant number of the followers.

The group in Los Angeles moved to MacArthur Park and encamped there for a few days before dispersing to other locations. Most of them moved to the San Diego colony. A handful stayed behind to try to rescue their meager belongings from "the Warehouse," as they called their Los Angeles slum home. Jordan hired private security guards to keep them out until they returned two buses that he had purchased for them. Even after they complied, he released only part of their belongings.

The Children of God seemed not in the least dismayed

about being kicked out of three of their locations. They explained that they now have more than forty other places to live. Nor are they upset by the fact that at the Coachella ranch alone they left behind more than $40,000-worth of improvements that they had made on the property. All they were interested in, they say, was gaining new members. In early 1970, when they set up shop on Jordan's properties, their total membership was no more than 150. Now it is two thousand. They estimate that half of these came in through the groups stationed on Jordan's properties. What is $40,000 worth of manual labor in comparison with a thousand new-born souls? Besides, the rank and file needed something to occupy their time when they were not reading the Bible and sitting in classes. The followers say they were getting stuck in the rut of a routine and God wanted to make them more dependent on him. So he chose this time to get them out from under Jordan's wing.

In retrospect, Jordan and his associates "found their teachings were not right; they were teaching hate. We tried to help them, but we couldn't." Added Jordan: "I never tried so hard in my life to get support from people for a project." What projects will he find next to substitute for the Children of God? It is reported that he already has feelers out to youth groups to occupy his building at Fifth and Towne in Los Angeles. The Coachella ranch will be used to train missionaries for Latin America.

What can one make of an evangelist who needed a year and a half to discover the teaching of hate in the group that he was bankrolling? It is beyond belief that he did not know all along what the Children taught. After all, their leaders were once his own associates, a fact that he diligently tries to keep secret. He must have thought that he could hide the radical nature of the sect from his supporters — at least until his mighty powers of persuasion could induce the sect to moderate its outlook. But the Children of God were not to be tamed or co-opted.

Jordan's disenchantment with the Children was quickened by pressure from the newly formed Parents Committee to Save Our Sons and Daughters from the Children of God Organization. The San Diego-based group charges that their children have been kidnapped, drugged, hypnotized, and brainwashed, and that the Children of God are part of a million-dollar extortion racket. The parents have asked the Attorneys General of the U.S. and several states to investigate the sect as subversive.

The Children seem to have gotten much the better of Jordan. They enlisted a thousand new converts and, with some of them, several new colonies in widely scattered locations — just what they wanted. In contrast, Jordan is left with three white-elephant properties, little to show off on his TV program by way of successful ministry, greatly reduced leverage in appealing for money, and a besmirching of his reputation as a judge of Christian works that merit the support of his faithful donors.

While the Children occupied Jordan's properties, the Texas Soul Clinic served as their headquarters and main training center, and the mission in Los Angeles served as their second largest colony and the front-line outpost from which they did their most successful recruiting. However, the colonies are stretched across the nation in cities like San Diego, San Francisco, Colorado Springs, Boulder, Detroit, Cincinnati, Austin, Dallas, Corpus Christi; in southern Kentucky and upstate New York; and in foreign areas, including the interior of Mexico, Vancouver, London, and Amsterdam. Itinerant "gypsies for the Lord" live temporarily in what they call "prophet buses," while trying to gain recruits and set up new colonies. By their estimate, five hundred new recruits joined in the first three months of 1971. At last count, they boasted more than two thousand workers in the field and claimed that three or four new disciples were being enrolled every week at each of the colonies.

* * *

The beliefs of the Children of God diverge at some significant points from the familiar fundamentalist line. They emphasize that Christians are to "forsake all" and "hate" their parents and families. They see themselves as the only Christians in existence who are "sold out one hundred percent" for Christ. Living communally is an essential ingredient in forsaking all. If a married man becomes converted, he must leave his wife and join the Children of God. His wife is welcome to join as well, if she decides to accept the teachings of the group. A
30

Bible passage that they delight in chanting in loud unison is Acts 2:44, 45: "And all that believed were together, and had all things common; and sold their possessions and goods, and parted them to all men, as every man had need." Though most interpreters of the Bible understand these verses to describe a situation that existed only briefly in the early church, the Children of God believe that this is an inviolable commandment of God for Christians of all times and places. That Christians have not observed this command is an indication of the carnality that has riddled the church since Pentecost.

Communal living is only one aspect of the total separation from the world that the Children of God attempt to implement. They are as violently opposed to the established church as any group could possibly be. One of their songs (inspired, according to them, directly by the Holy Spirit, as all of their songs are) says in part:

> O Lord, have mercy on me.
> I hate that damned old sound
> Of the church bells ringing
> And the people coming from miles around.

Attending school is just as bad. According to one elder, "Education is all just shit." Holding down a job means participating in the evil world order, so the Children of God do not work in the outside world. Churches, schools, and jobs are part of the Great Whore of Babylon, and to participate in any of these is to commit spiritual fornication with her.

The Children of God hold to a post-tribulationist view of the second coming. Their separation from the world order is a preparation for enduring the Great Tribulation. In their view, all other Christians will take the Mark of the Beast (666) on the forehead in order to buy and sell, and they alone will remain true to God, since they do not believe in trafficking with the world. There may be a few other Christians who at that time will realize the error of their previous carnality, but their only recourse then will be to join the Children of God. For in the Great Tribulation, the Christian church and the Children of God will be synonymous.

The daily regimen of the Children is tightly organized: 6:45, reveille; 7-7:30, snack; 7:30-10:30, work period; 10:30,

31

clean-up time; 11-11:30, breakfast; 11:30-2:30, classes; 2:30-4:30, "free" time (more classes for new converts, special projects for veterans); 4:30-6, more classes; 6-7, supper; 7-9:30, evening service of singing, inspiration, and testimony; 9:30-10:30, tribe meetings.

Scripture memorization is stressed: the goal is to learn three hundred verses in the first two months. Members copy verses and attach them to clipboards that they wear on chains around their necks. At every spare moment, they can be memorizing verses. After the initial training period, members must memorize at least two verses a day. They are outfitted with shoulder-strapped pouches into which their Bibles fit; the sword of the Lord is always at their side. Potential leaders are held in training for six months in what is called "a highly intensified BIBLE COLLEGE that takes a young disciple through several years of material in approximately six months."

Babes in Christ are given over to the care of an older brother or sister. They are never left alone. They are instructed to wake up their supervisor, who sleeps beside them, as soon as they awaken. Elders know where each member is at all times. There is absolutely no such thing as privacy for the Children of God. In fact, the doors have been removed from the toilet stalls. Discipline often is imposed for its own sake. Boys with long hair must cut it short. Those with short hair may be ordered to let it grow long. Every effort is made to destroy one's former identity. The break with the past should be as complete as possible. The new member must submit himself totally to the authority of the elder. One elder instructed a new brother, "If I told you to go blow up a bank, you'd do it, because the Lord is speaking through me."

Although the Children of God do not talk about it, there are reports that they are stockpiling rifles and other firearms for future self-defense — come the persecution. The Texas Soul Clinic had a fence around it, and guards were usually posted at the gate. Two large signs festooned the fence on either side of the gate. One quoted Romans 6:23. The other read: "The Wicked Shall Be Turned into Hell, and All the Nations That Forget God!! Not Much Time Left!!" A smaller sign at the guardhouse declared: "Friendly Visitors Welcome! Noon to Dark Only, Please! Honk and Step Out to the Gate!"

A silent vigil in Los Angeles

A yet smaller sign on the gate said, "No Trespassing." When a stranger approached, a voice boomed out over a loudspeaker: "State your name and business."

Like other Jesus People, the Children of God seek their recruits from among those in "the hip and drug sceen [*sic*]." They advertise "over 90% lasting (total) deliverance." They estimate that seventy to ninety-nine percent of their members come from the drop-out culture. They claim, correctly, to offer new recruits "a complete new way of life."

> We believe that it's not good enough to just rehabilitate a person from drugs for six or eight months, because if she or he doesn't have something really solid in their lives to fill the gap, they will eventually wander back to their old sub-culture life style. This is the great difference in what we are offering in Christ Jesus because our cure is lasting! Our young men and women are not just getting delivered from illicit sex, drugs, and useless lives. But they are being delivered *to something!*

The elders, who control the activities of the members, are quite young: there is almost no one over thirty in the group,

33

and some are as young as fifteen and sixteen. The most visible activity is witnessing. The witnesses go out two by two, especially to those seedy parts of big cities where the youth and drug cultures flourish. They are fantastically aggressive recruiters, as indeed they must be, since their main source of support is the money received when a new convert sells his earthly goods and gives the money to the elders. They are well enough versed in their system to argue circles around all but the most advanced of Bible students.

By far the most dramatic of their activities is engaging in vigils. As the Spirit leads, the "Prophets of Doom" (their term) don red sackcloth (symbol of repentance), daub their foreheads with ashes (symbol of mourning), place wooden yokes about their necks (symbol of bondage), and wear one earring (symbol of willingness to be a "slave of love" to Christ). Carrying wooden staves (symbol of divine judgment), they stand in protest at public events to denounce the unrepentant. Imagine the stunning impact when Jerry Rubin came to the campus of the University of California at Santa Barbara to make a speech! In marched a long line of sackcloth-and-ashes-garbed youths, staves and signs in hand, who stood stone-faced and silent. At a signal the whole line began to clank the staves on the pavement in unison and chant, "Woe, woe, woe, woe, woe." Rubin never had a chance. Other vigils have been held at a Texas-Arkansas football game, the opening of the Chicago Seven trial, the lying in state of Senator Everett Dirksen's body in the Capitol Rotunda in Washington, D. C. (because Dirksen sponsored legislative efforts to permit Bible reading in public schools), and various anti-war rallies.

Another activity, for which they find their inspiration in the Book of Jeremiah, is what they call "smiting." Harking back to their early publicity successes, this involves going into a church and more or less taking over the service, denouncing loudly the institutional church and calling for repentance and a one hundred percent commitment to Christ. Eyewitnesses have told us also of an activity called smiting with the Word of God, which involves taking a Bible and hitting another person on the head with it.

When the Children of God are not out on the streets engaged in one form or another of witness or demonstration, they are at their colonies working at their trades or studying the Bible, mostly the latter. Eight hours a day is the norm. Indeed, the only thing which they read is the Bible. All else is worldly wisdom to be shunned. The kind of Bible study they engage in is a narrow proof-texting that involves reading to find new passages which, however badly yanked out of context, support the already accepted notions of the cult. But they know their line, and they know it extremely well. No other group among the Jesus People has a system of theology down so pat.

The trades at which the Children of God work include electronics (to keep the musical instruments and sound equipment in repair), mechanics (to keep the "prophet buses" running), carpentry, secretaryship, kitchen supervision, general maintenance, Bible teaching, and printing, photography, art, and layout (to publish their own tracts and newspapers). One of the products of the printers is the *New Nation News,* the "Inter-Colonial newspaper" that is not for general public consumption.

The original idea was to divide the Children of God into twelve groups, named after the twelve tribes of Israel. Levi was to be the tribe of elders and teachers; Issachar was the tribe of mechanics (because, as was explained to us, "car" and "Issachar" sound alike); Zebulun does farming; Simeon food preparation; Dan ham radio; Reuben groundskeeping; Benjamin teaching of school-aged children. (Since there were soon more than twelve tasks that needed doing, new names were included and additional tribes added. Thus, Gilgal is the name of the KP crew.) However, this system, which reflects the rigidity of the whole cult, does not work out smoothly in practice. When elders transplant a brother or sister from one colony to another, there may be a pressing need for him to work at some trade other than the one at which he was originally working. Nevertheless, he retains his original tribal loyalty. Once a Danite, always a Danite.

Meeting a witnessing crew of the Children of God on the street is an unforgettable experience. *New Nation News* gives the group's own version of a witnessing expedition:

35

And God's children circled around a large candle, singing and dancing and speaking of the impending destruction, and the alternative to hypocrisy: dropping out of the System to live for Jesus.

In one case, we observed a young man chasing another down the sidewalk, waving a Bible in one hand, and shouting, "Don't run from the Spirit, brother!" On another occasion we confronted a girl who was obviously a babe in Christ and her male companion. He said that he had been a Catholic and a transvestite; just one year earlier he had walked on that very same street wearing women's clothes. He explained that the Spirit had taken away all of this upon his conversion. The girl asked us if we were saved. When we said yes, she took up her guitar and sang for us. We asked her if the Children of God spoke in tongues. She gave us an impromptu demonstration right on Hollywood Boulevard. We asked what she thought of the brothers and the sisters at Calvary Chapel of Costa Mesa. Her face turned to a scowl and she hissed, "Bullshit."

On one of our visits to the Los Angeles colony, we met this girl again. When we beckoned her to come over and talk, she was very hesitant. She did so nevertheless, all the time glancing anxiously at one of the elders. She sat down on a couch and immediately said, "I should be going to bed now. It's time for me to go to bed." She spoke hurriedly and very uneasily for a couple of minutes and then left. Apparently, she was not supposed to be in such an exposed position without a more experienced brother or sister. When one of us tried to ask some questions of a brother standing nearby, another brother, apparently a more experienced one, immediately jumped into the discussion and took over the whole responsibility of answering the questions and pressing the propaganda line. The conversation went on for an hour.

Then a group of brothers and sisters carrying guitars filled the little reception room and began to sing their songs. As the songs were being sung, a couple of the girls began dancing together. As other brothers and sisters came in from outdoors, they were greeted by both brothers and sisters with kisses, following the biblical exhortation to greet one another with a holy kiss. We were urged to join in the dances (imagine our

36

Children of God singing

embarrassed clumsiness!), first with just one partner, then with a group which formed a circle. The Children explain that their dances are the dances of Judah, that is, Jewish folk dances. Dancing is not prohibited, because David danced before the Lord and the Israelites danced for joy.

All of our conversations with the Children ended up as attempts by them to proselyte the "Egyptian slaves" — us. One of the elders quoted a verse from Matthew 24 to prove beyond a shadow of a doubt that there would be no rapture before the Great Tribulation. (One verse is always a sufficient proof-text for a doctrine. The proof-text for *that* idea is II Timothy 3:16.) When one of us said that perhaps the view of many Christians, that Christ will come before the Tribulation, was correct, he was asked where he had learned that.

"I think I first learned it from my church pastor."

"Well, no wonder. What can you expect from a church? You can only get false teaching from a church because it's part of the Whore of Babylon. How much do you give to the church? Even if you gave twenty percent of all your income, all you could expect is a twenty percent interpretation of the Bible. We forsake all and give one hundred percent, and we get the hundred percent right interpretation of the Bible."

We continued our questions. "Doesn't the Bible say that he who does not work should not eat?"

"We do work. We're ministers, and ministers are to be supported by those to whom they minister." Thus, new converts support the old by giving all their money to the group.

"What about Paul? He worked as a tentmaker."

"Paul was out of the will of God then. Look here, I can prove it. It's in Acts 18:3 that he worked as a tentmaker, but in Acts 18:5 it says Paul was pressed in the Spirit. Now there. That proves it. He felt guilty. Why else could he have been pressed in the spirit?"

The obvious answer is that Paul was "pressed in the spirit" because he felt the need to testify to the Jews that Jesus was Christ, as verses four and five indicate. But the Children of God cannot be reasoned with. They have their answers, and no "carnal Christian" will be able to explain the Word better than they, who are directly illuminated by the Holy Spirit.

"What do you think of polygamy? It was practiced in the Bible."

"I don't know what polygamy is."

We explained what the word meant, and he told us that that was not a very good thing, because the Bible said a bishop should be the husband of one wife.

"Doesn't that indicate that some people in the church other than bishops had more than one wife?"

Finally — no answer, except to say that that seemed to be wrong.

"Do you practice footwashing? After all, it's in the Bible."

The elder was bewildered — an extremely rare circumstance. "No, we don't. Jesus did it only one time. Maybe I should do it one time so that I'm following what the Bible teaches. I'll have to think about it." (On a subsequent visit, a girl volunteered to us that she had footwashed — one time, just like Jesus. The shepherd had tended his flock.)

"Do you smoke or drink here?"

"No. When I was first saved, no one had to tell me that smoking and drinking were wrong. I just knew. I guess the Spirit told me. You know, at the Alamos' they smoke. That just may be the little leaven that leavens the whole lump."

Upon being told that the King James Version was the only inspired Bible, we asked what the French and Germans read. They thought that there must be a King James Version in each of those languages as well. How do they know that the King James Version is more accurate than other English translations? First, they argued that if you look at the other Bibles, you see how different they are, and that proves that these translations are wrong. Pressed further, they explained that the Holy Spirit bore witness to them that the King James Version was true.

Our most interesting experiences in a Children of God colony took place late on Friday and Saturday nights. On one of our visits to the Los Angles colony, we arrived about 11:30. Those of the group not assigned to witnessing teams that night were seated in chairs and sofas lining the walls of the large main room of the mission building. All were busily engaged in reading their Bibles. As usual, we were placed in the charge of one of the leaders of the colony, in this case a sister, Helah. An ex-Roman Catholic, Helah had experimented with drugs, spent eight months in a nudist colony, hitchhiked all the way to New York and back trying to find something to give meaning to her life. She had been with the Children of God for a year and was soon to be married. She told us she would never have chosen him for a husband if she made the choice by herself and "in the flesh," but the elders had arranged the marriage (the Children want children), and now she was eagerly anticipating it.

While we were there, several of the other brothers embraced and kissed Helah. Most spokesmen for the Children insist that the group has no problems with sexual immorality. One brother admitted that they had had occasional problems, but these had been dealt with at once. When there was any difficulty, the offending Children were counseled and quickly repented of their evil ways. Since the Holy Spirit tells the elders who is doing or even thinking evil, they are able to correct the wrong. We were unable to find a satisfactory answer to the question of who checks on the elders.

We were greeted warmly, like old friends. Many of the Children had seen us before and offered us a "Praise the Lord" or some other sign of welcome. We were all served large portions of ice cream and cake, but nothing to drink. There was no other food in sight, but everyone seemed healthy and in good spirits. A spirit of camaraderie filled the room.

Each Friday and Saturday night there is a celebration. To the accompaniment of electric guitars and drums, everyone sings and dances in the Spirit. To see the Children in one of these uninhibited songfests is to see them at their very best. Spotlights are turned on the musicians; the lights are turned low in the rest of the room; and an eerie green light gleams in a corner. The loud music crashes through the room, overwhelming the senses. The Children clap with the music, sing enthusiastically, and dance the Hebrew folk dances, either in couples or in circles. Some of the young men seemed quite aggressive in seeking out a variety of girls to dance with, but it is not uncommon to see two brothers or two sisters dancing together. Most of the dancers form large circles. Though most of the dancing is anything but erotic, a few of the kids who danced alone employed the more erotic body movements popular in current dancing styles. The scene is not too much different from any rock concert and dance.

One of the songs was a rewritten version of the Beatles' hit "Lucy in the Sky with Diamonds." The words were changed to "Jesus in the Sky with Angels," but the musical rendition was well executed and very faithful to the Beatles' recording. Another of their songs conveyed a sense of chortling delight with the agonies currently racking America:

> *Three cheers for the red, white, and blue.*
> *You've turned your back on God,*
> *Now he's turned his back on you.*

One of their many songs that used the words of the Bible was, "What shall it profit a man if he gain the whole world and lose his own soul?" The song was interrupted by chants of "Woe." With each "Woe," a raised fist was lowered.

We stayed until 2:30 a.m. When we left, the celebration was still going strong. We asked Helah if they always stayed up late and slept late. She explained that some of the babes in Christ needed a lot of sleep, but that she usually got by with just an hour or two a night. "The Lord just seems to supply our need. As we grow in him we just don't need very much sleep." We did; so we left.

* * *

A frequent allegation against the Children of God is that they engage in kidnapping. Letters have appeared in the *Hollywood Free Paper* concerning this subject. In Volume 3, Issue 12 an open letter from the Inter-Varsity Christian Fellowship of Southwestern College, Chula Vista, California, was published. It read in part:

> The area is Chula Vista, the date is May 6th, and the time is afternoon. A white bus pulls up on Southwestern's Campus and unloads several youths who call themselves "Children of God", their mission — to convince youth that their way is the right way, which includes the selling of all earthly possessions, following them as captives, held and taken somewhere in Los Angeles, taught UN-CHRISTIAN DOCTRINES, guarded at all times, with fearfulness shaking their bodies, no sleep, no food, and ignorant that Christ's Mission was to save man-kind from sin. After L.A., they are bussed to Arizona, taught in a hyp-notical state, kept away from the sunlight, and filled with wickedness. These people pounce upon weak Christians, and pull them into an hypnotic state with their wicked eyes. These people are the "wicked forces of Satan" that produce fear, hate, greed and lust.
>
> The adults taken from our campus have not been returned. Parents are concerned and brokenhearted.

In the next issue a counter-letter appeared, signed "The Children of God" but written by Fred Jordan. It denied the charges and demanded a retraction:

> The fact is that members are always free to depart, live only in the fear (that is to say the love) of God, sleep regular hours and partake of wholesome and abundant supplies of food. . . . The church certainly does not teach "un-Christian doctrine"; in fact it teaches only the Word of God as revealed in the Holy Bible.

In the succeeding issue, Kent Philpott, a long-standing leader of the Jesus People in the Bay Area, wrote:

In 4½ years of street ministry and operating Christian houses, I have never encountered so dangerous a group as that Texas based group formally called "The Children of God". . . .

The fruit they have left as they have passed through various areas has been confusion, snatching away of people (at times people under age), creating factioning, demanding of followers the turning of all property and money (the elders become 'stewarts' [sic] of the property and money), an unhealthy subjection of followers to their elders and teaching, a hiding behind the Bible and 'spiritual' talk, violence when people oppose them (they call it 'smiting' those who oppose the 'Lord's annointed' [sic]), extreme legalism (i.e. any version of the Bible other than the King James is sinful to read), bizarre reactions (one whole family set out to commit suicide after a prophecy to that effect came out in one of their meetings), and seeing people as objects of material gain rather than a person. . . .

Their familiar approach is to go into Christian houses or other concentrations of Jesus People and try to attract new believers. They especially *use* prophecies and revelations as a 'tool' in that a person will be told through such a 'tool' that God has called them to belong to "The Children of God." They make a person feel like he is disobeying God if he doesn't join their group. . . .

Just recently in the Bay Area, two young believers had to literally escape from "The Children of God." One guy walked all night to get away. He said he was watched so closely that someone of the group even went to the bathroom with him. Another girl needed outside help to deal with the group after they had taken over her house.

Asked about the issue of kidnapping, the Children of God explained that the Bible teaches that the believer in Christ is a brother or sister of fellow-believers and that a Christian is to "hate" (never clearly defined) his father and mother and brothers and sisters. They say that they encourage weekly correspondence with the families they have left behind. Some parents come to visit their children at the colony. There is trouble only if a parent tries to take his child home. An elder told us of several encounters in which he tried to encourage a member not to return home and was beaten up by irate parents as a result. He described a dramatic tug-of-war in which he pulled on one arm of the youth while the father pulled on the other.

While they are sensitive about the charges of kidnapping, they have their own perspective on the issue. They see the unhappy parents of new members as the ones guilty of kidnapping. A recent issue of *New Nation News* tells of a Michigan father "kidnapping" his daughter from the Detroit colony:

> After arriving in Detroit she began having heavy trials as her religious friends plagued our doors and we had no rest until we let them in to speak to her; but she held her ground and didn't give place to their lies — not even for a moment. They went back to Ann Arbor empty handed, but there they began to plot a kidnap of their friend who had exposed their hypocrisy by dropping out of their idolatrous system. The kidnap was carried out by her parents and some religious demons, who unexpectedly barged into our building. Everyone was taken by surprise as the Kidnappers started throwing everyone around, and during the melee the old man grabbed his daughter.

A similar account comes from the same issue:

> A girl named Kathy decided to join after working for Youth for Christ for two years as their secretary. Her girl friend blew it, being a typical Mt. 10:36 (Man's foes shall be they of his own household), and ran home to tell mommy. Then a religious hypocrite showed up with a subverting crew and began spouting out his sales pitch to lure her back to the pit. The girl was torn between the two and she knew what she was supposed to do. The guy was a regular Jn. 8:44 (Child of the Devil) and refused to give her up to God's will. So after a vicious battle between the two forces, a policeman drove up, the guy ripped her off, and they drove away into the night. This guy better get prepared for a sea voyage with a Millstone tied around his neck like Jesus said in Mt. 18:6, 7.

It is certainly true that severing all ties, as the Children insist, has a calamitous effect upon the family that has been broken up. The Children believe that this is one of the prices of discipleship. They insist that members of the group are free to leave any time, although they are strongly urged not to. Loyal members do not. As one said to us, "What would it be like if I went home, and this guy went home, and that guy went? Our strength is in our unity; so we must stay together." Thus, parents come to visit their children on occasion, but children never go to visit their parents. The line between witnessing and kidnapping seems to have become blurred.

The Children of God have also been accused of hypnotizing,

43

but this seems not to be literally true. However, one of their techniques is staring the object of their witnessing right in the eyes. Those who encounter the Children of God repeatedly speak of "those eyes that look right through you." They consciously cultivate a piercing stare, which some observers may consider hypnotism. Indeed, for certain "victims" the effect may be similar.

There are at least four types of young people particularly susceptible to the Children of God. First are those who are at the end of their rope, who have tried all the "trips." They are worldly-wise and old beyond their years. Second are those with a fundamentalist background who do not have sufficient biblical knowledge to feel confident of their positions. Often they feel guilty about not being "sold out for Christ." Third are those who strongly need a sense of belonging. Their families and churches have not provided the security they crave. Fourth are those who come from excessively permissive backgrounds and feel a need for discipline. Obviously, these four types are not mutually exclusive; and the more of these characteristics that an individual has, the more susceptible he is to the Children. This is why many Jesus People in other groups are particularly vulnerable targets for "raiding" by the Children of God. Indeed, the Children have already realized some success in this area of proselyting.

What are encounters with the Children like? Our research has uncovered some fairly typical examples of young people who have joined and who have not joined.

A nursing student in Los Angeles was downtown shopping for shoes when she was confronted by some of the Children of God. She was nervous and tense at the time, aggravated by the fact that she could not find shoes that suited her. The Children said to her, "Why don't you come and live with us? We don't worry about needing to get shoes. We have plenty of shoes and plenty of everything else that we need." The girl had smoked marijuana and drank quite heavily. Although she was reared in a Christian home, she did not know the Bible very well, certainly not well enough to resist the seasoned proof-texting and typical scare tactics of the Children. They told her that she should not hesitate when God calls, that it was the Devil who was trying to get her to hesitate.

44

At their insistence, she went with them to the colony to talk further. She told them that she was planning to be a nurse. They said that they did not need doctors or nurses: "We ask 'Dr. Jesus' to solve our ills of the body as well as the spirit." If one becomes ill, the elders anoint him and pray. (Some wear glasses, and when pinned down about it mutter an evasive remark about "using the system for God." They practice natural childbirth. During the delivery the whole colony surrounds the mother, praying, singing, and speaking in tongues.)

They tried to talk the student nurse into selling all her belongings and giving them the money. When she asked if she could go home and talk to her parents about joining them, they urged her not to communicate with them at all. "Let the dead bury the dead," they said. She asked when she could see her parents if she decided to stay. They told her that they would send her to the Texas Soul Clinic for a few months, and after that she could return to Los Angeles. Only then could she communicate with her parents, if she wanted to. But they thought that by that time she would probably have no desire to do so.

All this happened the day before she was planning to leave for a week-long Inter-Varsity camp. She says that she fears if the Children of God had approached her a day earlier, she would have gone back to the colony the next day because she was so shaken and confused by the experience. In that case she might never have left. But she had been looking forward to the camp so much that she decided to postpone her decision to join the Children. When she tried to leave, they formed a circle around her and started praying loudly for her, asking that the Lord would take away all her belongings so that she would see that she was supposed to stay. However, when she absolutely insisted on leaving, they finally allowed her to go.

The student nurse was so wrought up by the whole experience that she feared that she was on the verge of suicide. This fear stemmed from her guilt feelings that she was not living right and so was unable to answer from Scripture the arguments that the Children had confronted her with. Her confusion was increased by the young people she had met in the colony. Many fellows in the group said that they had been

45

Repairing a prophet bus

draft-dodgers. One had made bombs, planning to blow up the world. Several girls had had illegitimate children. She later reflected that they were mostly "very messed-up kids." Their swearing bothered her.

The story has a happy ending: the week at the Inter-Varsity camp brought about a crucial change in her life, and she now "has her head together" much better than before.

Another typical account of a proselyting junket by the Children comes from a campus chaplain in San Luis Obispo, California. He tells of one student who was talked into spending the night in the "prophet bus." Noticing his watch, the Children asked him if they could have it, since "if he really loved the Lord, he would certainly be willing to give up his watch for the work of the Lord." In the chaplain's words, "It was only later that he realized that he had been the victim of a 'sanctified rip off.'" The Children of God had appeared during the week of final exams.

Obviously, they chose an excellent time to come to the campus. Everyone is uptight during finals week! I guess they went door to door in the dorms seeking witness opportunities. As for George, they spoke with him, talked him into going with them, and then refused to allow him to talk with any of his friends. This last point is what prompted one student to get hold of a campus chaplain. . . . The witnessing of the Children of God seems to rely on the right moment. Once they confront you with the "truth," they expect you to respond immediately without benefit of some thought or counsel.

One of the recruits gives a typical testimony:

I went to wild parties and nightclubs and tried to become a part of the New York night life. Again I was ignorant and everywhere I turned I was taken advantage of. In my job I finally realized I was only a slave, and seeing how lonely and humiliated I was, to be a nothing amid the tinsel of New York, I decided to leave. . . . In California, I lived with a New York girl friend and paced the streets for a job every day. Two weeks went by and I still didn't have a job. I was looking for some sort of new, different type of church to go to and was considering the Hari Krishna Temple, when one night I met some kids on the street, who talked to me about the Bible. They told me how much Jesus loved me and how only He could fill up that empty spot inside me, only He could take care of my loneliness — and all I had to do was ask Him into my heart. Their eyes shone with such love and concern and their voices came from the deep regions of their hearts. I fell in love with them, and fell in love with the Lord Jesus too. Now we're brothers and sisters, one big family that really loves one another and who are looking for kids like we were to tell them that they don't have to be alone, or be afraid, or have that empty feeling *ever* again.

Another tells of leaving college, where he was having difficulties, to work with Arthur Blessitt (see chapter three). While he was out on the streets witnessing, he encountered some of the Children of God and went home with them, never returning to Blessitt's center, His Place. He said that at His Place, "it was almost like asking Arthur Blessitt to come into your heart. Arthur Blessitt was just on one big ego trip." At the time we talked to him, he asked us to invite a mutual friend to come and visit him. He himself would not consider leaving to go to see her, because "our strength is in our unity." He professes himself to be totally happy with his new situation and feels that he is wholly within the will of God now for the first time in his life.

Another was attending Calvary Chapel of Costa Mesa (see chapter four), because "they were the most together." He changed his mind when he visited "the Warehouse." He is now a revolutionary comrade.

* * *

A handful of recent conversions have brought great joy to the Children. One of the converts is Jeremy Spencer, vocalist, lead guitarist, and composer for Fleetwood Mac, a British rock group. While in Hollywood performing on Sunset Strip, he left his hotel one night and never came back. The other members of the group thought that he had been kidnapped, but they finally traced him to "the Warehouse." He told his former colleagues that he would not return to the band. His musical mates were not the only mates he had left behind: he had a wife and two children residing in London. He told his old friends, "Jesus will take care of them." Since that time his wife, too, has become a convert to the Children of God, and they are back together.

Even more important than Spencer's conversion was that of David Hoyt. Hoyt, who had spent six and one-half years of his life in youth institutions and some time in the federal penitentiary for smuggling narcotics, sought truth first through meditation and vegetarianism. Then he became a devout student of a host of Oriental mystical religious teachers. From these he worked his way into Hari Krishna. One night he had a vision about Jesus, and through this he was led to a conversion to Christ:

> Everything was in full swing in the Krishna Temple when smoke began billowing out of the basement where I stayed. I ran down the steps with other Krishna people close behind but felt a supernatural power come over me as I viewed this large Universal Altar with every religion represented burning to the ground. Stepping close to the altar I grabbed the only remaining book that hadn't already caught on fire which was the Bible. No one had to tell me what was happening and I turned to a page that revealed that Jesus Christ, the True Light of the world, was setting me free.

48

Following his conversion, Hoyt, who is an exceptionally able and energetic fellow, established Upper Streams, a commune in Walnut Creek, California, and other communes in the Bay Area. After this he moved to Atlanta, where he established the Bread of Life Restaurant, Chamber Gates Lightclub, and the House of Judah and other communes, all of which were part of his Atlanta Discipleship Training Center. His conversion to the Children of God occurred in the summer of 1971. At least four of his communes and ninety of his disciples have followed his lead and joined the Children.

Hoyt sent out a letter in June 1971 telling of his latest shift and explaining the reasons why. Without going into much detail, he explained that he received a prophecy a month earlier showing him that the ministry in which he was engaged was in error. While trying to follow God's will wholly, it turned out that he, as the elder, was unable to do so. "I HAD COME TO THE DEAD END ROAD OF BEING A PROFESSIONAL PREACHER WITH A WELL RESPECTED MINISTRY BUT IN TRUTH AT THE AGE OF 25 I WAS TURNING INTO A HYPOCRITE AND PHARISEE." He came to see the shallowness of the Jesus Movement, in which, in his words, he was "of noted reputation." Now he saw that he was

> guilty of being deceived by the lightness of it all. I could no longer go along with *the phoniness of the bumper stickers and Jesus Freak t-shirts that did nothing but make Jesus another fad for the world.* Instead of all-out 100% total commitment to Jesus Christ it was a one finger sign pointing upward letting the world know that Jesus is cool. . . . The Lord helped me to see that *the charismatic and Jesus People Movement was already becoming corrupted within its first 5 years* of popularity and that we would not begin to dent the powers of Satan by a watered down gospel that was anything short of 100% dying to self and presentation of our life to God for His use and glory.

Hoyt also struggled against

> the temptation *not to offend anyone* and *make sure we pledge allegiance to our blessed and holy country.* . . . In reality *when you choose to follow God all the way an immediate break is made with being a nice respectable citizen* because when a person follows God they instantly become a stranger and a pilgrim walking on a foreign soil and bearing a much greater hope than that of physical comforts or worldly acceptance.

49

Hoyt says that he first became interested in the Children of God when he saw them on NBC-TV's "First Tuesday." Though he had heard bad rumors about them, he decided on the basis of that program to visit the Texas Soul Clinic and find out for himself. Though their grubbiness did not appeal to him, everything else about them did. He and his wife joined. Since that time he complains that his old friends have written him off "as being seduced by a seducing spirit" and have shown no charity toward him. At the same time, his attitude toward them seems somewhat less than charitable:

> Just recently a band of "Charismaticers" from our local area withdrew their support and contract for a park that we had pre-scheduled with the intent of reaching the lost because they did not want their name to be associated with *our strange sect that believes the Bible.* It is coming to the surface so clearly that people in religious circles are more afraid of having the boat rocked and really *don't have a real burden for souls.* . . . WE CAN BE MORE THAN A FADING REVIVAL AND A NICE SONG IN THE EARS OF CHARISMATIC WHITED SEPULCHRES!

Hoyt once entitled an article "No One Has All the Truth." He seems to have changed his mind.

If one learns about his past and reads what he formerly wrote, it is not altogether surprising that Hoyt joined the Children of God. The communes he had established had more in common with those of the Children of God than most Christian houses have. In a leaflet written shortly before he joined the Children, he answered a list of questions about his ministry. The one that received the longest answer was, "Do we make them obey God rather than their parents?" Explaining that this is a very delicate subject, he proceeds to elaborate on the corruptness of the average American home. His answer is, as expected, that the Word of God teaches us to honor the Lord first, though this does not mean that we should not honor our parents. At any rate, Hoyt's number-one problem in running his houses was the same as the number-one problem at the colonies of the Children.

Hoyt's conversion did not cost him as much as most conversions cost those who join the cult. He still has the position of authority in Atlanta that he previously had, and he now has more substantial outside support for it.

The most recent stars of the Jesus Movement to be picked off by the Children of God are Linda Meissner and Russ Griggs, leaders of important works in Seattle and Vancouver, respectively. Their defections came about in September 1971, just days before Fred Jordan evicted the cult from his premises.

Griggs became interested in the Children of God when he received a copy of the letter that Hoyt circulated announcing his joining the group. He traveled down to Los Angeles to find out for himself what the cult was up to. Like Hoyt he was impressed, and he delivered up his whole ministry — bakery, chicken farm, and training houses — to the Children. His enthusiasm infected Linda Meissner, though her affiliation entailed more laborious soul-searching than Griggs' did. She is married to a fireman who brought five children to their marriage, and her husband is unalterably opposed to the Children of God. Because of her stature, the cult has made an exception for her and will allow her to live at home, at least for the time being. While wrestling with her decision, she became the object of a high-level verbal tug-of-war. Carl Parks and Jim Palosaari, Jesus People leaders of Spokane and Milwaukee, respectively, went to Seattle to try to dissuade her. The Children countered with Hoyt and John ("Jethro") and Linda Treadwell.

Meissner was less successful than Griggs in taking followers along. According to Palosaari, only ten or fifteen of her disciples tagged along; the other fifty or sixty stayed out. The Children of God are now occupying the properties that Meissner and her Jesus People's Army leased. Two houses owned by churches in Seattle are still available for the now leaderless remnant of her work. She insists that, as president of the corporation, she is the "owner" of the Jesus People's Army and its effects, including the properties now in the hands of the invading Children, the *Truth West* newspaper, and the name of the JPA. The Children, like good revolutionaries, will continue to use the JPA name as a front in Seattle. Any gifts sent to the JPA will thus go to the Children of God.

Hoyt, Meissner, and Griggs had all gotten into a kind of empire-building that eventually involved them in fund-raising. These efforts included such "secular" enterprises as a restaurant, a bakery, and a chicken farm. Inevitably they became bogged down in sheer administrative details. These support roles detracted from their direct involvement in spiritual ministries; and soul-winning and discipling were the tasks to which they had originally devoted themselves and which they wanted to continue. To make matters worse, their followers, mostly from the counter-culture, did not always stick with them.

Linda Meissner recorded more than seven hundred conversions, but at the time when she joined the Children of God, she had fewer than eighty in her training houses. She felt helpless to perform her task as she had seen it in a vision: to raise up a great last-day army of zealots to sweep through the whole world for Christ. The Children of God, she concluded, offered her a ready-made army with which to fulfil her vision. David Hoyt founded eighteen communes and then watched them disintegrate one by one. These leaders were not enjoying the success that their initial enthusiasm had led them to expect. Something was clearly wrong.

Enter the Children of God. Their explanations of what was wrong seemed to tally with the evidence at hand. Meissner, Hoyt, and Griggs had been involved in the system. They themselves had compromised, and their communes housed even worse compromisers. What was needed was stricter discipline, and a prerequisite for that was dropping out of the system totally.

Old associates of the three asked them how the Children of God, with their uncooperative and unloving attitude toward other Christian works, could be in the will of God. They pointed out all the charges of home-breaking and other kinds of disruptive tactics. The reply was always that, whatever faults the Children had, at least they were getting the job done. They were growing at a spectacular rate. Their followers were sticking with them. And perhaps they could exert a beneficial influence within the group. It was a case of joining the Children of God or conceding defeat, and since they were committed to serving Christ, the latter option was out.

One of the Jesus People leaders who tried to talk Linda Meissner out of joining the cult was amazed to listen to Meissner and Jethro conning each other, neither recognizing

52

what the other was up to. Meissner expects to use the Children, and the Children expect to use her. The advantage seems to be all on the side of the Children: we have yet to discover an instance in which they have been outmaneuvered.

Can strong personalities like Hoyt, Meissner, and Griggs ever be docile enough to be meek disciples? Can they even bring themselves to accept a sharing of authority with other elders? In the past, for instance, Hoyt used modern versions of the Bible in his work. Can he now trade the modern "fellowship" for the King James "sup"? Perhaps these big-name recruits can be subservient for a while. But they are natural leaders, accustomed to calling the shots. How will they react when they are ordered to make a move that they consider a mistake?

If the liaison of the Children with Fred Jordan had gone on indefinitely, there probably would have been enough pressure to cause a split in the cult. Some elders would have begun to yearn for the purity of spirit that prevailed in the yesterdays of poverty and deprivation; they would have found the luxurious ranch in Coachella a trap that softened them and compromised their integrity. Since that threat of schism has been vitiated, the danger is now internal. The top echelon of elders has stayed together from the early days of the movement, and these veterans may be able to remain united. But what about the new leaders? Former associates of Hoyt, Meissner, and Griggs say that they cannot imagine that these three will stick with the cult. The veterans will probably not allow them into the inner circle of leadership; but even if they do, how can one hierarchy accommodate more than one "top dog"? The risks to unity are multiplied since each of these strong-personality extremists thinks to have direct access to God's truth through the special revelation of visions. It is a safe assumption that the Children of God will eventually undergo the splintering that always comes in groups with a cultic mentality and a highly authoritarian structure.

That there is a great yearning for spiritual reality among American young people is one of the main lessons to be learned from the Jesus Movement as a whole. The Children of God provide an answer that is so radical that it has a strong attraction for young persons who are in extremity.

Even within the Jesus Movement, the Children of God are an extremist group, but that is precisely their appeal. They cater to the "all-or-nothing" mentality prevalent among the younger generation. While discounting their charges that other Christian groups are really Satanically controlled, one ought not, it seems to us, charge them (as some Jesus People have) with being Satanic. They are genuinely serious about their spiritual lives. Although there are doubtless camp followers among them who say all the right things but whose real interests are in the security and sense of unity that come from being accepted into a family composed almost wholly of young people, it is only fair to record our opinion that the majority of the Children are genuine converts to Christianity, however eccentric and harmful the aberrations present in their thought and practice.

* * *

There is another voice crying in the neon wilderness of Hollywood Boulevard. More visible, though less thorough and less personal than the Children, are the omnipresent tract-pushers sent in a biblical two-by-two lock-step from the recently relocated Christian Foundation of Tony and Susan Alamo. Bristling with mimeographed slips of paper reading "Repent of your Sins! Jesus is Coming Soon!", the young missionaries from Saugus, fifty miles from downtown Hollywood, work their way against the flow of pedestrian traffic warning of the impending apocalypse. The doom merchants from Saugus are in no way physically striking. They adopt none of the more spectacular affectations common to Children of God vigils. Hair is short but shaggy and not trimmed; clothes are plain, almost shabby, and quite colorless. Missing, too, are well-known Jesus symbols — fish necklaces, One Way buttons, and assorted Jesus clothes bearing different gospel messages. Unlike the Children of God, these witness teams do not look well fed and well kept.

The method is apparently designed to stimulate curiosity, not discussion. The home-made tract provides enough information to make conversation unnecessary. It tells of the disaster awaiting the unrepentant, a warning that is brief and to the point; it displays the address of the Foundation and the scheduled times for the eight meetings held there weekly; it announces free shuttle-bus service from the corner of Highland and Hollywood every day of the week. The transaction between missionary and mission field seems calculated to make conversation difficult if not impossible. The Alamo witness teams move so quickly through the sidewalk crowds that it is virtually sure they will be gone by the time the recipient realizes that he has heard the voice crying in the wilderness and not just another sales pitch (a distinction no doubt somewhat blurred to many by this time). The evangelism of the Alamo witness brigades is limited to passing leaflets as quickly and as widely as possible, nothing more. No persuasion, no attempt at conversation, but simply an almost mechanized routine: "Repent!", followed by a tract that tells where.

"Where" is a converted restaurant on the outskirts of Saugus, an hour and a half trip by Christian Foundation "bus" — actually a number of vehicles ranging from new Volkswagen vans to an older, dilapidated open-air slat-side truck. Though billed as a shuttle service for visitors, the chief function of the vehicles is transporting the three shifts of witnesses who barnstorm Hollywood during the day. The morning crew arrives from Saugus and is returned when the afternoon shift comes to replace them. The afternoon team leaves the streets at six-thirty with any curiosity seekers who have been recruited and returns to Saugus. When the visitors are returned to the street around 10:30, the third string hits the boulevard until 2:00 in the morning. Each team is armed with the same tract, peddles the same repent-or-be-damned message, arrives and departs on schedule, and returns the next day to repeat the process.

The presence of the Christian Foundation teams on the bus makes the ride to Saugus interesting (albeit unnerving) for the curious. As the few visitors settle into the cramped space, the truck rolls off. The riders have absolutely none of the trappings that are associated with the Jesus Movement. Even the smiles are missing. There is little conversation — none at all between the returning witness team and the curious, and only smatterings among the team itself. What little talk there is centers on topics like the nearness of the last

55

days, the absence of a true witness to Christ in the established churches, and the ease with which young people could be persuaded to join the cause of Christ as opposed to the intransigence of adults. On our trip to Saugus we talked to one of the Alamo disciples for no more than half a minute. He could tell us little of the Foundation itself and would tell us almost nothing of himself.

There was plenty of Bible reading going on, not systematized, for everyone was at different points, but incessant. Those who had Bibles read them page after page, from the end of one book to the beginning of the next and then to the next. The trip was unusually quiet, considering that the truck carried an all-male cargo of twenty-five.

The atmosphere changes somewhat when the truck arrives in the large dirt parking area that surrounds the Christian Foundation. Welcome to the Foundation is provided by a large sign that proclaims "This is Tony and Susan Alamo's Christian Foundation." Standing around are a school bus and a handful of recent model station wagons, all painted red, white, and blue and emblazoned with a hand-painted "Tony and Susan Alamo's Christian Foundation." The building itself is an old, rustic restaurant, made surprisingly spacious by the removal of a few walls. The changes wrought by the Alamos and their disciples have restored what reportedly was a ramshackle building on the verge of condemnation to a measure of respectability, though the Foundation itself is still somewhat seedy. Occupancy by the Alamos and their followers has disguised the structure's former use; yet a few traces remain. Restaurant booths are now used more for Bible study than eating. A stuffed deer's head still greets those who enter, although its charm is somewhat dissipated.

Half an hour before the scheduled 8:00 p.m. meeting, the Foundation is alive with activity, conversation, and Bible reading. At the front of the meeting room is a slightly raised stage covered with electronic gear — amplifiers, microphones, speakers — and musical instruments of all varieties — trumpets, trombones, clarinets, drums, guitars, a piano, an organ, a harmonica, and even a flute. The din of the makeshift orchestra tuning up, coupled with rather widespread conversation, stands in stark contrast to the quiet ride from Hollywood.

56

Despite the increase in conversation, subject matter seldom varies and never strays from the spiritually significant: the world is coming to an end, Jesus is coming soon. That message is repeated in conversation after conversation.

The meeting area is cordoned into sections by a wide aisle between two clumps of folding chairs. The back section is reserved for those who live at one of the Christian Foundation's four communes around the meeting hall. The front section, somewhat smaller, is occupied by visitors arriving from Hollywood or, more commonly, on their own. The segregation is politely but firmly enforced by those overseers who have drawn ushering duty. The hall is filled to standing room only fifteen minutes before the scheduled start. The crowd, however, is 250-300, rather than the 400-500 circulated by the Alamo witness teams. Though it is not unusual to see middle-aged adults and very young children, the bulk of the congregation is 16-22. The group is as varied as any gathering of the Jesus Movement, the most notable factor being the presence of Blacks, both young and old, on more than a token basis. The number of them is admittedly small, under fifteen, but the Alamo Christian Foundation seems more attractive to Blacks than any other group labeling themselves Jesus People.

Without a signal of any sort or the appearance of anyone behind the podium, conversation, musical practice, and Bible reading cease precisely at 8:00 p.m. The hall is quiet but expectant. Tony Alamo, a small, well-groomed, middle-aged man, presides over the nightly gatherings at the Foundation. On the infrequent occasions when he is absent, an overseer conducts the meeting. Alamo opens every service with a word of welcome mingled with warning:

> Welcome to Tony and Susan Alamo's Christian Foundation. We believe that this is the House of God and ask that you refrain from talking during the service. If you have questions, an overseer will be glad to answer them afterwards. If there are other Christians here, we ask that you do not pass out any literature. If you have literature that you want passed out, please give it to Susie or myself or an overseer. We will screen it, and if it is in accordance with the King James Version of the Bible, the only inspired word of God, it will be passed out on the streets of Hollywood.

Despite the authoritative tone of the remarks, no penalty was prescribed for violating the dicta, either by talking or handing out literature. (Alamo told us later in a private conversation that violators would be asked to leave.)

The meeting begins with a rousing song service that would thrill any lover of the old-time religion. The music — said to be a fulfilment of the command to worship the Lord with singing and praises and accompanied by the orchestra and unbridled foot-stomping, hand-clapping, and dancing in the Spirit — is truly impressive. It is joyous; it is celebrative; it is nearly frenzy. And most of all, it is loud, almost unbelievably so. Thirty instruments and three hundred people singing at the tops of their voices in a space that would be comfortable for half that number make even shouting an ineffective means of communication. That is not enough for the Alamos. Though the natural amplification verges on the threshold of pain, microphones bracketed to beams in the ceiling pick up and magnify the uproar. The effect is that of a spiral, each voice gaining intensity in an effort to be heard over an ever-increasing level of sound. Volume, however, is a quality not confined to singing alone; it is foreshadowed during the invocation. The command from Alamo to pray evokes highly audible groans, moans, and plainly apparent speaking in tongues from nearly everyone in attendance. The prayers of the congregation are so loud that Alamo's lead, always in English, can barely be heard, if at all. Though the congregation begins its prayer on command, it often takes several amens, each louder than the other, to restore the quiet seemingly so valued in the opening remarks.

Music at the Alamo Christian Foundation, despite the volume and exuberant audience response, has much in common with established church musical programs. Unlike most of the Jesus People, the Alamos do not transpose gospel lyrics to new and more popular musical scores. The music at the Christian Foundation is quite reminiscent of Pentecostal and evangelistic services in backwoods rural areas. The songs are the same — "When the Roll Is Called Up Yonder," "Nothing But the Blood," "I'll Fly Away," "I Am a Pilgrim," and a magnificent, rollicking version of the "Hallelujah Chorus" done by a 150-voice choir with full orchestra accompaniment, directed by a jitterbugging, blue-suited director. Solos too fit the model; the booming, gravelly, blues-y female voice sliding through the measures of "In the Garden" — again, barely audible over the uproarious din. The music is rhythmic, exciting, and practiced. Audience response is somewhat mechanized: the congregation rises in unison and without command for the more martial of the gospel hymns and sits, likewise undirected but unanimously, for more soothing melodies.

Although long hair is not as prevalent at the Foundation as it is at most Jesus People gatherings, the Alamo disciples seem slightly incongruous against the old-time fundamentalist sound track. The words, the style, and the spirit of the Alamo brand of music would make even the most rigid fundamentalist beam brightly. The disheveled and often dirty and unkempt participants would, however, turn smiles to puzzlement. Most residents of the Alamo community show signs of what must be a Spartan existence. Shoes are worn to the point of obvious discomfort. Faces lack the vigor and the happy sparkle typical of more publicized versions of Jesus People. Levis are the common denominator among the men and are covered with the dust that surrounds the semi-arid Saugus area. The women are plainly and inconspicuously dressed, but are not markedly cleaner than the men. The mismatch is truly startling. The music and the mood are from the heart of "cleanliness is next to godliness" country; the appearance is distinctly from another world.

When the song service ends after an hour, the scene again is highly similar to old-time fundamentalist meetings. There are testimonies, brief, spectacular, and colored with the jargon of the Bible Belt, not Berkeley. Words like "sin" and the "pits of hell" are repeated time and again, as is the pitch to "come up and get saved." The Jesus trip of the hip Christian is totally foreign to the idiom of the Christian Foundation. Following the testimony time (for which people are recruited by the overseers, who also recruit kitchen help, cleaning help, and witness team members), the main attraction of the evening, the appearance of Tony or, more often, Susan Alamo in the pulpit, climaxes the service.

The contrast between the Alamos and their disciples is almost unbelievable. Tony, forty-ish and a few years younger than his wife, is a picture-book example of successful America. He

59

and Susie live, not at the Foundation or even nearby in Saugus, but in the hills of Studio City overlooking Hollywood. Their daily circuit to Saugus is made quite comfortable in a new chocolate-brown Ford LTD, a means of transportation somewhat different from the gutted old truck in which we traveled, along with the witness teams, from the Alamos' personally proclaimed (though they claim divinely commanded) mission field. Tony fits the image that his automobile demands: a nattily tailored suit of fine denim, white silk shirt with blue polka-dots matched with a carefully knotted silk polka-dot tie (blue on white), patent leather boots, pomaded hair gleaming with tonic, sun glasses, all accented by a fat, three-flap executive wallet thrust in the waist band of his pants, which already bulge with a stylishly plump potbelly. What Tony lacks in magnificence, his wife makes up in splendor. A platinum blonde, impeccably made up, Susie is as classy as Tony is flashy. Her clothes are carefully chosen — white skirt, contrasting blouse, and highlighting jewelry — and create an image quite reminiscent of Lana Turner.

Notwithstanding Tony's control of Christian Foundation services, his swagger, and the bevy of followers at his heels as he struts through the meeting hall, it is clear that the power, the dominating personality, the charisma, the cohesive force of the Alamo Christian Foundation are Susie's. She is cheered upon her late arrival at a Friday night meeting; her voice is commanding, her stage manner polished. She is the Foundation's resident theologian; her views are the views of the Foundation from her husband on down. Word for word, phrase for phrase, example for example, the teachings of Elder Susan are repeated by all.

Tony is, however, not without his impact upon the proceedings. His testimony, known throughout the Foundation, is a classic adventure story that combines elements of Horatio Alger and the Apostle Paul. Born Bernie Lazar Hoffman in (of all places) Montana, he was, according to his own claim, an incredibly successful Hollywood impresario. His promotional work for Sonny and Cher, P. J. Proby, and Earl McDaniel, made him widely known and rather wealthy. He had his own recording label ("Talamo"), which reached the heights of financial success when, in Tony's words, "I had the Twenty

Original Hits, twenty smash hits on one album, Oldies but Goodies for $2.98. I made loads of money. I was making more money than General Motors, and I was banking it in New York."

At the height of his success Tony "used to run around with a little dame and six motorcycle escorts," until one day during a business meeting he received an audible message from God threatening to kill him unless he gave up his lucrative business and began to preach the gospel. The impact of that voice has colored the Christian Foundation in every phase of its operation. Tony's conversion was the first step down the primrose path to Susan. The flamboyant career of a West-Coast promotion man apparently held little charm for Susan. "She's a dignified woman. She would pay no more attention to me than the man in the moon."

Unlike her husband, Susie has been both a long-time Christian and a long-time evangelist. Reared in a Jewish home (as was Tony), she had what Tony describes cryptically as "a very supernatural experience with the living God" at age nine. She lost some of her youthful enthusiasm through the routines of an established denomination and dabbled in a career in motion pictures with more guilt feelings than success: "She never really could get away from the love of the living God because it was written on the tables of her heart. She knew that it was just like the Lord letting her get a first insight into what sin was really all about." The anxiety led Susie out of the movies and into Pentecostal evangelism, where she has spent the last twenty years of her life. Her courtship with Tony is shrouded in evasive spirituality: "The Lord actually put us together, and it was a very natural way that he did." The miracle occurred in the mid-1960s, and the Christian Foundation was begotten in 1966.

There was some hesitancy about beginning the Christian Foundation. "We didn't ask for this work. . . . We didn't come in after somebody. God called us into this work." The Alamos began their first ministry as a pair of itinerant evangelists occupationally engaged full-time, but only after Tony obtained a heavenly dispensation permitting him to promote one final performer in order to demonstrate his sanity to his now doubtful (following his dramatic conversion experience) acquaintances.

61

Susie soon began a persuasive campaign to convince Tony to accompany her on tract-passing treks from their comfortable Santa Monica home to the streets of Hollywood. Tony finally gave in to the pressure: ". . . finally she said, 'Look, I'm going on the streets tonight, and I'm going to pass out gospel tracts. You can stay home.' I told her, 'Well, you don't think a red-blooded American man is going to let his wife go on the streets with those narcotics addicts and knifers,' and I said I'd go. I went out with her."

Quickly the Alamos attracted a following, and soon they were filling a rented house with nightly crowds braving cramped conditions to hear Susie preach. According to Tony, their following in the early years was (he claims it still is) ninety percent reformed, converted, and cured junkies. The figure may, like much of Tony's rhetoric, be a bit of hyperbole, but the claim of reaching the drug culture seems a valid one. With the help of the Full Gospel Businessmen's Association, Tony and Susan moved the fledgling Foundation to new, more spacious quarters. That house-made-church, too, was quickly outgrown. After some serious trouble with the police in a quarrel over the right to assemble, and in the face of local residents' suspicion of the growing collection of former drug users meeting in their neighborhood, the Christian Foundation, once again with the aid of the Full Gospel Businessmen's Association, pulled up stakes and reestablished itself on the present Saugus property in 1970.

* * *

Apart from the intellectual domination of the Foundation by Susie's old Pentecostal theology and jargon, Tony's theophany is directly responsible for a good deal of the dogma of the Christian Foundation. The hell-fire and damnation message of their tracts and preaching stems from the supernatural extortion Tony claims is responsible for his conversion:

> I knew that God was not just a God of love because he threatened to kill me, and I saw these God-is-love people, little cats running around with their phony little messages, not messages from the Bible, and I heard that God drowned the whole world and that didn't figure out to me. And that he barbecued Sodom and Gomorrah and that he was gonna come back and fry everyone else that didn't get right. So I figured, who's kidding who?

The ceaseless hammering at the fear of God is an obsession in Saugus. Tony castigates other Jesus People in no uncertain terms: "I don't like what they're preaching. They're preaching God is love. It's not true, and it's throwing a lot of people into the pits of hell." Though he refuses to disassociate the Christian Foundation from the term "Jesus People" (in fact, Tony claims to have started the movement), his remarks about the movement are highly contemptuous and reveal a lack of any true understanding of its characteristics: "All they [the Jesus People] have to do is confess the Lord Jesus Christ and you can smoke dope, you can commit adultery, you can do anything you want. It's a lie out of the pits of hell."

Tony's fear of the freedom granted by the doctrine of God's love is the basis for the numerous rules enforced at the Christian Foundation. He rejects the "Christian commune" label, for it is associated in his mind with lurid images of sexual orgies following devotional prayer. Segregation along sexual lines at the Foundation is total. Men and women live not only separately but far apart. Contact of any sort is strictly forbidden. Lewd clothing, a judgment made by Tony's trained eye, is outlawed, as is talking to members of the opposite sex except at meal time, and then only with a female-male ratio of three to one. Marriage is permitted with the approval of the Alamos, but only after a total separation of ninety days reserved for praying and fasting.

As would be expected, drugs, drinking, and social dancing are prohibited. (Cigarette smoking is not on the list of forbidden fruits. The exception can be traced to Tony's post-conversion experience of scorn and ridicule by an established church for his tobacco habit, in spite of his supernatural encounter with God. The sin is admitted by Susan but dismissed conveniently as a "sin of the flesh not of the soul," quite like overeating.)

Daily life is governed by "a very intricate system" of overseers and their underlings developed, hand-picked, and headed by the Alamos. The "best elders on earth right now," as they are affectionately known by their followers, are always just a long-distance phone call away, should any problem arise that exceeds an overseer's authority to handle. None of the members work outside the Foundation; neither do they attend school. Money to the tune of $15,000 a month is supplied by donations. The Holy Spirit is said to supply wisdom enough for all — to the extent of miraculously teaching the illiterate to read.

The King James Version of the Bible is the one inspired version of Scripture for the Alamos. Oblivious to its problems and ignorant of the strengths of some modern versions, the Alamos oppose adamantly any contemporary revisions — especially *Good News for Modern Man* — as "right out of the pits of hell." When questioned about the errors they allege to exist in modern translations, Tony spiritualizes vaguely:

> I can't really tell. The Spirit inside tells me that it's wrong. In several instances I have gone through a particular experience that is related in the King James, many times I've done it, and you take the modern-day version and the way it tells it there are so many mistakes it's unbelievable.

The popularity of the heretical modern Bible translations is a keystone in the Alamos' belief that the return of Christ is imminent. These are the very last days, although the rebuilding of the Temple at Jerusalem, says Tony, must be achieved before the return of the Lord. That removes none of the urgency. The problem is explained through the wonders of prefabricated buildings, or by a story concocted by Tony claiming the discovery of the temple by rabbis in Jerusalem. He admits that no man can know the hour of the second coming, but Tony gives the world twenty years at the outside.

The nearness of the return of Christ is the very reason for the existence of Tony and Susan Alamo's Christian Foundation. Claiming to be Joel's Army and a fulfilment of the prophecy of old men dreaming dreams, young men seeing visions, and hand-maidens prophesying, the Foundation fully expects persecution to begin shortly. Plans are already afoot to move the Saugus remnant further toward the wilderness in order to escape the torment of the Antichrist, who, according to Tony, is already on earth and will be raised up shortly. The Jesus People, with their God-is-love jargon, are going to be deceived, as the established church already has been. The Foundation, with perhaps a few others, will be martyrs for the faith.

In the face of the foreboding signs of the end — smog, pollution, and the tension in the Middle East — business goes on as usual in Saugus. Witness teams depart, services continue, as does the twenty-four-hour prayer chain. Tony and Susan have the message — Repent, Jesus is Coming Soon. As for the rest of the Jesus People:

> Ones that are not of the Lord will fall, will fall flat. This God-is-love movement is nothing new. That's been around since the Garden of Eden. "Thou shalt not surely die. God is a nice God. Do you think he'd put a nice tree like that in the garden and not let you eat from it? He's a God of love. Eat from it. Eat it." They ate it, and they did die, because God is the truthful one, and Satan, who preaches that God-is-love message, is the liar. They've got to fall. Who is God going to keep on this earth doing his strong work? Is he going to keep this God-is-love movement, or is he going to keep the bulldog who says, "I'm not afraid to tell the truth"? I could care less what you think about our message. I didn't write it. I preach it. My wife and I preach it.

* * *

Although the Children of God and the Christian Foundation are the most notable of groups deserving the title of "doom-saying exclusivists," there are smaller movements similar to these. A commune in Fresno, California, which goes by the name of "Christian Brothers," includes men and women who dress in white and usually carry a cross, either around their necks or in a holder like a sword sheath on their belts. They believe that salvation requires a distinctively anti-establishment life style. For them, too, the King James is the inspired version of the Bible, and they spend long hours memorizing it. The structure is very authoritarian; women in particular are most docile. Unlike the Children of God and the Alamos, the Christian Brothers hold regular nine-to-five jobs. They are as strong as any group on the preaching of judgment and damnation. In fact, though they occasionally give concerts as an effort to spread the gospel, they do relatively little in the way of evangelism, at least in comparison to the two groups previously discussed in this chapter. When they do witness, they are quite cold and unfriendly. They emphasize the doom and judgment which will befall everyone but themselves.

A similar group is located in Montana. To our knowledge, this group has no official name. They are reported to be even more gloomy and somber than the Children of God, who are quite capable of expressing an infectious joy on occasion. They, too, see themselves as the only ones who are truly the remnant.

And then there is Leon. Leon heads up a small group — at last count, thirteen — who have traveled nomadically throughout northern California, but who have now stayed for a whole year in Eureka. Leon used to belong to the Children of God, but they say that he drifted into heresy and left. The Children consider him farther out than themselves. Some Jesus People who consider the Children of God far out view Leon as a "good brother," but they admit that he is a little "trippy." Specifically, Leon apparently has more than one woman as his bed-partner, but whether this is a case of polygamy or serial monogamy is unclear. While his legal marital status is unknown, all agree that he "has a thing about women." Leon practices something akin to the smiting by the Children of God. He has been known to break up meetings in rural churches by standing up and speaking without being asked to. His denunciations are usually phrased in florid King James English. We have been unable to confirm rumors that he and his followers have engaged in vandalism of these churches.

three

THE HOLLYWOOD SCENE

Straights, Streets, and the Superstar

RECOGNIZED LEADERS IN THE JESUS MOVEMENT ARE HUMBLY vague in citing its earthly origins. All are quick to point to the Holy Spirit's supernatural outpouring of power, but hedge when asked to name the first physical manifestation of that power, adopting instead a theory of widespread spontaneous generation. At any rate, its growth has been inexorable and concentrated around focal points of enthusiasm, first on the West Coast but now becoming nationwide.

Vancouver and Seattle bivouac the all-volunteer Jesus People's Army. Berkeley, in the forefront of any cause not in the mainstream of technological America, looms to the south. The almost giddy excitement of Atlanta bubbles far off to the east. But from the first hesitant evangelistic voices quivering on street corners to the present peak of success, the rebel capital of the Jesus Revolution has been Hollywood. The choice was as natural as it was unpremeditated. California, a mecca for freaks of every variety, provided fertile ground for the movement to flourish: a virtually limitless population of dopers, drag queens, and revolutionaries, growing larger by the day. The atmosphere, notwithstanding the apocalyptic smog, was congenial. Reputed to be tolerant if not totally open and accepting, California would be an easier context in which to do God's work than the smug confines of the rest of established America.

67

In the midst of metropolitan Los Angeles, Hollywood is compact and full of everything that the world has to offer, including Jesus People. The Hollywood representatives are as varied as the several blocks of shops, peddlers, and entertainment that line Hollywood Boulevard and — now to a lesser extent — Sunset Strip. There are those who adopt the name and claim the fame of the revolution, while violently denouncing established Christianity, established America, and any possession that smacks ever so slightly of being of the world. There are those who preach doom and separation. But the Children of God and the followers of the Alamos are only two hues in Hollywood's evangelistic rainbow. Sidewalk preachers offer a wide range of exotic options. Nearly everywhere one can meet turned-on young Christians mouthing newly coined (though unoriginal) slogans like "Jesus Is the Bridge over Troubled Water."

Despite the variety of the movement along Hollywood's sidewalks, the obvious mainstay of revolution is the stereotyped Jesus Freak popularized and romanticized by the mass media. The image is long-haired; the message, Jesus Loves You; the congregation, an alienated but not hostile group of former junkies, ex-pushers, and reformed whores. The picture that emerges from *Time* and *Look* is not altogether inaccurate; it in fact does characterize, superficially at least, the Jesus People of Hollywood.

However spontaneous the movement's origins were and however direct the line of communication between the Jesus People and heaven remains, the course of events in Hollywood continues to affect and alter the spread, growth, and character of the Jesus Revolution. Hollywood is not without its hierarchy of saints. Early in their history the Jesus People of Hollywood factionalized, not into hostile camps but into groups loyal in varying degrees to one elder, teacher, prophet, or what have you. The result was not gaping schism, but a hip version of the somewhat friendly rivalries of neighborhood churches on opposite corners.

The story and the character of Jesus People in Hollywood can be traced to the top of the factional hierarchy, to two men similar enough to attract followings that blend readily with each other and yet different enough to remain distinct and separate.

68

That story begins with the saga of the showmanlike preacher Arthur Blessitt, Minister of Sunset Strip, now in self-imposed exile, and continues with the magician-turned-editor drama of Duane Pederson and the *Hollywood Free Paper*.

* * *

Flamboyant, sensation-seeking, and with a flair for public relations, Arthur Blessitt arrived in the midst of the then thriving Sunset Strip via Mississippi, Montana, and Nevada in 1965. Blessitt's ascendancy antedates by at least a year the beginnings of any other manifestation of the Jesus Revolution. His California headquarters, named "His Place" in a burst of evangelical cleverness, opened several months after he began his campaign of sidewalk evangelism. It has moved several times in the intervening years, but it is no longer the thriving redemption center pictured in *Turned On to Jesus* (Hawthorn, 1971), a book billed as the "fascinating story of Arthur Blessitt." Full of inflated rhetoric that makes Blessitt the Paul Bunyan of a spiritual tall tale, the book records a typical evening during the heyday of His Place:

> It became *the* place to go. It was *in*. Hundreds trooped through our door each evening. On Friday and Saturday nights it was so jammed we had to empty the crowd into the street every few hours to permit a patiently waiting new bunch to enter. . . .
>
> The toilet service became one of our His Place traditions. Whenever a doper gives his heart to Christ, we move him straight to the john. Once I counted eighteen bodies squeezed into our little bathroom. "I don't need this anymore. I'm high on the Lord" the typical convert declares. He pulls out his cache of grass, reds, speed, or acid and drops it into the bowl (p. 143).

The days when His Place housed "the hottest head in town" appear to be at an end in Hollywood. The Strip itself is withered; the action has shifted to Hollywood Boulevard. His Place is now closed or empty except for Mike Ooten, an associate of Blessitt, even on a midsummer Friday evening. Ooten blames the virtual desertion of the Strip and Blessitt's headquarters on the Los Angeles Sheriff's Department. In its prime the Strip became a target for the strict enforcement of anti-loitering laws. Burly cops four abreast prodded and hassled the

69

street populace until Sunset's sidewalks became less than hospitable. The exodus to the Boulevard, thus, left His Place stripped of its clientele, empty, a mission walled off from its mission field.

The explanation, despite its plausibility, is typically Blessittesque. The account of Blessitt's career as the Minister of Sunset Strip is one of woe and harassment from united vice lords and establishment police. His book opens with a melodramatic courtroom battle between good, in the person of Blessitt, and evil, in the flimsy guise of a conspiracy of night club owners. The issue, in Blessitt's mind, "boiled down to a single vitally important question: Was there room for Jesus Christ on the Sunset Strip?" (p. 2). That battle as well as several others, including run-ins with city zoning boards, resulted in the temporary closing of His Place. Not easily discouraged, Blessitt grappled with the power of City Hall. Each time he succeeded in reopening over the opposition of club owners financially damaged by his evangelism. The police, too, are accused of harassment. After quoting the first of the Bill of Rights, Blessitt (with ghost-writer Walter Wagner's stylish improvisation) describes the beginning of the Sunset anti-loitering campaign:

> After the Bible they [the first Amendment to the Constitution] are the most cherished, hallowed words I know. But as far as the Los Angeles Sheriff's Department was concerned, they might never have been written. A confluence of behind the scenes power, its instrument the snappily uniformed sheriff's deputies, was gathering for the destruction of His Place (p. 209).

The saga of Arthur Blessitt in Hollywood and the history of His Place are told in *Turned On to Jesus* in terms of a conspiracy of the "straight" world of drunks and devotees of topless entertainment to rid themselves of the nuisance of a highly successful gospel night club. The persecution theme is central in Blessitt's account of his own life. From a seminary president accused of forcing him to decide whether he would "rather be ignorant and on fire than be a scholar and spiritually dead" to vice lords, corrupt police, and stodgy preachers, the establishment, he says, has sought to harass, intimidate, or confine the Minister of the Sunset Strip. Despite those efforts and even the

70

success of some of them, Blessitt has triumphed time and again. Even the anti-loitering campaign of the Sheriff's Department, blamed solely by Ooten for the demise of Hollywood's His Place, was viewed early in 1971 as a vindication of Strip evangelism:

> Though His Place might vanish like a vapor that didn't mean the hippies would disappear. In fact, we were the only ones effectively weaning the hips off the strip. Some kids had been busted a dozen times by the sheriff and warned to keep away from the strip but they returned like homing pigeons (p. 223).

Blessitt's victory was somewhat empty by the summer, as was His Place. He himself is no longer in California; the Strip ministry is seemingly in its death throes; and despite delusions of grandeur about the attractiveness of His Place to street people, hopes of revival are not promising. What remains of the ministry Blessitt had on the Strip has been altered in the face of the exodus. The transition, according to Ooten, holder of the recently coined title, "Teacher of His Place," is one from evangelism of the unsaved to teaching those who are already Christians. Its success has not been overwhelming; a turnout of less than five is not unusual, and the total of two — Ooten and a former Baptist youth pastor — on a Friday night in June seemed quite typical. Blessitt himself has been unable to adapt to the changing situation and to the possibility of a ministry less spectacular, less adventurous, and less successful (in terms of numbers of conversions, the only measure Blessitt knows).

Presently the Minister of Sunset Strip is busy changing labels. Next up: minister to the world via Times Square. Blessitt lost none of his evangelistic one-upmanship during his decline on the West Coast. Competing with neighbors sporting topless entertainment, the New York version of His Place, complete with peephole, is advertised by a marquee bearing the announcement of "Totally Naked." All the peephole reveals, however, is another bit of Blessitt's genius — a mirror captioned by the words, "Man stands naked before his God." New York's millions seem less than captivated, despite claims of thousands of converts (where hasn't Blessitt added thousands to the kingdom of heaven?).

Blessitt's new plans include a two- or three-year trek around the world bearing the same wooden cross with which he once

71

Arthur Blessitt

trudged across America. The New York ministry has never really gotten off the ground. Rather than facing failure, Blessitt has opted for a cross-dragging ministry in which there is neither success nor failure, just publicity. Upon his arrival at the airport in London, BBC representatives whisked him off to tape interviews for British television.

Thoughout his career as the evangelist to America's misfits, Blessitt has sought to be a figure with whom those on the fringes of society could identify. The journey from small-town USA to Hollywood is full of cultural shock, even for one as tuned in as Blessitt. Nevertheless, he adjusted well:

> I also let my hair grow longer and learned a quick lesson in dress. A collar or a business suit wouldn't get you anywhere. The first time I walked into a trip room I wore a tie and suit. The heads panicked. They thought I was a narc (narcotics agent) out to bust them. After that I switched to turtlenecks and psychedelically patterned slacks or bell bottoms and sandals. Then came the beads (p. 110).

Blessitt became one of the first to adopt the argot of the street for his evangelistic pitch. If the jargon of the "Jesus trip," "Jesus the everlasting high," "dropping Matthew, Mark, Luke, and John," "dealing reds" (Blessitt stickers, not pills) had its origin in one man, it was Arthur Blessitt.

Throughout, Blessitt has sought good Christian adventure. From the beginning he has gone where sin, if not at its worst, was at least at its most sensational. *Turned On to Jesus* is full of page after page of detailed description of assorted dens of iniquity. The sensationalism reaches its maudlin height in the bathetically comical rendition of Blessitt's struggle with and triumph over a group of semi-nude female nymphomaniacs. He is hooked on excitement. The allure of California was too much for the small-time sin of Montana; the wickedness of Times Square won easily over the mundane teaching ministry in Hollywood. The histories of Blessitt's various ministries are almost transient. His Place began with great energy, but as the thrill dissipated, the ministry waned and he moved on.

* * *

Blessitt's absence has not affected Hollywood's remaining population of Jesus People. Perhaps because His Place never fully aligned itself with the movement (to be sure, Blessitt was on the street and out of the established church, but the apocalyptic and charismatic character of the revolution never was prominent in his preaching), the abdication of its psychedelic leader has gone unnoticed and largely unmourned. The movement, which did not exist when His Place first opened its doors, grew up around the Strip outpost and soon had its own leader, its own gimmicks, and its own following. Of the manifestations of the Jesus Revolution that followed in Blessitt's three-year-old footsteps, by far the most successful and widely known is the *Hollywood Free Paper,* organized, edited, published, and advertised by Duane Pederson.

Pederson and Blessitt seem at times mirror images. A transplanted Minnesota farm boy, Pederson, like Blessitt, has little in common with those whom he seeks almost desperately to emulate. The life of the street — the danger, the alienation, the drugs, the depression — is really unknown to the kingpins of Hollywood's Jesus Freaks. Pederson's own career in evangelism began inauspiciously when he won the lead role in a college play and overcame the stammering that had plagued him since childhood. Entertainment soon became his life. Skilled at sleight of hand, he found himself absorbed totally in the world of a nightclub magician.

Apparently the glamour held him only briefly, for "several years later totally disillusioned, and no longer starry eyed with wonder at the glare of footlights and the smell of grease paint, I was working the nightclub circuit. My little dreams were beginning to disappear. I had long since learned that applause did not provide total satisfaction." While Pederson's disillusionment with the life of a magician was no doubt genuine, his recounting of its depth and street people-like quality is sheer fantasy:

> So I tried to retreat from the world of harsh reality through drugs, booze and about everything else. But none of these things did the job I hoped they would. Each escape effort failed. Each return to reality found me lonely. I still lived pretty much in a world of fantasy. I was nowhere. I honestly believe that the deep love I have for street people — and all the others that might be called "society rejects" — is because I have experienced everything they have (*Jesus People*, p. 12).

Pederson, like Blessitt, measures success in arithmetic terms. The conversion count and the success which those numbers are supposed to represent are never far removed from Pederson's conversation. Despite a quick disclaimer — "We aren't counting or keeping score and trying to nail down numbers. . ." (p. 79) — Pederson's autobiography repeatedly mentions circulation increases and describes two instances in which the *Hollywood Free Paper* is credited with responsibility for 600 and 2000 conversions respectively. Even now Pederson's only yardstick of success is circulation. The *HFP* has grown steadily and rapidly since the production of the first edition in 1969. Present circulation is 425,000, and with local inserts of news and announcements the paper is printed in several cities across the country: Chicago, Kansas City, and Cleveland among them. The goal is a circulation of a million within the near future.

The beginnings of the *HFP* are still somewhat hazy, though Pederson attempts to chronicle the paper's history in *Jesus People*. Armed with only the idea of a Christian underground newspaper imitating the then less established *Los Angeles Free Press,* Pederson records his initial fund-raising campaign in a few fuzzy-detailed anecdotes that he sums up typically enough: "In a very real sense, God provided the money for that first issue" (p. 17). Missing from the account is any mention of the help lent by Hollywood's First Presbyterian Church. Following his first edition, Pederson approached First Presbyterian, well known for its concern and involvement in the Hollywood youth scene, with a proposal for a partnership. The church had just opened an outreach coffee house, the Salt Company, and was toying at the time with the idea of printing an underground paper to accompany their in-person evangelistic efforts. Pederson's project dovetailed neatly with that, and it was adopted, coaxed along, and underwritten by the congregation.

In spite of the aid rendered by a bulwark of established Christianity, Pederson has little complimentary to say about the church. He often alludes to churchgoers as the "religious folk" chastised and condemned by Jesus. Nevertheless, he does continue to receive financial support from quite a few church Christians. His castigation of the church ignores the fact that his survival can be attributed to the establishment, but it blends neatly with his fabricated revolutionary self-image: "My ideas seem to be so radical and far out in left field that they're totally unacceptable to any of the religious world" (p. 70).

The union between the *HFP* and organized Christianity was brief and somewhat stormy. The bone of contention was not Pederson's idea of Christian presence on the streets through the underground media but the *HFP*'s intellectual level. The church's objection was only to the paper's shallow and simplistic treatment of the gospel and its ramifications. Pederson disagreed, claiming the simple, undecorated, unexpanded message, "Jesus Loves You," was all the *HFP* needed. Pederson, with the assistance of Lawrence Young, a printer and long-time ally of evangelical causes in the Los Angeles area, garnered enough financial support to set up shop on his own.

The controversy over the intellectual and cultural level of the *HFP* has plagued Pederson since direct relations with Hollywood Presbyterian were severed. Repeatedly phrasing his articles in what he supposes to be the language of the street, Pederson sees the particular ministry of the *HFP* as aimed at the drug culture. This purpose accounts for its teeny-bopper quality: "We gear our thing to the dope scene, and this is, according to all statistics, in the junior high and high school age bracket." About the continued criticism of the paper's admitted low level, Pederson says, "I'm not concerned about that because each one of us has a different ministry, and I feel our ministry is where it's at and encourage anyone else to do what they should do."

If the *HFP* is where it's at, it is at the "Jesus is the Answer, now what was the question?" level. Crassly, Pederson capitalizes on the issues of the day. One issue blares, "Free the Prisoners," but there is no mention of the implied subject — the plight of American prisoners of war. The article is devoid of any concern for social issues at all. The plea is for individual salvation for prisoners of sin. The fundamentalist aversion to the hated social gospel and refusal to involve oneself in social problems except on an evangelistic basis is further evident in another misleading headline. "How Moral is War" skirts the problem of war for Christian ethics by purposely ignoring it: "Nope we're not talking about Viet Nam, we're talking about personal warfare inside of the individual. Dig?"

The *HFP* is filled with endless streams of unexplained slogans awkwardly strung together to form copy. "Jesus Is Better Than Hash," one article proclaims, and goes on to propose the ever-present Christ-is-the-Answer solution to the "nitty gritty fragmentation we experience on the inside":

> Well, we're not rapping about positive thinking or playing religious games. Nope. That's just as phony as the drug trip. We're rapping about a Person — Jesus Christ. And if you can dig Him (that means to depend on Him to put your head together) then you're in for some heavy surprises!! He'll turn you on to a spiritual high for the rest of forever.

Perhaps the most common phrases in the *HFP*'s evangelical sloganeering are those dealing with "spiritual ecology." Man's arch-nemesis is "soul pollution" begotten of his own evil desires: "The point is, God creates perfection; man creates pollution. Why? Because man's on an ego trip and God is not. Dig?" Admittedly, neither concern for social issues

76

instead of the gospel nor deeply philosophical treatises on the ontological status of man's existence should characterize a newspaper to be used for evangelistic purposes. But the imbalanced, misleading, and simplistic presentation of (in Pederson's words) "only one creed: Jesus Christ" without accompanying doctrines and responsibilities is no more than a half-truth. It leads to a nondiscriminating acceptance of all things claiming a Christian label — as seen in the slogan, "If You Don't Dig the Jesus People, You Can Bet Your Eternal Life You Don't Know Jesus" — and damages the development of viable programs for concerted Christian action in social issues.

HFP's simplistic evangelism has been emulated by a myriad of Jesus People newspapers. Yet few (an exception is the unabashed *HFP* imitation by the San Diego-based *Logos*) are as disjointed and as shallow as that from Hollywood. The *Maranatha* from Vancouver has included some articles on social issues of interest to the counter-culture (e.g., "Year of the Pig," "The Revolutionary System"), and, although total integration of Christianity and culture is not achieved (articles are commonly bisected into problem and Christian solution), the mere mention of social ills is a welcome relief from *HFP*'s fixation with the magnificence of "dig?" *Truth* from Spokane, Washington; *Goad,* the *Stars and Stripes* of the Jesus People's Army; and even the obscure but cleverly titled *Fish Rapper* all display more depth, more integration, more ability with the English language than does their Hollywood ancestor. Also in a higher class than *HFP* are *For Real* in Los Angeles, *Street Level* in Milwaukee, and *The Ichthus,* billed as the paper of the East Coast Jesus People, in Cherry Hill, New Jersey.

Perhaps the best of the Jesus papers is Hollywood Presbyterian's sequel to *HFP, The Alternative,* though the characterization of the staff as Jesus People is both uncomfortable (to them) and misleading. Its essential purpose is to present the gospel in intellectual and cultural terms in sufficient depth to be at home in the university. *The Alternative* talks of Francis Schaeffer and C. S. Lewis, men unread by and unfamiliar to most of the movement and its media. The newspapers of the revolution dismiss such mental exercise as "man's wisdom." For them the creed is Jesus. Nothing more need be said.

In an effort to expand his ministry, Pederson has endeavored to establish training programs for the souls won through the evangelism of *HFP*. He founded the Jesus People Church, Inc., for the purpose, according to an article in *Truth* (March 1971), of giving "a tax exemption to his efforts in the Jesus movement." Though Pederson is harshly critical of established religion, and in fact claims the most vehement opposition to his efforts has come from the major denominations, he is quite willing to take the tax shelter offered by incorporation as a religious body. The *Truth* article goes on to note that the Jesus People Church "has ordained five ministers empowered by the state to perform marriages and function as do ministers of long established denominations."

Other Pederson efforts have not been as successful as the *HFP*. Advertised prominently in its pages is the apparently nonexistent Hollywood Free University. A staff member admitted that the entire scheme was totally unknown to him. Nor could he tell us much about the recently established Jesus People Training Centers listed in the *HFP*. Though claiming that the sessions dealt with various Bible topics, Pederson's associate was at a loss to list the topic covered in even one of the sessions and admitted that attendance was only five to seven people per session.

The most successful subsidiary of the *HFP,* and one that is crucial to its financial life, is a mail order poster and bumper-sticker shop known as the Emporium, operated by a young convert who supports himself by collecting unemployment checks. For some time the sale of "One Way" posters, "I'm High on the Love of My Jesus" bumper stickers, and a few photographic blowups of the smiling visage of Duane Pederson augmented donations and kept the *HFP*'s head above water. The mounting costs accompanying the increase in circulation, however, have been a burden that the Emporium thus far has been unable to bear. A letter recently circulated from headquarters asked those who had purchased material to consider either purchasing more or simply mailing a donation, a sign that all is not well. Finances are a sore spot with Pederson; he characterizes things only as "very tight," a trait, he claims, of all young organizations.

An important dimension of Pederson's impact on Hollywood is the series of Jesus concerts that he promotes in the Hollywood Palladium. These popular and well-attended rallies appeal to both Jesus Freaks and church youth. Pederson's role is that of emcee and evangelist. He has played a similar role at Jesus festivals elsewhere in California and other states. Next to his paper these concerts are his most successful venture.

Duane Pederson has been and will continue to be a crucial figure in the Jesus Movement. He is closer to the image of the Jesus Freak — in attitude, not appearance — than is Arthur Blessitt. Pederson admits to a charismatic experience, a subject not mentioned by Blessitt. References to the apocalypse are sprinkled through the *HFP,* a subject missing in the hip sermons of the Minister of Sunset Strip. Pederson, however, has been out-"Jesus Peopled" by the following to which he proudly points as the measure of his success. Though charismatic, he is not as charismatic as most; though convinced that these are the end times, he is less convinced than most; though anti-established church, he ordains preachers. Still, the *Hollywood Free Paper,* with few exceptions, is viewed as the newspaper of the Jesus Movement, and Duane Pederson is its leader.

* * *

The message of the Jesus People in Hollywood is not confined to the biweekly collections of spiritual epithets produced by Pederson and his staff. There are many mouths in many places answering every question with the single reply — "Jesus." There is a marked revival in the time-worn but until recently declining practice of tract-passing. Perhaps the most effective, clever, and talented figure in the movement is singer and composer Larry Norman. Norman, who is in his mid-twenties, has been composing for more than fourteen years. He is much closer in appearance to the media-formed image of the Jesus Freak than either Pederson or Blessitt. But despite his long blond hair and ersatz Uncle Sam clothing complete with red, white, and blue shoes and pullover shirts with stars and stripes, Norman lacks the bubbling enthusiasm often assumed to be a common trait. He admits this lack of feverish emotionalism readily — "I've always lived by my mind not my emotions" — and feels no need to effect a more effusive manner. His stage performances are criticized by some as being somewhat snobbish; what passes as snobbery, however, is often but a collected calmness lacking in other musical groups of the movement.

After a career in popular rock that included a million seller ("I Love You" with People) and an offer (declined) to play the lead in the Los Angeles version of *Hair,* Norman began singing Jesus music of his own composition at Hollywood Presbyterian's Salt Company. He was soon rising rapidly as the poet laureate of the Revolution. His association with Hollywood Presbyterian was a close one, but a gentleman's quarrel over the emphasis of his songs caused the partnership to split and the participants to go their separate ways. The dissolution came as a result of a piece specially composed by Norman for a march and rally sponsored by the church. The song, "Right Here in America," is concerned with persecution of Christians in places like Cuba, Russia, and China, but the point is

> *And to think it might happen right here in America.*
> *I know you think it's not true,*
> *But it's happening to Christians right here in America.*
> *Wait till it happens to you.*

The church's objection was to the harshly anti-church sentiment Norman expressed in the words:

> *I'm addressing this song to the church,*
> *'Cause I've been to your churches and sat in your pews,*
> *And heard sermons on just how much money you'll*
>   *need for the year,*
> *And I've heard you make reference to Mexicans,*
>   *Chinamen, Niggers and Jews;*
> *And I gather you wish we would all disappear;*
> *And you call yourselves Christians when really you're not,*
> *You're living your life as you please.*

The church and Norman determined that each was emphasizing a different theme, and they severed the tacit union between them. The departure, however, was friendly, as attested by Norman's continued residence in a church-owned home across the street from the church complex.

80

Larry Norman

Norman's music reflects — with less shoddiness and repetition — some of the same characteristics seen in the *HFP*. Still, on occasion, his lyrics display the over-simplification that typifies Pederson's efforts. "Stop marching for peace and start marching for Jesus/And peace will take care of itself" is quite parallel both in method and in tone to the *HFP*.

Many of Norman's compositions are thoughtful and appealing to those on the fringes of the counter-culture. Perhaps his best is "Forget Your Hexagram":

> *Forget your hexagram — you'll soon feel fine.*
> *Stop looking at the stars;*
> *You don't live under the signs.*
> *Don't mess with gypsies*
> *Or have your fortune read.*
> *Keep your table on the floor*
> *And don't listen to the dead.*
> *You can't hitchhike your way to heaven.*

Many of his songs reflect the common concern among the movement with the nearness of the end times. "I Wish We'd All Been Ready" is a cut that appears on both of his albums, "Upon This Rock" and "Street Level."

> *A man and wife asleep in bed,*
> *She hears a noise and turns her head.*
> *He's gone.*
> *I wish we'd all been ready. . . .*
> *There's no time to change your mind;*
> *The Son has come and you've been left behind.*

Norman is a good musician, though he has been criticized as being somewhat imitative. Both his albums sell well among record-buying segments of the movement. In general, they are well-executed examples of evangelical Christianity in the garb of contemporary music.

In addition to his musical message, Norman writes an occasional column in the *Hollywood Free Paper*. Set off markedly in tone, content, and grammar from the rest, Norman's copy raises questions that seem beyond either Pederson or Blessitt:

> Why are we who are in the movement, so quick to encourage the act of conversion and then consistently neglect follow up? If we do not provide fellowship during the first few months of growth, the convert's hope in Jesus often dissolves or is displaced by lack of direction. And if we allow new Christians to fall away a first time, it will be difficult to renew them to repentance a second time. Is there no burden within the established church for the movement of street Christians, the Jesus People, the Jesus Freaks? Where are the workers and elders needed to help the new flock grow strong and scripturally sound? (*HFP*, Vol. 3, Issue 10, p. 4).

In both his prose and musical poetry Larry Norman is mature, perceptive, and aware of the movement's shortcomings as well as its strengths. Still, he is recognized by most Jesus People as a leader of the movement, though he seems a bit uncomfortable with the fame that his talents have brought him. His reputation is more widespread than Pederson's, and he is probably as widely known as Arthur Blessitt. He is Hollywood's most talented Jesus spokesman, and the movement at large is hard-pressed to duplicate his ability.

While Norman is the movement's premiere musical figure, virtually every coffee house and church has its indigenous musical attraction. Guitar-playing and singing are as popular among the Jesus People as they are in the youth culture as a whole. The better performers are invited to the Jesus festivals. Some of the groups featured in Duane Pederson's programs are Phoenix Sunshine, Harvest Flight, Dove Sounds, Philharmonic, and The Open Door. A couple of the top performers are jazz-style pianist Tom Howard of Minneapolis and the hard-rock combo, Ron Salisbury and the J. C. Power Outlet. Salisbury, a Nazarene college student, has a mature understanding of the possibilities and needs of the Jesus Revolution. Calvary Chapel of Costa Mesa sponsors a large number of Jesus rock groups of varying quality, the best among them being the Love Song and Children of the Day. The Chapel is now releasing records that feature several of the groups. Even the Alamos have a record featuring their orchestra and best singers. The Children of God include some of the best Jesus musicians, but record companies have refused to give them contracts, according to the Children, because of the virulently anti-establishment content of their lyrics.

four

THE HIP CHURCH

The Making of a New Establishment

DISENCHANTMENT WITH THE ESTABLISHED CHURCH IS, AS WE have noted, a hallmark of the Jesus Movement. Disenchantment is, in fact, a mild word to describe the feelings of groups like the Children of God toward organized religion in general. They commonly use four-letter words to convey their disdain for anyone and anything associated with even the off-beat varieties of organizations designed to channel and facilitate man's worship of the Almighty. These structures of men, they say, are not only obsolescent, but downright displeasing to the God who is not confined by the pious hypocrisy of the establishment.

While few groups are as vociferous in expressing this as the Children of God, all Jesus People share the feeling that the established churches have lost significant contact with the Jesus of the New Testament, or at least have failed to communicate the gospel, especially to the young. The church is viewed as just another social organization with a facade of piety whose main task is the care and feeding of drowsy, apathetic members who are nothing more than copies of their non-church-going, establishment-oriented neighbors. These church-conscious citizens may frequent the local church on Sunday morning instead of the nearby country club, but they are just as far removed from the life-transforming Jesus as their friends

84

on the greens. They are doped on a lifeless church routine: sing the hymns, listen to the preacher, pay the tithe, and go home. Next week: repeat performance. "It's a drag, man." So say the Jesus People.

* * *

Some of the Jesus People have discovered and left their imprint on a new kind of undenominational "hip" church. One of the first and most widely publicized of these new-breed churches is Calvary Chapel of Costa Mesa (actually located in Santa Ana, California). The story of Calvary Chapel is likely to produce envy in the heart of any evangelical pastor concerned with that much-discussed segment of the population, "today's youth." For Calvary Chapel is perhaps the most successful attempt in America today to accommodate the diverse needs and spiritual searchings of the youthful products of the counter-culture — all within the framework of traditional, church-oriented evangelicalism. However, Calvary Chapel is far from traditional in many crucial ways.

In the late sixties a group of fairly ordinary adults who had been meeting on Sunday afternoons with the Rev. Charles Smith for Bible study purchased a plot of ground in Santa Ana with a school building on it. In 1969 the present sanctuary was constructed on the old school site with the labor of young people and some adults. On the Wednesday night before the windows were installed, a dozen young people met in the unfinished building for the first Bible study. A little more than two years later, during the summer of 1971, more than a thousand people, most of them under twenty-one, had joined the original dozen for a typical Wednesday night Young People's Bible Study. And the same kind of phenomenal attendance is in evidence on Monday, Tuesday, and Friday nights as well — the evenings devoted primarily to the spiritual feeding of the church's young people.

People have come to Calvary Chapel — sometimes from hundreds of miles away — primarily to see the Jesus People and "what the Lord is doing" in this part of Southern California. Since the church has been featured in major articles in *Look* and *Time* and on at least one network telecast, it has

85

become something of a tourist attraction within the evangelical subculture, and its pastor has become a celebrity of sorts.

Chuck Smith is a balding, personable man in his mid-forties with an infectious smile. He looks more like the traditional corner grocer than the pastor of a hip congregation that (some say) numbers in the thousands. (Outsiders seem more interested in numbers than do members of the staff, so it is almost impossible to find accurate statistics of membership, attendance, conversions, and baptisms. An older member of the church told us that as many as 150 converts are added to the church weekly. Pastor Smith told a TV audience that upward of five hundred young people a month are baptized in services held at nearby Corona del Mar beach.)

Sunday morning services are held in triplicate, with Smith speaking at all three. Attendance at the first two services is four or five hundred. The eleven o'clock service regularly overflows into an adjoining outside patio. To get a seat inside the building on Sunday night, the would-be worshipper is advised to bring his supper in a sack and stake out his sanctuary spot well in advance of the 7:00 p.m. starting time. The seating capacity of the main sanctuary is approximately 425, and on Sunday night the overflow patio crowd of several hundred sit on backless benches under the open sky or stand around the edges of the assemblage.

The midweek Bible studies are a fire marshal's nightmare and a Jesus Freak's dream. Not only are the pews packed with the faithful, but the aisles and any other available spaces are filled with young bodies, many of whom sit cramped for an hour or more before the service begins reading their Bibles, quietly chatting with friends, and checking out the most interesting looking members of the opposite sex who file into the chapel. Most of the midweek attenders appear to be in junior and senior high. There is a sprinkling of straight adults in the audience.

The young people are attired in the garb of middle-class California casual types: long dresses, levis, football jerseys, T shirts (some with "One Way" inscribed on the back), patched blue jeans, and hot pants. Nearly all carry a Bible. The format of the service varies little from night to night, and the music is a combination of old-time choruses and the new hip evangel-

A new convert and Chuck Smith

ical sound. The entire youthful congregation joins in singing "Pass It On" or a similar song that often includes swaying with the music, arms interlocked. Individual soloists perform, accompanied by a guitar, and share music received "from the Spirit." Some of the musical groups — like Country Faith and Blessed Hope — are somewhat more enthusiastically received and enliven the tempo of the evening. As each song ends, members of the audience point their forefinger heavenward in the Christian sign meaning that there is only one way and it is through Jesus Christ. After approximately two hours of music and testimony, the Bible study begins. In another forty-five minutes or so the meeting is dismissed, and the young people go to their Orange County homes — or to Christian communes.

These youth meetings combine 1950-vintage Youth for Christ rallies with 1970 rock festivals. The jargon of the hip youth culture is pervasive: words like "heavy," "right on," "far out," and "for sure" are as prevalent as long hair and tie-dyed shirts. Yet our impression was that these young people are more earnest and sincere than their predecessors. It is hard to conceive of a Youth for Christ rally a couple of

87

decades ago in which a majority of the audience would have sat for hours waiting for a very simple Bible study to be conducted and for the charismatic gifts to be demonstrated.

For some — perhaps many — of these youths Calvary Chapel represents a kind of social center and a place where the action is. But beneath the typical adolescent exterior, one cannot help detecting a seriousness about their spiritual search. Many first-time visitors to Calvary Chapel remark about the atmosphere of love and acceptance. Along with the power of the Holy Spirit, this climate is credited by nearly everyone associated with the church as explaining its success. Smith feels that other churches have failed the youth generation by their rigidity and insistence on old ways and patterns that do not communicate to today's kids. He stresses the need to flow, to change, to adapt. The truth of the gospel remains the same, he says, "It's just put on new garments."

From the very beginning the church was a spiritual haven for those whose life style included long hair, beards, beads, and headbands. "We're not all supposed to be thrown into hell because we are different or odd or weird," says assistant pastor L. E. Romaine. "So whatever God sends in the back door — homosexuals, bisexuals, hippies, or straights — we tell them about the love of Jesus and that he died for them because they're worthwhile."

The garb of the new hippie converts was too much for some of the oldsters in the early days of Calvary Chapel. One is reported to have denounced the long-hairs because their bare feet were getting the carpet dirty and their levi rivets were scratching the pews. When Smith sided with the street people, some of the straight people left the church. Today shoulder-length locks and braless teeny-boppers cause hardly a stir among the straight adults who have remained to become pillars of the church, especially financial pillars.

Regardless of their background, hang-up, or attire, young people are accepted by the adults at Calvary Chapel, and, in turn, they love and respect those adults. "They're liable to hug you to death," says Romaine, who came to Calvary Chapel after twenty-three years in the military service. "I walked in here with my military white side walls and encountered more long-hairs and beards in six months than I'd seen in years.

88

Overflowing love: a baptismal embrace

They hugged me and threw their arms around me. They didn't
know who I was; their love just overflows." This kind of behavior is characteristic of the developing hip church. The people are flexible not only about the clothes considered proper
for worship, but about demonstrating Christian love for their
brothers and sisters. Before or after a service it is not unusual
to see individuals rush up and hug one another as well as
shake hands in "soul" fashion.

Smaller groups of believers sometimes meet following concerts or public meetings for informal, devotional gatherings
called "afterglow" services. Often they will form a big circle,
heads lifted upward, softly singing and praying. After closing
into a tightly packed prayer huddle or concluding the session
with reverent singing of the Lord's Prayer, small groups slowly
scatter or cluster off to the side, some speaking softly, others
laughing joyously. To them, Jesus is "so heavy man, it's
beautiful."

They have no hang-ups about touching each other. To some
critics, this type of emotional response smacks of an evangelical encounter group for lonely people. That observation may
not be altogether incorrect, for the participants say that they
have found a community to which they can belong. They have
encountered the person of Christ and are no longer lonely.

89

Romaine explains, "They were looking for something, and the amazing thing is that what the hippies were searching for and, in fact, expounding is the thing the church has, love — the love of the Lord Jesus Christ."

To provide an atmosphere of Christian nurture and a place to live for the many homeless street people who found Christ at Calvary Chapel, Smith and the church began establishing Christian communal houses in the area. These houses have become a form of missionary outreach into the community. They maintain an open door policy: any skeptical policeman is invited to come in any time. Not all outsiders can be convinced that the houses are not centers for sin. We talked with a middle-aged mother near an exit of Calvary Chapel one night. She was looking for her runaway daughter who she was certain had been taken in by these people. As far as she was concerned, these co-ed houses were simply convenient fronts for sex orgies.

Those who are familiar with the Mansion Messiah, Philadelphia House, and the rest of the houses know otherwise. A Calvary spokesman makes it clear: "They are Christian houses for young people who are trying to get established in the Word." Members stay an average of two to six months. Each house has an elder in charge (usually in his mid-twenties), assisted by several deacons "that the Lord is raising up." Many young people have left the houses to establish similar communes elsewhere. Sometimes they are sent out in groups of eight or ten as they are "led by the Lord."

Police officers occasionally find it difficult to believe that some of the converts have indeed left their old ways. Occasionally, Smith or another staff member is asked to assist in matters of cop-commune relations. One morning at 2 a.m. the police were making a routine search for a runaway. Everyone was lined up, arms against the wall. One girl glanced at the investigators and said, "You know, officer, Jesus loves you and I do too." The police know that the young people are serious when they say things like that; yet they do not quite know how to respond to ex-dopers who are now carrying Bibles and rapping about Jesus. For the most part, however, relations with the police department and neighbors are cordial, and problems encountered by the houses are minor.

There are many more straight people, young and old, attending Calvary Chapel now than in the past. The street people are still there, but one is left with the impression that most of the young members are from middle- and upper middle-class Southern California suburbia. Most of them live at home with their parents, two or three cars, a backyard barbecue, a dog, and maybe a pool. They are attractive — clean, well clothed and fed, and, in the summertime, well tanned. This is a far cry from the crowd at the Christian Foundation of Tony and Susan Alamo.

The mood in the new establishment is summarized well in words of a song familiar to anyone who has heard Love Song, one of the excellent musical groups associated with Calvary Chapel:

> *Little country church on the edge of town —*
> *Do-Do-Do-Do-Do-Do-Do —*
> *People comin' everyday for miles around*
> *For meetin's and for Sunday school.*
>
> *And it's very plain to see*
> *It's not the way it used to be.*
>
> *Preacher isn't talkin' 'bout religion no more;*
> *He just wants to praise the Lord.*
> *People aren't as stuffy as they were before;*
> *They just want to praise the Lord.*
>
> *They're talkin' 'bout revival and the need for love;*
> *That little church has come alive,*
> *Workin' with each other for the common good,*
> *Puttin' all the past aside.*
> *Long hair, short hair, some coats and ties,*
> *People finally comin' around.*
> *Lookin' past the hair and straight into the eyes,*
> *People finally comin' around.*

The picturesque waters of Corona del Mar State Beach have been the location of some of the most widely publicized baptismal services in all of the Jesus Movement. Each month hundreds of converts (and an occasional bystander who suddenly feels the urge to take the plunge) participate in this informal and inspiring rite. The attitude of Smith and his staff toward water baptism would make most evangelicals blanch. They view the act itself quite seriously, but the mechanics of mass-production immersion at these services manifests the

91

Personal attention during mass baptism

hang-loose approach typical of the hip church. There are no instructional sessions preparatory to water baptism. The pastor and other staff members informally remind the people that if they have accepted Christ as Savior and if God has "laid it upon your heart to be baptized," then "the Scriptural thing to do is to be baptized." The church offers no baptism class and no membership class. "We don't have a class for membership because membership to this body is accepting Jesus Christ as your personal Lord and Savior."

Reportedly, as many as a thousand people have been baptized in a single service (some attired in bikinis, as *Time*'s photographers were quick to discover). Often people from other churches will join in the mass baptismals. Despite the apparent mob scene, the staff insists that each candidate is personally "ministered unto." At the outset of an ocean baptismal, Smith makes a few introductory remarks. As the candidates enter the water, they are told individually the sig-

92

nificance of what they are about to do and the "scriptural under-writing" for it. "So the instruction is on a personal basis, which is better than sitting in a class. . . . This is what the people are looking for, a freedom from that box."

Occasionally, one of the ministers will encounter a candidate who has never accepted Christ. He is returned, unbaptized, to dry land and encouraged to talk to someone who can introduce him to Christ. If this seaside evangelism is successful, the convert returns to the water once again for the now-sanctioned baptism. We talked to a girl who went to a baptismal service to observe, but then on impulse "felt led" to be baptized. She admitted that she never attended Calvary Chapel before or after the beach baptism.

One of the star attractions at Calvary Chapel is Youth Minister Lonnie Frisbee, whose conversion we mentioned in chapter one. He has played a central role in the accelerating youth ministry of the church. On the nights when he preaches, many people feel that Calvary Chapel takes on a more dynamic evangelistic and charismatic tone than on other nights. Frisbee seems more preoccupied than the other pastors with charismatic manifestations, and one gets the distinct impression that he is more or less "kept in line" by the older staff members. Soul-winning is his chief vocation. One sometimes gets the feeling when talking to him that he is not at all interested in one as a person, only as another potential convert. If he determines that the person he is talking to is already a believer, his main concern is to have him experience the Baptism of the Spirit and speak in tongues.

In October 1971 Frisbee announced that he was leaving Calvary Chapel and California. His immediate plans are to join Bob Mumford, a popular, Florida-based charismatic teacher for a period of intensive Bible study.

Most of the people at Calvary Chapel emphasize the tongues experience less than Frisbee. For them, as their weekly bulletin proclaims,

> . . . the only true basis of Christian fellowship is His love, which is greater than any differences we possess and without which we have no right to claim ourselves Christians. We look for His love in our lives as the supreme manifestation that we have truly been worshipping Him.

Those words are more than mere rhetoric on a church bulletin. At Calvary Chapel they are the essence of the corporate Christian experience. If any single word could characterize the mystique that is Calvary Chapel, it would be "love," Christian love.

Will Calvary Chapel change as it grows larger? A new sanctuary seating 3300 is under construction. Will an impersonality inevitably accompany this growth? Although God's Holy Spirit is clearly providing guidance at Calvary Chapel, the very human persons who comprise the congregation will surely have to confront the issue of size as this prime example of the hip church pioneers the making of a new establishment.

* * *

Another example of the emerging hip church is Bethel Tabernacle, in a lower middle-class neighborhood of North Redondo Beach, California, housed in an unimposing structure that looks very much like a Kingdom Hall of the Jehovah's Witnesses. Over the main entrance to the simple, rather small building is a neon sign proclaiming "Bethel Tabernacle." Another neon sign over a second door reads "Full Gospel." This church is the spiritual birthplace of literally hundreds of teen-aged runaways and youthful participants in the drug scene. It has received nationwide attention in the media, including a feature article in the February 9, 1971, issue of *Look* magazine.

From the inside, the building looks more like an enlarged Quonset hut than a church sanctuary. Simple electrical fixtures are suspended from the ceiling, and acoustical tile partially covers the walls. Several hundred old movie-theater type seats, drooping forward from decades of use, are fastened to the linoleum-covered floor. The aisles, the raised platform, and the front of the sanctuary are covered with a fading red carpet. The pulpit furniture, four chairs in Danish modern decor, seems strangely out of place. Behind an older, plain wood pulpit stands a small table containing miscellaneous paper, an overflowing Kleenex box, and an aerosol can of insect repellent. On the plain communion table in front of the platform stands a vase of garishly colored artificial flowers. On the wall behind the platform hangs a crude wooden cross constructed of old timbers formerly used as vehicle stops in the church parking lot.

The appearance of the sanctuary on a weekday afternoon is

94

somewhat untidy. Scattered over the floor are an abandoned sandal, a well-worn moccasin, pieces of paper, and other small items. Lying about the auditorium are tambourines, which are used to add zest to the strongly evangelistic services. From time to time during the afternoon, young people amble into the church, some of them entering prayer rooms in a section of the building behind the main sanctuary that houses Sunday School classrooms. On any given afternoon several young parishioners can be heard praying in tongues in these various rooms. Others merely wander into the sanctuary to use the pay phone in the tiny narthex. Some of the young people apparently come to the church to pick up personal mail. The incongruous spot where such mail is left, along with other church mail, is on the pulpit, a popular rendezvous for the casually attired youth who seem to use the church as a kind of hangout.

Bethel Tabernacle is a substitute home for literally scores of ex-dopers and young transients who have encountered the zealous missionaries from this hip church. Now their lives revolve around the activities of the church. Bethel's leaders stress total commitment to Christ. Those fully committed are described as "one hundred percenters" and constitute the "spiritual core" of the church. They are expected to attend all the officially scheduled services: Tuesday, Wednesday, Friday and Saturday nights, and twice on Sundays. On the other nights of the week, they go out as witness teams anywhere within a twenty-mile radius of the church, not to distribute gospel literature, but to hand out little cards with the name, address, and phone number of the church and information about services.

The young man responsible for the influx of hippies and the new style of evangelistic outreach in the church is Breck Stevens, its twenty-year-old assistant pastor. The story of Stevens' conversion and previous activities follows a familiar Jesus People pattern. Coming from a Catholic background, he rebelled against church, parents, and society. At sixteen he left home to become a hippie. He used all kinds of drugs (including heroin), experimented in witchcraft, pushed dope for a year, and was finally jailed. One night while he was strung out on drugs, a woman came up to him and said, "Jesus loves you," and gave him a card directing him to a Teen Challenge center. Through the ministry of that organization, he was converted in a Huntington Beach coffee shop in 1968 and returned home to be reconciled with his parents. He stumbled across a listing for Bethel Tabernacle in a telephone book, visited the church, and was immediately impressed with the pastor, Lyle W. Steenis.

According to Stevens, Brother Steenis preached "full surrender, holy living, total commitment, fasting, prayer, Bible reading, and witnessing," a no-nonsense approach that appealed to Stevens. After a few visits, he asked if he could bring some hippies to Bethel. He brought twenty-one long-hairs the next week, and at the end of the service all of them came forward to receive Christ. This marked the beginning of a new era for this old-time Pentecostal church and was a turning-point in Steenis' twenty-five-year ministry. Hippie types started to stream into the little white church in Redondo Beach, but the adult congregation did not rise up and call them blessed. In fact, some of the members went out into the parking lot and tried to run them off. The pastor sided with the hippies ("I'll whip the next guy who tries to run them out") and announced to his congregation: "Those doors swing both ways. If you don't like what's going on here, you can leave the church." More than two hundred adults did just that. As Stevens tells it, they were "gospel-hardened," and didn't have a "burden for souls." Not hippie souls, in any event.

The young people kept coming, twenty-five to a hundred per night. In a few years' time thousands have encountered the ministry of Bethel Tabernacle. Between five and thirty youth are converted at every service, though Stevens admits that many "fall away." Hundreds of runaway kids have been returned home, in accordance with the law. Those who have jumped probation and AWOLs from the service turn themselves in. Drug addicts (Stevens estimates that eighty-five percent of the young people at Bethel Tabernacle have used drugs) are "delivered" immediately from their habits, with no withdrawal symptoms.

It is not difficult for the new converts to come off drugs and stay off, according to Stevens, but the temptation to commit sexual sin is another matter. The biggest hang-up of youth today is premarital sex, he says, and the people at Bethel do their best to avoid it. "Many young people still have a sex problem, even though they carry a Bible and love Christ."

96

Contact between the sexes is strongly discouraged by the church leaders. "The kids here don't have time for dates" — which is understandable in that they are expected to go to church six times a week, witness whenever possible, and spend an hour or two each day in prayer, in addition to attending school or working or both.

Other Jesus People are criticized by the Bethel leadership for what they see as a disturbing preoccupation with physical contact between boys and girls. Embraces, whether for reasons of spiritual ecstasy or otherwise, are not permitted at Bethel. Commenting on a widely distributed TV documentary on the Jesus People, Stevens exclaimed: "These ministers of God on television in front of forty million viewers hugging girls after baptizing them! The Bible says it's good for a man not to touch a woman." (In his thinking, this proscribes holding hands until marriage.)

Girls may come to church barefooted and dressed in jeans, but no miniskirts are permitted. Anyway, Stevens explains, "God tells a person how to dress; we don't have time." Young people at Bethel "are not interested in impressing anyone with looks or fashion." Nor are they ever tempted to take a sip of wine or beer. "No one in this church wants anything to do with it."

If they have little time to date, they have even less time to watch television. "Sometimes it'll take new converts a couple of weeks to get off their television. After a month or so, they're so busy they don't have time for sin." The same goes for movies, dancing, and comic books. "Idle time is the devil's workshop — we believe that," asserts the youthful assistant pastor.

The Bethel ministers also teach that Jesus rock music is not biblical. They point to $5000-worth of "psychedelic albums and Jesus rock music" that has been discarded in a huge pile in one corner of the church. This music has been thrown away "not because they've been told they have to, but because God lays it on their heart." What's wrong with folk music and Jesus rock? "Singing was never used in the early church or by the apostles to spread the Gospel." Congregational singing in the context of a service of praise and worship presents no problems. But folk and rock groups are not allowable means of witness and Christian entertainment. Stevens, who once played the guitar himself, feels that a person can be caught up in the emo-

97

tionalism of the music and thus be prevented from having a true spiritual experience.

Another reservation that Stevens expressed vis-à-vis the Jesus Movement is the prevalence of hip jargon in a spiritual context. He does not like the use of such language, for "it lowers Christ to a worldly level. Jesus is not a cool cat; He's not hip; God's not groovy." Also, he is bothered by cartoons and the indications of commercialism in the Jesus newspapers. "We're going to have a few wolves in the Jesus Movement who want to make money and take advantage of sincere young people."

Strict adherence to the Bible is the name of the game for this strongly charismatic church. All nine gifts of the Spirit are said to be in operation in accordance with scriptural patterns. Personal evangelism in the simple old-time way is the chief mission. The people at Bethel have no desire to join with other groups or churches in the movement for combined rallies. Again, it is pointed out that the New Testament does not prescribe such joint ventures. It is recognized that other groups have particular ministries that God is using, including the Billy Graham Evangelistic Association. But when it comes right down to it, the Bethel people have little interest in what is happening beyond their own sphere of witness. "God has given us a ministry here — we don't have time to think about other places."

* * *

The Sierra Madre Congregational Church in Sierra Madre, California, is a fairly traditional church that has "come alive" in the Jesus Revolution that is bringing renewal to many older, established churches. It has been well respected over the years in its quiet suburban town near Pasadena of twelve thousand conservative Californians. Despite its stability as a community institution, the church's history has been marked by theological turmoil and congregational upheaval. Before the Rev. Richard J. Anderson arrived in the spring of 1968, many parishioners conceded that the church was dying. Attendance at Sunday morning worship services was about sixty-five, and the youth group was holding seances and experimenting with Ouija boards. Agnostics were teaching Sunday School, and the content of the upper grades curriculum was more political than theological. The orientation of the church had been largely social action.

98

Anderson described his new congregation as a "very desperate group of people" who wanted to know about Jesus Christ. "They asked me when I came to teach them who Jesus Christ was, how to study the Bible, and how to pray."

This church, especially its pastor, has had an amazingly effective ministry to local hippies and other young people during the past year or two. The nearby Sierra Madre Canyon has been a Bohemian enclave for more than two decades. As the drug culture began to spread in the early sixties, the canyon became known throughout the San Gabriel Valley as a center of it. Many of the canyon hippies were living in cars and campers, and some have broken into the church and slept in the Scout room. Others have come to the church asking for food and clothing. Anderson has provided blankets and clothes and has bought them food or given them a hot meal. Sometimes he has had a person's car repaired and has paid for it.

These acts of kindness and Christian love led to a new and challenging ministry for the young pastor. He began to visit the canyon on a strictly informal basis, sometimes being invited into a house or commune. Several of the canyon residents expressed a desire to hear some Jesus music. With a dozen Jesus People Anderson presented an informal concert in a garage equipped with $3000-worth of sound equipment. The response was remarkable. People who had been on hard drugs were dramatically converted to Jesus Christ.

Anderson and several other people in the area have formed Refuge in Jesus, a corporation apart from the church that tries to combine the efforts of a number of churches and individuals in a joint ministry to the canyon people and other young transients in the community. Every night it sponsors Bible study in a public park across the street from Anderson's church. Between thirty and sixty people attend these informal sessions, with the number swelling to well over one hundred for special concerts.

Sunday morning attendance has grown to about three hundred. Even on warm summer Sundays, the church is filled to capacity. Although there are far more adults present than at a similar service in Calvary Chapel or Bethel Tabernacle, there are always a sizable number of local street people and canyon hippies. Several "street urchins" (Anderson's term for eleven- to thirteen-year-olds who are essentially homeless) are usually

99

there, too. Most of these young wanderers come from broken homes in town, and occasionally some of them will break into the church during the week.

Anderson is articulate and extremely personable. One observes similar behavior here as in Calvary Chapel. Says Pastor Anderson: "I embrace anyone who's at the door. A lot of them are older people, and I don't mind this at all. It's very genuine, like meeting a relative. At our concerts this has happened too — a kind of a melting together of people."

His informality is reflected in the worship services. "I like a certain amount of form, but in terms of communicating, I sometimes walk right down in the middle of the congregation and talk to people right across the pew. Anything that really helps to communicate, I'm for." Commenting on the worship service, Anderson says: "People tell me, and I sense it too, that there is a spirit of love and informality here. There's also a spirit of dignity. God is here and you feel awestruck by His presence."

Anderson says that he is not terribly interested in the institutional church or its future — a statement that would make many of his colleagues cringe. His life is clearly not tied to a denomination and its retirement program. And he feels that any church, traditional or otherwise, can benefit from the Jesus Movement if it is "open to learn things in the New Testament that we've always kind of brushed over and to receive all that the Holy Spirit is doing today." Such a church will be caught up with what is happening, he says, and it will be like catching a wave and riding it in. "I sense a tremendous ground swell of the moving of God's Spirit and I think anyone who wants to go with it can, Catholic or Protestant. I think it's possible to get very negative toward it and fearful and in a sense to have it pass you by — sitting on your board out at sea."

Anderson is frequently asked whether the Jesus Movement is real or just a passing fad. He is emphatic in his response that the Jesus People he has encountered are sincere and more committed than most older Christians who ask about the sincerity of the young people.

> I compare the commitment of these young people whom I know very well with what I have known in young people over a twenty-five-year period of working with youth. I am so much more delighted with the intensity, the ability, the love of Scrip-

ture, the zeal, the stability, and the gentleness of these Jesus People. I am so deeply impressed that I don't spend time worrying whether it will last.

The Sierra Madre Congregational Church is not as well known — in terms of the Jesus Movement — as Calvary Chapel and Bethel Tabernacle. Indeed, it is a slightly less clear-cut example of the emerging hip church. But it does demonstrate the possibility of ministering to the counter-culture without minimizing other, more traditional functions of the church. It could serve as a prototype for future youth ministries by conservative churches reluctant to emulate the almost exclusive youth orientation of Calvary Chapel and Bethel Tabernacle.

five

THE CHRISTIAN WORLD LIBERATION FRONT

Old Wine in the New Left

DESPITE ITS NAME AND ITS AFFINITY FOR THE HIP SUBCULTURE that has flourished in the San Francisco Bay Area since the heyday of Haight-Ashbury, the Christian World Liberation Front is not just another radical leftist group in some kind of Christian disguise. It is in fact far removed from the New Left in many respects.

The Christian World Liberation Front is an organization of evangelical Christians with a unique ministry to the street people of Berkeley and the students of the University of California campus there. It was one of the first groups identified as Jesus People and Jesus Freaks by the press. In July 1969 the organization began an underground newspaper called *Right On*, the first and, many observers feel, the best Jesus paper. Employing the hip vernacular of the street people, the paper brings the revolutionary message of Jesus Christ to a population of radicals, activists, dopers, and ordinary university students — a subculture overlooked and often scorned by many churches and straight Christians.

In addition to publishing the newspaper, CWLF is engaged in an extensive literature ministry including pamphlets, tracts, leaflets, and comic books, as well as manuals like a freshman orientation handbook designed for students and a medical

102

handbook that details basic first aid techniques and discusses how to plan a nutritious diet on a shoestring budget. All of the literature contains the same simple message of the gospel of Jesus conveyed in the hip language so familiar to members of the youth culture. An excerpt from *The 2nd Letter to the Street Christians* conveys the flavor of their hip version of Scripture:

> Dig it! God has really laid a heavy love on us! He calls us His children and we are! The world system doesn't recognize that we're His children because it doesn't know Him. Right on, brothers and sisters, we *are* God's children even though we're a long way from being what He's going to make us. Don't get hooked on the ego-tripping world system. Anybody who loves that system, doesn't really love God. For this whole gig — the craze for sex, the desire to love everything that looks good, and the false security of believing you can take care of yourself — doesn't come from our Father but from the evil world system itself. That world system is going to be gone some day and along with it, all desire for what it has to offer; but anyone who follows God's plan for his life will live forever. (Dig it! This whole plastic bag is exactly what Jesus liberated us from.)

The CWLF feels that the liabilities of such rewriting of the Bible — the loss of the subtlety and beauty of the language and the estrangement of the Jesus People from historic Christianity — are outweighed by its great asset — the possibility of direct communication of the gospel to the hip subculture.

After the politically radical Berkeley Liberation Movement distributed a pamphlet describing its aims and objectives in revolutionary jargon, the CWLF published a pamphlet of their own. Identical in size and format, the two pamphlets were a universe apart in content. The frontispiece of the leftist pamphlet featured an illustration of Chairman Mao and leaves of a marijuana plant along with the quotation: "Let a hundred flowers bloom." The equivalent page in the CWLF pamphlet contained a sketch of the head of Christ and a quotation from him: "You will know the truth and the truth will set you free." Both pamphlets listed a thirteen-point platform. Side by side, they read very similarly:

Berkeley *Liberation Program*	*New Berkeley* *Liberation Program*
1. We will make Telegraph Avenue and the South Campus a strategic free territory for revolution.	1. He will free all who come to Him from bondage to the crippled self, the maimed world, and the scheming devil.
2. We will create our revolutionary culture everywhere.	2. He will enable all who come to Him to develop their inner talents, abilities and resources to the fullest.
3. We will turn the schools into training grounds for liberators.	3. He will turn the schools into training grounds for liberation of the inner self.
4. We will destroy the university unless it serves the people.	4. He will destroy the powers that bind us as we turn to Him, the only One who truly serves the people.
5. We will struggle for the full liberation of women as a necessary part of the revolutionary process.	5. He will provide for the full liberation of men and women as a necessary part of the revolutionary process of building His family.
6. We will take command responsibility for basic human needs.	6. He will take responsibility for basic human needs.
7. We will protect and expand our drug culture.	7. He will make drugs obsolete.
8. We will break the power of the landlords and provide beautiful housing for everyone.	8. He will bring a new spirit of concern and cooperation among people who turn to Him and trust Him for moment by moment direction.
9. We will tax the corporations, not the working people.	9. He will continue to show His concern for the poor and oppressed people of the world.
10. We will defend ourselves against law and order.	10. He will eliminate fear of tyrannical forces and powers.
11. We will create a soulful socialism in Berkeley.	11. He will create a soulful Christianity in Berkeley.

104

NCLE SAM · ESUS WANTS YO

CWLF banner at a peace march

12. We will create a people's government.

12. He will govern perfectly.

13. We will unite with other movements throughout the world to destroy this racist-capitalist-imperialist system.

13. He will unite Berkeley Christians with others throughout the world to demonstrate His alternative to the present world system in all of its manifold manifestations.

While the radicals shout, "All power to the people," the Jesus People proclaim, "All power through Jesus." At a Ho Chi Minh memorial service sponsored by leftists, the usual shout of "Ho, Ho, Ho Chi Minh, the NLF Is Gonna Win!" echoed from the crowd. From the voices of a small group of Street Christians came another chant: "Ho, Ho, Ho Chi Minh, Jesus Christ Is Gonna Win!" At a peace march and rally in April 1971, CWLF distributed a special edition of *Right On* and other Christian literature to most of the 150,000 participants. In addition, CWLF set up a free Kool-Aid stand for the thirsty marchers, marked by a sign that read: "Whoever drinks of this water will thirst again: but whoever drinks of the water that I'll give him will never thirst — Jesus Christ."

The rhetoric and evangelistic methodology of CWLF have been immensely effective and have brought considerable publicity to the Berkeley Jesus People. But their activities extend beyond the dispensing of a cup of Kool-Aid in his name or the street corner distribution of *Right On*. Their concern for man goes beyond the individual conversion experience, as essential as that is. They offer help to distraught drug users and have been involved in a free food distribution program. They have provided hospitality in Jesus' name to hundreds of homeless and friendless young people. They have established crash pads for kids off the street and recently opened a Christian youth hostel on famed Telegraph Avenue. For $1.50, young people can spend the night, eat a hot breakfast, and talk with Christian workers if they wish.

In addition, CWLF operates several houses (they prefer that term to "commune") in the Bay Area with names like Agape House and House of Pergamos. In addition to providing a place for transient youth to sleep, these houses are residential way stations for many new converts. Some are run by older Christian couples who provide a family setting for those who often have never known what a real family is like. Many of the young people come from broken homes and have never really experienced friendship. What they really need most of all is a Christian family, and the houses provide just that — Christian friends and Christian community. Some stay for only brief periods; others stay for several months and then go to another part of the country, often to establish a similar ministry; still others stay on to become a part of the permanent CWLF staff.

CWLF also sponsors a ranch for young Christians called Rising Son Ranch. It is located in the mountains far to the north of San Francisco near the largest concentration of hippie communes in the West. While the ranch does have an evangelistic outreach to these neighboring communes, its main purpose is to enable young Christians from the Berkeley area to "get out of the scene and enable them to grow in Christ, to really dig their roots down into Him." Three married couples are on the staff there, "real strong Christians." They spend their time

106

conducting Bible raps and generally helping the young people "get their heads together." The young people work on the ranch and are welcome to stay as long as they wish.

Most staff members feel that street people who accept Christ tend to settle down and establish roots rather than continue to wander about. "Street Christians" are babes in Christ who are "still into the [hip] scene someplace." As they mature in their Christian faith, they continue to break the ties with their former way of life. Not that they become "establishment" or cut their hair, but they do change their life style noticeably. Teen-agers who have come to Berkeley for a summer and become enamored with the whole scene are encouraged by the CWLF staff to return home, especially if they are still in school.

Almost every night of the week, CWLF-sponsored Bible raps are held throughout the Berkeley area, often in the various Christian houses. On weekday afternoons, staff members conduct Bible seminars on the university campus. This growing teaching ministry of CWLF is singled out by staff workers as one of the most pressing problems. With large numbers of new Christians in the community, the lack of sufficient qualified teachers is keenly felt. Local churches could be of assistance, staff people say, "but most church people don't want to dirty their hands because of preconceived characteristics of the hip subculture."

* * *

The CWLF has its beginnings in the work of Jack Sparks, an Indiana farm boy with impeccable establishment credentials — a bachelor's degree from Purdue and a master's and doctorate from Michigan State. He taught statistics at Penn State, where he was associated with Campus Crusade. Some time during the fall of 1968 he and his wife, along with several other Christian couples, began to feel a need to get through to the youth culture of America, especially the more radical segment of that culture epitomized by the Berkeley scene.

Under the auspices of Campus Crusade, Sparks and his wife and three other couples — Pat and Karry Matrisciana, Fred and Jan Dyson, Weldon and Barbara Hartenburg — moved to Berkeley to initiate a pilot project. They spent time on campus, talked with people, and began to pray that God would show them how to be relevant, how to share with people, how to make a Christian impact on the cutting edge of the counter-culture. Sparks explains in the March 1971 issue of *Vanguard*: "We have sought to drop into the lifestyle of the changing youth culture and — insofar as we see that culture not violating biblical standards — to adopt the culture and thereby have an increased opportunity to build a body of believers" (p. 22).

Adopt the culture he did! He let his hair and beard grow, lost about twenty pounds, and began dressing in jeans and work shirts. Those who know him well say his attitudes have changed, too. He used to be very academic and introspective. No more. His intimates say he is "for real," not just dressing up to play some phony role. He is a sincere, humble man of vision, with a sense of urgency.

When Sparks dropped into the hip Berkeley scene, he dropped out of the straight world of Campus Crusade. He and his associates felt a need to be free from the Campus Crusade bureaucracy and to develop a particular kind of literature suited to the specialized ethos of Berkeley. And an establishment-sounding organization like Campus Crusade did not go over well in Berkeley.

On the other hand, CWLF did not go over well with some of Sparks' friends back East. He lost considerable financial support from individuals disenchanted with his revolutionary rhetoric and hip life style:

> An old and dear friend from Pennsylvania called me aside this summer and said, "You're cutting yourself off from the good people of America. The way you live and your hairstyle and your dress and the kinds of activities that you're carrying on are cutting you off from the people who are the backbone of this country, and I'm no longer able to support you if you continue that." I said, "I'm sorry I have to disagree with you, but biblically I can't support your stand and I have to continue the way I am." And this was a man who had been supporting us extensively (*Vanguard*, March 1971, p. 22).

While the "good people of America" may have deserted him, his organization continues to grow. The bills are paid and salaries met (most of the time). Financial support comes from individuals and some churches familiar with the work of CWLF, who believe that Sparks is on the right track in the way he seeks "to be God's people in Berkeley and to truly represent Him right here, regardless of what that might mean to people from without."

CWLF does not attempt to saturate evangelical churches around the country with their representatives. Sparks takes few speaking engagements, although staff members occasionally minister in local churches. "One of the things we try to avoid here is building men into names. We try to spread our leadership, build up our younger people."

One of the established churches working most closely with CWLF is the Walnut Creek Presbyterian Church, which sponsors a kind of auxiliary called Friends of CWLF. A shopkeeper who attends the church sometimes has a few CWLF girls model clothes at a fashion show for members and friends of the church. The girls are given opportunity to share personal testimonies and relate the ministry of the CWLF. This kind of bridging of the gap between straight and hip is all too rare in the Jesus Movement.

Probably straight Christians are most confused by the CWLF's use of revolutionary-sounding language and hip jargon. Even the organization's name, Christian World Liberation Front, is an obvious takeoff on the name of the radical Third World Liberation Front. The CWLF has no problem with this: "Jesus liberates and the world needs Jesus. The entire world needs liberating; so what's more fitting than Christian World Liberation Front?" They have no qualms about using rhetoric and jargon familiar to those in the hip and radical scenes so that the culture-free gospel of Jesus Christ can be disseminated. "What's truly needed is the sense of the power of people getting into a cultural context and being God's people there," says Sparks.

Some outsiders accuse CWLF of espousing liberal and radical political causes. Actually the organization bends over backward to avoid any kind of political label. As an organization it is clearly apolitical, though individual staff members are free to align themselves with any socio-political orientation that they wish. The staff admits that the youth associated with CWLF tend to be more liberal than conservative; the same is probably true of most of the permanent staff.

In an interview in the *Wittenberg Door,* Sparks was asked: "How much do you align with radical concerns?"

> That is not an easy question to answer. Because that depends on every situation. Every situation must be evaluated in itself, with respect to many of the problems that the political radicals see with American society. And I'm really with them because the problems are indeed there. But I can't align myself with their solution. And this is where, quite often, we get called counter-revolutionary around here. And we are counter-revolutionary. It took me a long time to find out that we really were counter-revolutionary. You see, I've always thought of counter-revolutionary as someone who is against the people who are into the revolutionary thing. But this isn't really true. That is, that isn't the only thing. If what you're into contributes to the build up of a violent revolution, then you're a revolutionary. But we're talking with people about love and peace and a relationship with God. And that's counter-revolutionary. And so, they're right when they call us that. . . . We can have common cause with respect to specific issues, but we cannot ally ourselves with anybody who needs a platform. And so, because of that, nobody is satisfied with us. The conservatives aren't satisfied because we don't ally ourselves with their political platform. The liberals aren't, the radicals aren't — nobody is. And that's the way it must be (August 1971, p. 9).

On the other hand, an article in the August 1971 *Ramparts* tried to link CWLF with right-wing causes. The author had spent several hours with CWLF people, and "he kept trying to pin us with some sort of right-wing thing." He attempted, unsuccessfully, to get a statement that CWLF accepted financial support from several well-known wealthy rightists. The *Ramparts* article pointed out that CWLF, along with other Jesus People in the Bay Area, did demonstrate at a West Coast conference of the Students for a Democratic Society and that they were bodily evicted from the session. CWLF also demonstrated at the Russian Center in San Francisco over persecution in Czechoslovakia. They have been seen picketing the topless-bottomless fleshpots of San Francisco's notorious North Beach district, and they have joined other Jesus People to picket Glide Memorial Methodist Church in downtown San Francisco, noted for its homosexual weddings and unorthodox worship services or "celebrations."

110

In May 1971 a group of CWLF young people joined members of a Presbyterian band of Jesus People known as the United Presbyterian Liberation Front (UPLF) to demonstrate in behalf of personal evangelism and discipleship training at the 183rd United Presbyterian General Assembly in Rochester, New York. During the one-week conclave, singer Larry Norman and members of UPLF appeared on radio programs and presented two Christian rock concerts. The UPLF appeared before various committees, passed out leaflets, and made a twenty-minute presentation before the entire Assembly.

Such militant excursions are not the main thrust of CWLF's work, however. It is the ministry in the Christian houses, the teaching ministry on- and off-campus, and the distribution of *Right On* and other printed materials that make up the bulk of their activities.

Right On appears to be increasingly directed at the large Berkeley population of college students rather than at the street people. As Jesus papers go, it is unquestionably the most solid in content and intellectual in appeal. Unlike other underground papers in the Jesus Movement, it publishes thought-provoking, substantive articles on current issues from war to women's lib. The evangelistic appeal is there too, of course, but so are well-written movie reviews.

CWLF increasingly sees the need for emphasizing content and instruction; so they are establishing a tape and book library. CWLF may possibly develop into something like L'Abri, Francis Schaeffer's Swiss retreat house that has gained renown as a "mission to intellectuals." Sparks has visited L'Abri. There is also talk of instituting a Christian "Counter University" in Berkeley, offering courses in various disciplines taught by Christian professors who would present Christian perspective as an alternate to the overwhelmingly secular orientation of the University of California.

The editors of *Right On* reflect the educational level of the policy-making staff of the CWLF. David Gill was a history major at the University of California and holds a master's degree from San Francisco State; Sharon Gallagher is a graduate of Westmont College and a sociology major. All of the policy-making staff are college graduates; some hold advanced

111

The staff of "Right On"

degrees. That places CWLF in a different category from all of the other Jesus groups we have discussed.

Another characteristic which distinguishes CWLF from most Jesus People is that they are not charismatic in orientation and teaching. CWLF has no official stand on the question of tongues-speaking and related phenomena. There is no official encouragement to seek speaking in tongues, though the experience is recognized as a valid spiritual gift, a tolerance lacking in many evangelical churches outside the Jesus Movement. States one staff worker: "There are brothers and sisters who speak in tongues who come to our meetings. Fine. If they start laying their trip on us, that everybody needs to, we'll show them from Scripture that it's not so."

We have repeatedly observed that Jesus People are disaffected from the organized church. While many of the people who are

112

part of CWLF share these misgivings and questions about the role of organized religion, most attend traditional churches occasionally, some regularly. Whatever their individual practice, all would probably agree that real fellowship takes place not in formal, structured services or meetings, but in the life-to-life relationship of brothers and sisters who have compassion for each other. This kind of fellowship, as Jack Sparks puts it,

> . . . begins with brothers and sisters who meet together and collectively put themselves on the line of being salt and light in the context they live in. I suppose that that could happen within a church. . . . I do not think that the kinds of meetings which are now held in lecture halls [church sanctuaries] will last in this country. . . . That is not where the fellowship and worship is going to go on (*Wittenberg Door*, August 1971, p. 15).

CWLF actively supported a Billy Graham Crusade. To entice members of the youth culture to go to hear this establishment evangelist, widely known for his friendships with U.S. Presidents, the First Presbyterian Church of Berkeley and CWLF formed a "Committee to Investigate Billy Graham." Each night of the Crusade they chartered a bus to transport young people from Telegraph Avenue to the Oakland Coliseum and back.

CWLF has had little success in the area of a witness to minority groups. Like Jesus People everywhere, CWLF counts very few Blacks among its ranks. This has been a source of concern and embarrassment. A former office of the organization was situated in the middle of a ghetto, yet virtually no Blacks responded. Some Puerto Rican Americans transplanted from New York City and several Mexican-Americans are part of the CWLF community.

While the rest of the evangelical world looks on in quiet amazement or with raised eyebrows, the Christian World Liberation Front is busy going about its business of bringing men and women into "the Father's Forever Family." Our judgment is that it has an edge on other Jesus groups in terms of intellectual and spiritual maturity. It is an organization to watch as future chapters in the story of the Jesus People unfold. Sparks summed it up well: "We have really sought to be God's people in this place and we're trusting Him to open up the creativity of us and the kids that we work with to demonstrate His love and His concern for the people who live here."

six

THE REVOLUTION MOBILIZES

Jesus People on the Move

ALTHOUGH THE JESUS PEOPLE ARE NATIONAL NEWS, MOST COM-munities are without a Jesus People outpost. The movement clearly bears the stamp of California. The Jesus Revolution is only the latest of several manifestations of the youth culture spawned in the Golden State. It may be the case that, culturally speaking, as California goes, so goes the nation. But not right away — and not without some modification, usually moderation.

The Jesus People label is probably more widely dispersed than the Jesus People themselves. The label has a romantic popularity among many Christian young people who would like to share in the sense of being on the cutting edge of the youth culture, so they adopt the label without realizing what it originally referred to. An example of this kind of appropriation may be seen in *The Ichthus,* which calls itself the paper published by The East Coast Jesus People. It employs words like *ethos* and *catalytic,* words much too sophisticated for Jesus Freaks.

> We speak from the viewpoint of historic Christianity. We comment on the world we live in and its activities in light of our beliefs, and attempt to articulate the good news of Jesus Christ as it relates to the problems of life in the second half of the 20th century (June 1971, p. 1).

115

That is a far cry from the simple gospel approach of most Jesus papers. In our opinion, it is a far superior outlook, but it is not an accurate reflection of the Jesus Movement.

One widespread effect of the Jesus People and the publicity they have received from the media is that an outspoken witness for Christ has gained a new social acceptability. Being an old-fashioned, Bible-believing Christian is no longer a source of embarrassment or shame. Peer pressure is no longer adamantly against it. There is a new freedom to witness. It used to demand courage to speak out; now it is much easier, especially if those who do so describe themselves as part of the spiritual revolution treated respectfully in the secular press. This new social acceptability of bearing a public and outspoken witness for Christ is one of the best effects of the Jesus Revolution. In the long run, it may be *the* best effect.

In this chapter we shall examine the enclaves of Jesus Freaks outside of California that seem to us the most important ones. Like the rest of the counter-culture, Jesus People are notoriously transient. Bases of operation open and close with dismaying rapidity. Papers are often published irregularly. Even communes quickly come and quickly go.

We shall restrict ourselves here to ministries that seem to us clearly to deserve the Jesus People label. Our focus will be on some of the more stable works, ones that seem to have a good chance of staying around for a while. Ministries that seem to us to belong on the fringes of the movement will be discussed in chapter seven. Here our intention is to give a sense of the diversity now developing on the national scene.

* * *

Duane Pederson's book, *Jesus People,* dashed off with the help of Bob Owen, is of little value for the history of the movement except as a chronicle of the *Hollywood Free Paper.* Pederson does make two references to the origins of the movement: a lengthy recounting of how he christened the then-nameless collection of long-haired Christians "the Jesus People," and an obscure reference to what he takes to be the movement's human originator — Linda Meissner of Seattle: "As far as I am able to determine, it began as the Holy Spirit began to work through a gal named Linda Meissner in the Seattle area" (p. 83).

Despite Pederson's fleeting attention to Seattle and its prophetess, Linda Meissner cannot be so easily or quickly dismissed. This Joan of Arc of the Jesus People's Army was no mere imitator of what went on in Hollywood. There were similarities in abundance. Slogans, techniques, style — virtually all of the action in Seattle meshed neatly with the Pederson-Blessitt Hollywood scene. But this seems to have been spontaneous rather than imitative. Meissner was in America's streets while Pederson was still pulling rabbits from hats. Further, she knew more of street life than he, and though she cannot deliver herself of the kind of flashy rhetoric that Blessitt's picturesque spiritual anecdotes use, her experiences were far closer to the street world than the quick incursions into the world of sin of the "Minister of Sunset Strip."

To be sure, Meissner's newly pledged allegiance to the Children of God (see chapter two) clouds the picture in Seattle and, indeed, the whole Pacific Northwest. Still, the revolutionary faction that she began has shaped the movement's growth in important ways. Her story caught the fancy of many local leaders of the revolution, and the Seattle contingent has been imitated for both good and bad largely out of attraction for Meissner and her claim of supernatural authority. Because of this, the road traveled by Seattle and its leader is perhaps a clue to the path that the revolution may take in many of its now scattered manifestations.

Meissner's story begins, like Pederson's and Blessitt's, in rural America. "I was raised on an Iowa farm, drove tractors, milked cows, and dressed chickens." Her family attended a "modernist Methodist church" where she was taught that "God was somewhere 40,000 miles away and, of course, the days of miracles were over." In what is an almost standard conversion account, her rendition includes the early crisis and the spiritual solution:

> . . . through a crisis of my mother's illness, in which she almost died, I cried out to God — "if there's a God, come to me" — and I had a real born-again experience. . . . As a result of this I discovered at least one teeny miracle: I knew God wasn't 40,000 miles up in the sky.

Meissner's disenchantment with the established church (though she still claimed to attend her "local assembly" until joining the Children) was much earlier than either Pederson's or Blessitt's and apparently can be traced to the modernism of her younger years. Her introduction to the world of Christian activism came at the hands of David Wilkerson and Teen Challenge in New York City. Wilkerson's program in the then unexplored wilderness of the drug world gave her the kind of awareness of the world of the street that still eludes some self-appointed Jesus People leaders. Further, the secularism of the city convinced her of the reality of the supernatural:

> God wasn't dead after all, the days of miracles were not over, heroin addicts did come clean, were totally delivered, prostitutes and skeletons were made into brand new people. It happened a few times and we saw it happen again and again. It was beautiful. I was living in a small Book of Acts again in my New York City days.

Through sojourns in the West Indies, Mexico, and finally in Hong Kong, Meissner's burden for America's hip generation became unbearable, and her disaffection with the institutional church grew. "Something began to happen to me inside, and as a straight little darling, I began to turn into a revolutionary." Meissner returned to the States, but not without a direct visitation from God that overcame her hesitancy to leave Hong Kong. The story, as she tells it, is one of the few detailed recountings of the spiritual beginnings of the movement:

> I told him I wanted to stay down there and help those people because they were so sick they couldn't go to doctors. Not like Americans, they have a sore throat or something, they were really sick. And I thought God could heal them (I wasn't a faith healer) but I didn't know what to do . . . and I wanted to stay there. And God said, "By whose spirit?" In a very distinct manner he talked to me. He said if you were the greatest speaker in the world, one person alone could never get the job done. And if everyone you prayed for were healed, one person alone could not get the job done. And he said you come back to Seattle, Washington, and by yourself . . . be obedient to what I tell you. I will raise up a mighty army of young people, and you'll go forth and speak the words of life, and he said they'll all go forth and bring healing to the people.

Though she did not know what the future held, she returned.

God spoke to her again in Phoenix, Arizona, while she was brushing her teeth:

> I knew I had to pick up a piece of paper and write. These are the words that came: We are in a time of war, time when the spirit of the Antichrist is about and in and out. How can there be any doubt that the coming of the Lord is nigh? Even now, the Spirit has groaned and sighed. Hear their cry, hear their cry, a hundred million people dying. Who doth go against Satan's blow, who doth know, who doth know? Arise, behold the earthquake. Alarm. Alarm. Do no harm. Which way? Which way? Behold a bridegroom cometh. Go out and meet him. Yet empty-handed while thousands thirst far below, none of my grace to know. Ah, the pain, the pain of death, the death eternally separated from God. Fear not, my little ones, thou shalt be the forerunners, thou shalt go across the earth, great newsbearers. Day Star. Amazed, amazed that I should know these that thou bestow.

Still the fledgling prophetess hesitated, perhaps uncertain because of the somewhat garbled content of the revelation. But after a year and a half of struggling with her spiritual call (marked by the constant intervention of verbal messages from heaven), Meissner relented. "When I was really sure that I had really heard from God and it wasn't any brainstorm, I walked into the city of Seattle, Washington, alone."

She was not alone long. She began groundwork for the revolution that she was soon to lead. As a traveling evangelist Meissner crisscrossed the city, speaking at local churches and school assemblies. The charismatic character of the movement showed itself from the beginning. After relating that "anywhere from fifty to seventy-five percent of the audience would accept Christ," she says of her evangelistic success at various speaking engagements: "And of course with this came a great outpouring of the charismatic renewal, and I saw massive numbers receive the Baptism of the Holy Spirit. Seventy-five, fifty at a time. One hundred at a time, whatever." The year 1967 was spent literally sharing the vision and planting the revolutionary seeds, but even then Meissner began to attract a following of "street people who had been converted." She engaged in a slow but steady recruitment of the Jesus People's Army. Though her efforts at evangelism went on full-time through 1968, her following had not expanded beyond a small group of long-

119

haired associates with whom she met for Bible study and prayer.

The birth of the Jesus People's Army in 1969 signaled the beginning of the prophesied spiritual revolution:

> By 1969 we had what we called the Corps. There can be no spiritual revolution without a Spiritual Revolution Corps, and I began to see that there was a little group that began to come together, to work together. . . . People began to come to me in that year and say, "You are working too hard. Is there anything I can do to help?" I contacted a few friends I had . . . and told them I would be at such and such tonight, and they'd pack the place out.

Still short of followers (she admits, "We didn't have any workers"), the movement began to spiral, especially in Seattle's schools. With typical revolutionary verve and in characteristic language, she describes the revolution's sweep through the classroom, ". . . prayer meetings began to be organized in the school. The Bible began to hit the high schools; it was very, very heavy."

Since the heavy appearance of the Bible in Seattle Lincoln High School, the revival has, in Meissner's estimation, "spread like wildfire." It is impossible to trace the direction of the flow of influence, whether north to south or south to north, after 1969. Before the birth of the Corps, Meissner was virtually unknown outside Seattle and Hollywood was being evangelized only by Arthur Blessitt and the Alamos. It seems doubtful that either city's evangelists were known to their opposite numbers. Meissner still knows nothing of the Christian Foundation, and both she and Blessitt were obscure before they were offered the public relations help of the media.

The year 1969 was a critical year for Jesus People. Hollywood was suddenly flooded by experiments in hip Christianity — the Salt Company and Larry Norman were on the rise, the *Hollywood Free Paper* first appeared in the streets, His Place was in the spotlight, and the Alamos were on the move. Seattle, too, was replete with replacements for institutionalized Christianity. In addition to the explosion of converts and charisma at Lincoln High School, the Seattle version of the Salt Company — known as the Catacombs — opened its doors to an average of two thousand a week (Meissner's own estimate), communal
120

houses were founded, and the newspaper *Agape* published its first edition — just after the initial appearance of *Right On*.

Prophets of both kingdoms, north and south, are hesitant to admit the possibility of cross-fertilization. To almost everyone bearing the name and claiming the fame of the movement, its independent manifestation among nearly isolated individuals is the proof of its supernatural origins. To Pederson's affirmation of the divine generation of the revolution, Meissner adds:

> Then [after the revolution in Seattle was in full swing] I began to find out that there were a lot of people like me all up and down the West Coast. The same thing was happening in Portland, Berkeley, San Francisco, San Diego, and we were all taking the same steps at the same time. We all moved to commune houses together, coffee houses together, newspapers together. . . .

This divine source theory does not, however, rule out claims to originality on the part of the human leaders. Most of them, Meissner included, are well aware of chronology and point, often proudly, to revolutionary inventions that they patented just before they were simultaneously discovered by the movement at large. Blessitt has his gospel night club; Pederson his term Jesus People and his newspaper. Meissner? "We found we had the first march. We found out in Hollywood they had a march, five thousand strong. So everyone was moving in marches."

Meissner has expressed camaraderie with Jesus People elsewhere, though it is unclear how her recent enlistment with the Children of God will affect her enthusiasm. "Arthur Blessitt is a very good friend of mine. He's coming here for a city-wide rally. *Hollywood Free Paper* — I love them to death. The Christian World Liberation Front — some of my best friends in the world. Right on. David Hoyt is fantastic. My opinion of all of them that I know is really great. Yep, Jack Sparks and all of them. I love them all." The presumed spontaneity of the movement is central in Meissner's endorsement of her fellow-revolutionaries: "It seems that if any of us are moving in one direction, we're all doing the same thing at the same time. We don't have any organization to tell us that, so it's really darling."

Meissner's seeming willingness to spread the credit for the

121

revolutionary fervor was but a meager attempt to hide the factionalism, jealousies, and conflicts that had come to plague the Jesus People's Army. Along with the authority she had from her claimed theophany, Meissner had given the JPA an extremely authoritarian structure that made it plain that she was the chosen vessel for the Northwest. In 1970 the tranquil acceptance of this structure was shattered by the rise of a handful of elders unwilling to bow to her superiority. The most significant of the JPA's young Turks was Russ Griggs, a doctor's son and a commune organizer in Vancouver, who began to challenge Meissner's authority.

The battle for the allegiance of Seattle's and of Northwest's long-haired Christian soldiers soon stripped Meissner of her unquestioning cadre of followers. She succeeded in propagating the picture of the JPA as one revolutionary force united under her banner, for she was known throughout the movement as the captain of Seattle. The decision of Meissner and Griggs to join the Children exposed the divisions buried by her "we are one in the Spirit" verbiage. Few of the JPA's soldiers followed her to the Children of God. Tacoma, long listed by her as a personal satellite, was totally unaffected by her abdication.

Still, Meissner's departure has by no means unified the Seattle movement of the JPA. Seattle-area churches have organized the Seattle Presbytery, a steering group of twenty to thirty charismatic pastors, in an effort to stabilize the erstwhile JPA and salvage what is left of Meissner's once glorious revolution. The Presbytery is destined to run into difficulties. Meissner claims ownership of *Truth West* (a sequel to *Agape*), but that claim is hotly disputed by her one-time followers. She continues to receive donations earmarked for the JPA, but, as might be expected, the money has found its way to the Children of God. Naturally, incensed cries of foul are heard throughout Seattle.

The Children of God hope to capitalize on Meissner's fame and take over the JPA as a whole. It is doubtful that they will succeed, for Meissner's influence seems weaker than was previously imagined. Still, the recruitment of her by the Children is a significant feather in their communal cap, and their inroads in Seattle and Vancouver have been major. Whether the rest of the Pacific Northwest will follow the Meissner lead as slavishly as it once did — or at least seemed to — remains to be seen. The best guess is that it will not.

* * *

Perhaps the best insurance against a blitzkrieg of the Northwest by the Children of God is Carl Parks, the commander of the JPA's legions in Spokane, Yakima, and Walla Walla, Washington, and Coeur d'Alene, Idaho. Parks has attracted a sizable following in Spokane and the surrounding area; but, despite his leadership role, he is not engaged in building a Jesus People empire. His own story has some similarities to the conversion of Tony Alamo. Holding a job that was rapidly making him wealthy, Parks sensed an urging from God to resign his position or lose his salvation. His decision was not long in coming: in the face of a promotion that would have vaulted him into the upper echelons of his company, Parks chose "not religion but total surrender to Christ." But Parks' experience differs significantly from both Alamo's and Meissner's. At the time of his calling, he was a lifelong Christian who, by his own admission, "had never rebelled against God," but who paradoxically had "done everything you can name." Nor was the divine message to him a theophany; and this lack of direct verbal exchange with God still characterizes Parks' life, an absence that he good-naturedly dismisses as inconsequential.

What did happen to Parks was apparently sufficient: he determined to live only by God's leading. The somewhat mystical character of that resignation to the divine call is apparent in his account of the beginnings of his ministry to Spokane's hip community: "I walked out the door; and my wife asked me where I was going, and I said, 'I really don't know. I'm just going to see if the Lord leads.'" The ministry began in what Parks characterized as "an opium den." Excited by the seeming willingness of the den's resident heads to listen to his "no heavy rap" presentation of the gospel, Parks began to frequent the place and soon had attracted a following.

Parks denies that there was any outside influence — from Seattle or elsewhere — in his early activity. Characteristically, he claims an independent and spontaneous use of his ministry. That claim is no doubt genuine, but the isolation of Parks' little band was short-lived. The Spokane movement soon

123

meshed with Meissner's then small JPA, though Parks carefully maintained — and still does — his distinctions from his western counterparts. Today he is more sensitive than ever to those distinctions. He points out quite emphatically that his band is now known as Jesus Freaks, not the JPA, a change occurring since Meissner's abdication.

The most visible — and perhaps the best — product of the Parks-commanded troops is *Truth*, the corps newspaper published in Spokane. Meissner once characterized the paper as a "fantastic tool," an opinion in which Parks concurs. He explains:

> *Truth* is not just a newspaper. We actually print it with a lot of thought behind it to be used as a witnessing tool. When we explain how we print it — the psychology behind it — it becomes very much alive to them [the new recruits in the JPA] how you can go out in the streets and use the *Truth*.

Parks' contention that there is a psychological base behind *Truth*'s publication is doubtful in view of the paper's simplistic tone, which is more reminiscent of Duane Pederson and his *Free Paper* than of Marshall McLuhan and communications theory. The paper is, however, both more substantial and more dressed in true counter-cultural garb than its California counterpart. Typical of *Truth* psychology (not to mention its style) is "The Parable of the Parsley and the Acapulco Gold":

> To what can we compare the Kingdom of Heaven? . . . Do you smoke dope? Have you ever smoked bad dope? You know, full of stems, maybe mixed with parsley and catnip. Yeh, you burn your throat, and the only way you can get high is hyperventilating.
>
> Let's say you just bought a lid for fifteen bucks. Bad dope. You're sitting there, puffing away. Maybe you're getting a little high hyperventilating. Maybe you're getting a little bummed out because it's a burn.
>
> I come tripping up to you, and I have a big sack of Acapulco gold. Say it's one of those plastic garbage sacks full. And I say, "Man, if you'll just throw down that lid, I'll give you this Acapulco gold, free. It's already paid for, but the only way you can get it is to throw down your lid."
>
> What would you do?
>
> Well, that's what Jesus is saying to you. He's just saying, "Man, if you're getting a little tired of your trip, of getting burned. If you just give up your trip and accept My life, I'll

give it to you free with all the love and all the joy and all the peace that comes with it."

You know, only a fool would smoke parsley when you could have Acapulco gold (May 1971, p. 14).

Truth's readers are far more discerning than Pederson's — if one can judge from the letters to the editor. *HFP* correspondence is confined, except for occasional exchanges with the Children of God, to glowing renditions of conversion stories and the movement's triumphs. *Truth* is the object of some dissatisfaction among its circulation. The inclusion of a picture of ex-Beatle George Harrison prompted responses from several readers: "After reading your *Truth* newspaper, and one particular article about George Harrison, I find it necessary to chastise your very poor judgment in even putting his picture in your paper. Mr. Harrison sings about HIS sweet Lord 'Hari Krishna', then so that must be his Lord. It's certainly not Jesus Christ. (Praise God)" (May 1971, p. 15).

Truth frequently recounts the Jesus Movement's history. The March 1971 issue made a refreshing and unusual attempt to create historical awareness by running a brief account of the Jesuit Order by John Leira, S.J., entitled "Jesus People, 1540?" The main thrust, Parks intimates, is still personal evangelism, but there are more genuine news stories in the pages of *Truth* than in most Jesus papers. The July 1971 issue included articles of significant length by William Willoughby, who has written for *Christianity Today*. Perhaps the measure of the paper's success is the circulation figure, set at 100,000 — a figure that is more important when it is realized that in Spokane *Truth* is sold for donation, not leafleted or stacked in the Christian education buildings of turned-on churches. All in all, *Truth* is one of the best Jesus papers. It is printed in two colors, carries a wide selection of good pictures, and runs more news stories about the Jesus Movement nationwide than any of its competitors. Articles are generally well written and, for a Jesus paper, noticeably free of misspellings and grammatical *faux pas*.

The tone of *Truth* is a bit misleading when used as a gauge of Parks' revolutionary leanings. Parks' upbringing as the son of an evangelist shows through in both his theological and social outlooks. His positions on issues that are central to the revolution's dogma are, in general, more moderate than the "hard line" advocated by the Seattle movement.

The most striking difference between Parks and Meissner is over the role of spiritual gifts. Parks' position can best be described as semi-charismatic; Meissner reiterates a Pentecostal position:

> Jesus says you will receive power when the Holy Spirit comes upon you, and of course when anyone becomes born again and saved, they have the Spirit. But Jesus spoke in Matthew — rather John [the Baptist] — "I baptize you with water, but Jesus will baptize you with the Holy Spirit," showing us there are two baptisms. . . . I speak in tongues. It changed my life from a bashful farm girl to a powerful revolutionary.

Parks apparently adheres to mainstream two-baptism Pentecostalism, but soft-pedals the result. Sensitive to the divisiveness that is frequently the bedfellow of charismatic experience, Parks approves of private experiences but flatly outlaws public demonstrations: "I have experienced the gifts of the Holy Spirit. We [his group meetings] don't speak in tongues. I speak against public speaking in tongues."

Parks' ministry in Spokane is multi-faceted. Seventy disciples live in the communes: the House of Abraham for men, the House of Sarah for women, the House of David for the band, and three houses for married couples. The Voice of Elijah, Inc., operates the I Am coffee house, which claims ten to forty conversions every week, and the Jesus Free Store, which sells nothing but accepts donations in exchange for merchandise in accordance with the recipient's ability to pay. The Wilson McKinley rock band performs at the I Am and at various evangelistic outreach efforts. Once a month the whole Spokane entourage invades another town for a week-end of evangelizing. On nights when the I Am remains closed, the group gathers for several hours of Bible study taught by Parks. Always the primary activity is street-witnessing, featuring the dissemination of *Truth*.

Like Tony Alamo, Parks is not really at home among his long-haired followers, despite all of his attempts to sound hip. His social outlook is expressed in a little booklet, *A Woman's*

Sidewalk witness to straights

Life, written by his wife Sandra (and apparently not proof-read by anyone):

> Discourage any contentions between you and any of the guy's, even if they start to show it. Show them you are above that. The men in our group are for the most part not interrested in the average pretty girl. They arn't even interrested in the average Christian pretty girl. They know they need virtuous wives. A wife that will not keep their eyes off of Jesus. They want to be virtuous men. And so if you want a husband from this group you will first have to become a virtuous women.

Nevertheless, Parks' ministry is solid and has a maturity lacking in Seattle. He is willing to meet the challenge of the Children of God and has taken a group of his disciples to Los Angeles to acquaint them with the Children as brothers rather than threats. The balance and moderation of Parks' ministry and its toning down of hostility to the established church seem the best defense against the march of the Children's fanaticism. These traits also safeguard against aberrations that might otherwise be generated from within.

With the exception of the deeper inroads of the Children, the movement in the Northwest is, at this stage, quite parallel

127

to its Hollywood counterpart, particularly to Pederson and his newly incorporated Jesus People Church and Training Center. The Jesus People's Army is now officially a nonprofit corporation — Youth Outreach. The Voice of Elijah, Inc., is the title of the Spokane operation. Perhaps the structure required to maintain a nonprofit corporation will better withstand the Children's crusade.

* * *

Another locality with a strong Jesus People ministry spawned by the JPA is Milwaukee. The most direct link between Wisconsin and Seattle is Jim Palosaari, the director of Milwaukee's Jesus Christ Power House. Palosaari, following his disillusionment with the campus radical scene in San Francisco, was converted through Russ Griggs and became a prominent figure in the cluster of Seattle-Vancouver communal houses, spending his time in Meissner's Army organizing new communal barracks for the Corps. The return to Milwaukee was, according to Palosaari, a response to an unmistakable divine calling. In February 1971 Jim and his wife Sue opened the movement's first Milwaukee commune. Palosaari's apprenticeship under Meissner stood him in good stead in the Midwest.

The Power House, open six days a week for Bible study, testimonies, and occasional music from a Palosaari-organized band, The Sheep, is the Milwaukee movement's central gathering point. Palosaari's communal efforts have grown quickly, and the original handful on Frederick Street has grown to fifty disciples in two houses. The Milwaukee revolution is at once charismatic and apocalyptic. The emphasis is on tongues, but healing and other associated phenomena are frequently experienced. A favorite spiritual anecdote concerns a girl whose hearing doubled in strength: miraculously she could hear a watch from twice the normal distance.

An interesting difference between the movement in the Southern California bastion and that in the Northwest (including Milwaukee) is highlighted by Palosaari. The JPA's version of the movement is slightly removed from the Pop Christianity of Hollywood. Though the language is from the same subculture, Carl Parks' "Parsley and Acapulco Gold" (page 124 above) parallels the argot of the drug world more closely than do Pederson's "dig" and Blessitt's "I'm dealing reds." And the proliferation of posters, bumper stickers, and buttons is less prominent in JPA country. Distaste for mere sloganeering is strong in Palosaari and his disciples. Palosaari openly denounces the ever-increasing variety of Jesus decorations as "faddish" and worries aloud over the lack of training and discipline in the movement. The absence of true discipleship, says Palosaari, is endemic in Southern California, and he claims that the lack has resulted in young people being saved and then subsequently drifting back into drugs. Palosaari encourages converts to sell their goods, but does not require "forsaking all." Residents at his communes abstain from both work and education to concentrate on evangelism; but, like Meissner, he warns against abandoning surrounding society in the search for a Jesus culture. That, he says, is the movement's basic error; an isolated Jesus People simply could not last, for the continuous religious celebration that such a society would engender would soon lose its spontaneity, and the "fad" would come crashing down.

To combat the shallowness of much of the revolution, Palosaari has recently opened what is termed a "Believers' Discipleship Training School." The school is scheduled to run a forty-week gamut, alternating seven-week sessions of classwork with three-week practical exercises in witnessing and recruiting disciples on the streets of cities other than Milwaukee. The trainees are given only enough money to reach their destination for these three-week sessions and may not ask for any other money, trusting that the Lord will provide. The opening session of the school attracted seventy of Milwaukee's revolutionaries, a number that pleasantly surprised Palosaari. The Believers' Discipleship Training School is unique in the movement — no other school is in actual operation, despite the myriad of promises. Palosaari has closer working relationships with organized churches than do most Jesus People leaders, and quite a few of his trainees come from churches rather than as new recruits for his communal houses.

Milwaukee's connection with the Northwest is maintained through mailed copies of *Truth* that occasionally find their way to the streets, but more commonly *Truth* is digested, condensed, reworded, and republished in *Street Level,* "The

129

Jesus People Paper of Mid-America," edited for a time by Sue Palosaari. A former English major at San Francisco State College, she set somewhat higher editorial standards than most Jesus papers. *Street Level,* in addition to news of the Northwest, carries testimonies, announcements, and its share of advertisements, including billings for CWLF workshops and Duane Pederson's *Jesus People.* Also, there are hints — some subtle, others not so subtle — at the movement's alleged persecution. In an article in the May 1971 issue, *Street Level* vented its persecution complex:

> Milwaukee has managed to accomplish what few other American cities have been able to achieve: Freedom from Religion.
>
> If you question this statement, just pick up your phone and call the City Park people and request some of the facilities that are supposedly available to the citizenry. Put a request in, for instance, for a rally where free Jesus rock would play and testimonies would be heard from people whose lives have been changed; who were once alcoholics, addicts, prostitutes, radicals, who now want to be productive and share the love of their Savior, Jesus Christ.
>
> I believe you will receive the same reply that we did, "I'm sorry, we don't like to get involved in that sort of thing. We don't allow religion in our parks."
>
> Yes Milwaukee, keep it up and you will truly achieve Freedom from religion along with Russia, Bulgaria, and Red China.

Street Level does share the fascination of most movement journalism with simple spiritualized object lessons presented in what is said to be the language of the street. For example:

> You know there's a remedy, a cure to our world wide indigestion. It's a heavy fact to realize that we haven't made any more progress than old Adam and Eve — but when we finally wake up and take stock of the fact that we're sicker than any medicines or philosophies of clear headedness, or magic rites, or religious rituals can cure. . . . well . . . the Head Gardener is still around and He'd like you to taste of just one more fruit . . . guaranteed to cure all of the poison in your system. Non-toxic, without additives or preservatives, a pure non polluted fruit straight from the garden — Jesus Christ, the Tree of Eternally pure Life (May 1971).

Palosaari freely admits that his ministry has ties with that in Seattle; that is, he is not as concerned as some within the movement to demonstrate independent origin. Still, Palosaari and his disciples are no mere automatons. Perhaps because its leader is a "second generation" Jesus person, the Milwaukee work is more eclectic than most. Palosaari has pieced together his work — borrowing freely from his experiences in the Corps but adding bits of Hollywood and the Children of God — into a unique mix. It has a stability exceeding that of most works; and like Carl Parks' Spokane operation, it offers reason for hope for a gradually maturing and moderating Jesus People ministry.

* * *

Chicago has recently begun to feel the zeal of the revolution. The long failure of the movement to take hold there has gained the Windy City a Nineveh-like reputation among the Jesus People of Milwaukee. Chicago is *the* great mission, full of excitement, danger, and potential converts. *Street Level* trumpets the battle cry:

> One hundred years ago September Chicago went up in flames. Now once again the "city Billy Sunday couldn't shut down" is feeling the first licks of a fire that will rekindle the embers of hearts, as the Holy Spirit of God begins his searing cleansing work. . . . Chicago, maybe Billy Sunday couldn't shake you, but hold on! The Holy Spirit of God is coming soon (July 1971).

The Milwaukee revolutionaries are not, however, the first to visit the Chicago mission field. The *Hollywood Free Paper* is reproduced there, and a Jesus People Directory assembled in California lists several communes in the Chicago area for the benefit of sojourning Jesus People. Virtually all of the directory's Chicago listings, however, are erroneous. Either the premises have been vacated, or the occupants refuse to identify themselves with the Jesus Movement. The list includes the Chicago 15, a group of Roman Catholic priests and seminarians active in the Resistance; old, established ministries like the politically oriented Quaker House; and the Reba Place Fellowship, a Mennonite commune in Evanston. There are Jesus People in Chicago, not included on this list, but massive revolution is still somewhere in the future.

The Chicago ministry that most clearly fits the Jesus People

131

label is an Arthur Blessitt-like street evangelism led by Sammy Tippit, a twenty-four-year-old Southern Baptist from Louisiana. "God's Love in Action," the name chosen by Tippit and his crew of seven, lacks the showman's flair once evident in His Place, but like Blessitt's the ministry is simple gospel witnessing, nothing more. Tippit dispenses stickers like Blessitt's "reds," but bearing his own monogram instead. He concentrates his efforts on street people, though his fascination with them is markedly less than that of the Minister of Sunset Strip. A typical night's work finds Tippit donning his "God Is Love" jacket and heading for the streets of the Old Town, New Town, or the night spots on Rush Street, where he doles out his fistful of tracts and button-holes passersby.

Though he vigorously rejects the commune label, Tippit and his staff members live together in a flat in a run-down neighborhood of recently migrated Southern whites. This quasi-communal existence and their emphasis on simple evangelism are the main ties that God's Love in Action has with the movement's more revolutionary wings. Tippit is unconcerned with both tongues and the apocalypse, and neither he nor his wife Tex nor their associates come out of the counter-culture.

Tippit and three others were recently arrested for obstructing the sidewalk during a tract-passing session on Rush Street. In protest Tippit began a fast at the Civic Center and, according to reports, neither ate nor slept (if he had, a loitering charge would have been added to his record) for twenty-five days. It was all to no avail, however, as the trial (a jury trial, at his request) was scheduled for late October 1971. Already the arrest and vigil have received extensive coverage by the local news media.

The absence of a strong Jesus Movement has deprived Chicago's newspapers of what is, at present, exceedingly good copy. The void has, however, been filled; where Jesus People do not exist, they are simply invented. The labeling can produce some bizarre results. The Chicago *Tribune* has classified "The Process," a group that openly delves into the magical world of the occult, as Jesus People. Tippit's gang and the Processeans occasionally meet on the streets, and they acknowledge each other with the respect due a worthy antagonist.

The only other Chicago-area contingent of Jesus People is

132

a work in West Chicago headed by Ron Rendleman. It is essentially geared to the creation of a mature discipleship outside the auspices of the institutional church. Counting Rendleman among the Jesus People is not entirely wishful thinking, for his ministry is charismatic and he is indeed convinced of the imminent return of Christ. But despite his distaste for organized Christianity, Rendleman is not willing to cast the church totally aside. Rather, he sees a unity superseding both the evangelical subculture and revolutionary ethos: "The Lord wants the Jesus Freak on his right hand and the conservative on the left, and the left and right will break bread together." Rendleman's ownership of a farm (now used to house his disciples) and occasional employment as a television actor make him an exceptional Jesus person. Neither he nor his followers are counter-culture products. A typical disciple is a Wheaton College dropout who characterized his Alma Mater as spiritually sterile, too devoted to human learning.

In spite of Rendleman's straight-society credentials, Edward Plowman of *Christianity Today* characterizes him as a "street Christian." If Rendleman is that, he is one of the few concerned with mature discipleship, one of the even fewer who hedges his condemnation of the church, and the only one to own a farm of his own. Rendleman's chief claim to fame lies in his group's activities during a Billy Graham Crusade in Chicago. When some Satanists decided to disrupt the altar call, Rendleman and his troops confronted them politely but firmly, and successfully resisted their disruptive tactics.

* * *

Jesus People are scattered elsewhere across the nation, though other ministries seem less substantial than the ones we have discussed in this chapter. Kansas City, Missouri, has a Christian commune, the House of Agape, which houses some twenty-five disciples. Its elder is a twenty-two-year-old former drug user named David Rose, who was converted in California and later moved east to spread the good news of the revolution. Florida has a small, new string of communes organized by Don Pauly, who previously had established a cluster of communes in and around Pasadena, California, which we shall look at further in chapter eleven.

Many cities have witnessed invasions of the spiritual revolutionaries. Sacramento hosted a march on the Capitol Building in the spring of 1971 on a government-decreed Spiritual Revolution Day. Salem, Oregon, was the site of a large Sweet Jesus Prince of Peace Rock Festival. Stanford University is one of a large number of locations at which similar Jesus rallies have been staged, this one cleverly labeled the Sweet Jesus Roll Away the Stone (or Rock) Concert. San Francisco, which has some claim to being the birthplace of the whole Jesus Revolution, is not without its resident Jesus Freaks. Right in the heart of Haight-Ashbury is the flourishing Harvest House Ministries, Inc., featuring an underground paper, a health food restaurant, and several communes; it will be treated at greater length in chapter eleven.

But many corners of the nation are seldom frequented by Jesus People. Despite the coverage of America's religious press, which heralds the movement as a "shore to shore wave of witness" (*Christianity Today,* May 7, 1971, p. 39) and which describes it as "taking on the characteristics of the great revivals of the past" (*Eternity,* August 1971, p. 6), the revolution has yet to reach every village and town. The myth of the omnipresence of Jesus People is largely the creation of the movement itself with a helping hand from the media.

The greatest teller of spiritual tall tales is the *Hollywood Free Paper.* The Jesus People Directory that fills its back pages with nationwide manifestations of the movement is as inaccurate as it is long. Most of what passes in the *HFP* as bona fide revolution has moved with no forwarding address, is reported to exist at addresses that do not, or displays none of the attributes characteristic of Jesus People, knows little of the revolution, and denies its alleged membership in the movement. Many of these listings are established church-organized programs that have little in common with the movement. While not hostile toward the revolution, ministries like "The House," sponsored by a Baptist church in Wilmington, North Carolina, have had virtually no contact with the movement except through what they read in magazines.

To be sure, there are manifestations of the movement throughout the nation that are as revolutionary as any on the West Coast. The bulk, however, are outposts, like Milwaukee, of the movement's fatherland. The Children of God with their colonies now as far east as New York, Ohio, Kentucky, and Georgia are by far the most national of the revolution's subgroups. A chain of thirty-seven communes known as Shiloh Houses (see chapter eleven) is the only other organization with a similarly nationwide scope. The movement is slowly moving from west to east. Arthur Blessitt, the forerunner of the Hollywood explosion, is now on his tour of England and the world, Milwaukee's sphere of influence is expanding, Chicago is characterized by Ron Rendleman as being in the same situation in which Hollywood was two or three years ago, and the Children of God have plans for more converts and more colonies. The revolution has indeed mobilized, but the blitzkrieg of California and the Pacific Northwest has not and apparently will not be repeated.

seven

AROUND THE EDGES

Helpers, Hangers-on, and Hucksters

THE JESUS REVOLUTION, AS WE HAVE SUGGESTED, IS NOT A
monolithic collection of long-haired ex-dopers who are per-
petually high on Jesus and ready to journey to the mountain
top there to speak in tongues until the apocalypse. That image
has its flesh-and-blood counterparts, but there are also the
alienated evangelicals with hair still short, only recently intro-
duced to the world of charisma. The movement is slowly being
infiltrated by varieties of people ranging from establishment
exiles to capitalists in Jesus People clothing. None of these
are really spiritual revolutionaries, but they do make it difficult
clearly to define the limits of the Jesus Movement.

* * *

The periphery of the movement is presently supporting a
growing number of teaching ministries. The most impressive
are those headed by ex-staff members of Campus Crusade for
Christ. Several disaffected former associates of Bill Bright —
among them Jon Braun, Hal Lindsey, Bill Counts, and Gordon
Walker — share the flourishing anti-institutionalism common
to the movement, but they lack other trappings characteristic
of the Jesus People. None of these newly organized missions
is actively charismatic. Nor, Lindsey's celebrated best-seller

The Late Great Planet Earth notwithstanding, are they obsessed with mankind's impending doom.

The details behind the exodus led by Braun and emulated by others from Campus Crusade in 1969 and 1970 must be pieced together, but the account by Walker, former director of Campus Crusade at Ohio State, seems to capture the essential ingredients. According to Walker, the conflict began to develop shortly after he joined Crusade's staff. In his early years as a staff member, he says, the Crusade was "sort of like a big family," particularly among its full-time personnel. The rapid growth of the organization, however, changed all that.

> Two basic conflicts began to develop. . . . One was an administrative-type conflict, and the other was theological. Administratively, of course, everything was focused on Dr. Bright. It became quite a frustration to some of us to get things done, because there was such a holdup sometimes. That was one aspect of a much larger problem.

More significant than that friction, which could be dismissed as a simple personality conflict, was what Walker describes as the "battle of law and grace." For Walker the struggle was centered in the church as a representative of organized Christianity:

> The whole issue of the church was a big issue to me personally. I began to see the church is not an organization but an organism. The whole issue of organization itself became an aspect of the law-grace-church issue. If you have an organization, you have to operate on law. There is no other way.

The issues involved in the resignations of disenchanted Crusaders were ones that would gain sympathetic ears throughout the developing Jesus Movement. Both Jesus People and ex-Crusaders, chafing under the burden of institutionalism, had decided to serve Christ outside the confines of organized Christianity. Walker says: "I decided when I left Campus Crusade I would never work through another religious organization, that I would serve the Lord in the simplest way I knew how." Other exiles apparently had geared their futures in the same manner, for Lindsey, Counts, and Braun are all engaged in expanding "unorganized" ministries dotting the edges of the Jesus Movement.

The best known of these works is the J.C. Light and Power House, administered by Lindsey and Counts. Nestled in the

137

plush hills of Westwood, the Light and Power House is a live-in arrangement equipped to handle up to forty residents. The accommodations are closer to an apartment or dormitory situation than to communal living. Members of the co-ed house either hold jobs or attend school and pay $125 a month for room and board. The latter is taken in family-style meals. Each member has a three-hours-per-week chore requirement. There are no curfews, with residents free to come and go at their choosing. Alcohol and drugs are forbidden on the premises; smoking cigarettes is frowned on but permitted. In-depth Bible studies are mandatory but held only once a week, infrequently by comparison with similar ministries.

The fame of the house in the Los Angeles area no doubt results from Lindsey's authorship of *The Late Great Planet Earth*. Though admitting that prophecy is taught frequently, Counts claims that "a stronger emphasis is with the grace of God." Counts himself soft-pedals the apocalypse, though for him, now seems more likely than later:

> I would say Christ conceivably can come back five hundred years from now and not now. However, if he does come back five hundred years from now, it would be because what God will do [is that] he would stop some of the processes now in motion and bring them to a halt. In my opinion, the chances are better that he will come back soon than that he won't.

The Light and Power House further distinguishes itself from the more fanatical segments of the Jesus Movement by denying that the presumed nearness of the second coming is call for Christians, all of them, to fling themselves into full-time personal evangelism. Says Counts:

> I would never accept it from people if they say, "I'm going to drop out of school because Christ is coming and there's no use being in school." Now they can drop out of school if they want, but I won't let them get away with that reason.

The chief function of the Light and Power House is to "give some biblical depth to the spiritual movement that is going on." Both Lindsey and Counts reject the label Jesus Freaks, contending instead that the House sits on the fence supposedly dividing hip Christianity and the establishment.
138

They criticize both sides. House residents seldom attend neighborhood churches. As Counts analyzes it:

> Most churches simply are not in touch with the needs of where people are; so they prove irrelevant. They don't meet their needs; so they don't go. I don't know of any church within easy driving distance of this place where his [the resident's] needs are met enough that he felt it worth going.

About the Jesus People he says: "The movement that's taking place is experience- and emotion-centered. And if they don't bring in more in-depth teaching of the Bible, it cannot last."

As a result of their dismal experience with Campus Crusade, Counts and Lindsey have given up trying to sell organized religion to the younger generation, though both continue to attend establishment services regularly. The lack of elders in the movement is a major concern of both: "We're trying to crank into this thing [the Jesus Movement] some people who have had a year of in-depth Bible teaching so it will have some stability, so it won't just be superficial." The House is attracted to those segments of the Jesus Movement which conduct some sort of biblical study. Calvary Chapel of Costa Mesa is appealing to House residents (though the Pentecostalism is shunned) and, according to Counts, would be attended heavily if the distance (about forty miles) were not so great. The spontaneity and freedom of the hip church, without the charismatic influence and with more and deeper Bible study, seem to be the aims of the J.C. Light and Power House, though a regular worship service is not part of the master plan.

In the fall of 1971 a less structured two-year alternative to seminary was inaugurated. This "biblical training school" is to involve small numbers on a full-time basis in a course designed to circumvent the normal three-year period of seminary training. Unlike the balance of House residents, training school students do not attend classes or work elsewhere, but merely pay the monthly room and board fee. Counts outlines the training school's curriculum: "In the first year it's a strong survey of biblical doctrine and the biblical books, and the second year it will be mostly Greek." Administered by Lindsey and Counts, the school, it is hoped, will provide a more workable training for full-time Christian service than is now available.

139

Rapping about the Bible

Though the goal of the J.C. Light and Power House, the forming of a revitalized Christian ministry, may square with that of the Jesus Movement as a whole, the method of Lindsey and Counts is quite removed from the mainline Jesus Movement. Rather than relying solely on the miraculous intervention of the Holy Spirit, the Light and Power House prefers more traditional patterns of instruction. Though the curricula of seminaries dwarf the efforts of their work, Lindsey and Counts do see the need for relying on more formal training rather than deferring to a supernatural transfer of knowledge from heaven directly to the soul.

More closely related to the chief elements of America's spiritual revolutionaries are the efforts of Grace Haven Farm in Mansfield, Ohio, directed by Gordon Walker. Though his location separates him somewhat from the centers of the movement,

140

an appreciation of the movement is central in Walker's thinking. He characterizes Jesus People glowingly as people who are "completely free in their mind at least of the religious establishment and totally committed to Christ as his personal savior." Walker views his ministry quite simply: "I think our work right now is to get some people grounded in the Word." Walker, his wife and five children, another ex-Crusade family, and a handful of live-in helpers work the two farmlands donated by a wealthy Mansfield businessman. The farm is moving toward self-sufficiency in food production; other expenses, including salaries of forty dollars a month for live-in help, are provided by unsolicited donations. The farm is used by groups for retreats as well as for regularly scheduled weekly meetings. It functions much like a Christian camp.

After leaving Campus Crusade and promising himself freedom from religious organizations, Walker moved his family from Columbus to Mansfield, where he hoped to conduct Bible studies and classes on an informal basis. Soon the Walkers began to attract a small following — Crusade refugees at first, but later including exiles from more varied backgrounds — seeking a haven in which to do some re-evaluative thinking. Walker was hesitant about the prospect of a live-in ministry:

> What began as a trickle became a stream of people coming —
> students and non-students — just to rap. Some wanted to live
> with us for a while — three months. We really didn't want to
> get into this — people living with us — but we felt the Lord
> was definitely doing something because we were not going out
> to get people to come, they were just coming.

The coincidental development of Grace Haven as a small community rather than merely a family residence has attracted a more varied population than the Light and Power House. Lindsey and Counts, for the most part, attract a following quite similar to themselves both in background and in outlook. Power House residents are university students or graduates. They share dissatisfaction with the stultifying effects of the institutional church. Walker's farm, on the other hand, is, as he says, "one of the most varied ministries I've ever seen." Ex-addicts, depressed preachers, reformed revolutionaries, and deserters of the Crusade's army have at one time or another sought shelter at Grace Haven. The farm claims close ties with

141

the Jesus Movement, and Walker admits the presence of a charismatic influence, though maintaining firmly, "We don't want to be identified as part of the tongues movement." Despite Walker's feeling that the bulk of his ministry is to Jesus People, its location in Ohio gives Grace Haven little contact with the more full-fledged manifestations of the movement, as illustrated by Walker's evaluation of the Children of God as "a good group of people,"

Though their methods vary, the messages of Counts, Lindsey, and Walker, fashioned in the same crisis over law and grace, are identical, almost to phraseology. Walker agrees with Lindsey's published views on prophecy, but like his West Coast counterparts he does not assign the apocalypse a prominent place in his ministry. Grace Haven operates in an atmosphere of freedom, encouraging variety and spontaneity. His own conviction is that "God's garden has a lot of variety in it. I really feel it's characteristic of God that there is such a variety of life on this planet and in the Body of Christ." Some of that variety he finds among the Jesus People, though he is somewhat apprehensive over the lack of depth that he feels is manifest in much of the revolution. Like the Light and Power House, Grace Haven seeks to minister to the movement's weaknesses:

> We have carried into this whole thing the strong emphasis on the grace of God, the unconditional, unlimited love of God for those who don't deserve it. We emphasize the doctrine of justification by faith, the priesthood of the believer, and total forgiveness. These are things we teach about, and I feel it has given it a deeper tone or quality than other things that have sprung up. A lot of it [the Jesus Movement] is rather shallow; it's not deeply grounded in Scripture.

The fourth of Campus Crusade's well-known refugees, Jon Braun, also is operating in the hinterlands of the movement, though not as actively as the founders of the Light and Power House and Grace Haven. Braun's ministry (he denies having a leadership role in it) is located in Isla Vista, California. It has only an informal organization. The group is named the Brothers and Sisters only because those labels are used by participants quite frequently. However, it is larger — 125 to 150 frequent its gatherings — than either of the other offsprings of

Campus Crusade. Braun characterizes the group as a collection of disaffected followers of the institutional church — he prefers the term "secular church" — in need of a restful haven in which they might breathe new vigor into the spiritual life suffocated by the restrictive confines of organized Christianity.

Although they are, by their own choosing, almost totally isolated from the movement all around them, the Brothers and the Sisters are closer to the Jesus People in some details of both style and attitude than either of their more organized counterparts. Similarities — the lack of a true apocalyptic outlook, for example — between these fringe groups are present; but differences, particularly over the importance of Bible study, are many. For Braun the guiding of the Holy Spirit is indispensable if the Bible is to be considered in any sense inspired. The Brothers and Sisters have discarded the traditional evangelical concept of propositional revelation in favor of a more Barthian, as-the-Spirit-leads position. As a corollary Braun and his followers have abandoned any effort at rational apologetics, preferring instead to pin their hopes on an almost mystical illumination by the Spirit. The writings of Watchman Nee, works influential throughout the movement, are an admitted source of belief for Braun and his compatriots. The Isla Vista meetings are far more rambunctious than studies held at the Light and Power House, no doubt because of the group's orientation toward worship rather than teaching. Singing is boisterous, spirited, and genuinely spontaneous. The gatherings are held in the living room of a large house, and the hospitality of the Brothers and Sisters is warm and sincere.

Despite their similarities to the Jesus Movement, the Brothers and Sisters have remained distinctly separate from the more active manifestations of the revolution. Isolating themselves from both mainline and fringe groups by ignoring the evangelization of the world and proselytization of the establishment ("All in the Lord's good time," says Braun, who fully expects the Spirit to work great things through the group sometime), these refugees are not at all interested in fulfilling the same needs which burden the residents of the Light and Power House and Grace Haven.

* * *

Musicians at a Jesus concert

Disenchanted Crusaders are not the only ones inhabiting the middle ground between revolution and establishment. In the face of all the movement's anti-institutional propaganda (which at times descends to unabashed name-calling — the Whore of Babylon is a favorite label), America's organized religious institutions are climbing on the bandwagon of the Jesus People.

Hollywood Presbyterian Church has perhaps penetrated the movement more successfully than any other representative of the establishment. As early as 1968, before the recruitment of the Jesus People's Army of Seattle, before the advent of the *Hollywood Free Paper*, before Chuck Smith flung open the doors of Calvary Chapel to bid the hip world enter, Hollywood Presbyterian Church opened the Salt Company, one of the first coffee house ministries, and perhaps the most successful one. For some time the church sponsored a musical group of its own, also called the Salt Company, who made several concert tours in California.

Hollywood Presbyterian's act was imitated by groups throughout the country. Many have now been abandoned, but the Salt Company has passed the test of time. It is now one of several semi-autonomous youth ministries that operate under the church's sponsorship. Music styles have changed from the handclapping rhythms of hepped-up versions of "Do Lord" to a subtle, more sophisticated, reflective blues. There is still little hard rock, due to the small confines of the performing room. Hair, once discretely shaggy, is now openly long; and communal-type houses, used as temporary residences as well as crash pads, have sprung up under the church's sponsorship throughout Hollywood. Witness teams, perhaps a misnomer, engage in public relations on Hollywood Boulevard.

Hollywood Presbyterian is still somewhat of an alien in a strange land. Despite the hoopla surrounding the Salt Company, there is far more substance to it than the clever bumper stickers and colorful buttons might suggest. Not that the gimmicks of the movement are derogated — smiled at, perhaps, but not belittled. Rather, they are simply assigned to a different level. Illustrative of the Salt Company's relationship to its movement-oriented neighbors is the comment of a teen-ager there about the *Hollywood Free Paper* — "Oh, that's all right for elementary school."

Like the ministries of Counts, Lindsey, and Walker, the various outgrowths of Hollywood Presbyterian attempt to infuse the surrounding revolution with a deeper, more intellectual dimension than the movement itself seems interested in. The friendship between the church and the ex-Crusaders is more than theoretical: summer 1971 saw Hollywood Presbyterian host a Summer Bible Institute conducted by Don Williams, the church's college pastor, in conjunction with Hal Lindsey and Bill Counts, with guest lectures by Gordon Walker. The church's relationship to the movement is that of ally not enemy. Williams explains:

> They need to find the full body of Christ. They need to know of Christ's Lordship over all of life. They need grounding in the Word of God. Their gifts to us are zeal, and love in true community. Can we receive from them and give to them? (*Christianity Today*, Aug. 27, 1971, p. 7).

145

The closest Northern California counterpart to Hollywood Presbyterian is Palo Alto's Peninsula Bible Church. After years in the coat-and-tie world of middle-class American Christendom, PBC has broadened its ministry from the routine Sunday morning worship service. Its efforts include seven Sunday School classes for college students on the Stanford campus and new programs designed to integrate the Jesus revolutionaries into the life of the congregation.

The most impressive of these efforts is the Body-Life service held each Sunday evening. The atmosphere is relaxed and friendly. Instead of a pulpit, there is a single microphone in front. The music is a casual mixture of traditional hymns and contemporary music accompanied by guitar. The congregation too is a mixture of the traditional and contemporary; ties and suits, slacks and shorts are all well represented, as are long hair and short hair, shoes and bare feet. The service includes the traditional elements — congregational singing, announcements, offering, sermon — but it has new elements, too — the sharing of recent experiences, an encouragement to take money (up to ten dollars) out of the offering plate as it passes if one has need, announcements of needs of members of the congregation that other members might be able to fill. The idea is that laymen, not just the paid staff, should be meeting the spiritual and physical needs of others in the congregation. And it works. Middle-class, middle-aged straights, who used to visit only with their own kind, now invite long-hairs into their homes for fellowship. When a hippie is converted, he may be put up temporarily by such a couple. Young people feel so much at home with some of the church's adults that they drop by unannounced and uninvited for brief chats. A full hour after the conclusion of a Body-Life service, almost all of those in attendance are still in the sanctuary, milling around and visiting informally.

One of the laymen in PBC has an outstanding ministry of his own. Lambert Dolphin, a bachelor in his late thirties, has opened his home to young people who need a place to stay. A few stay for an extended period; most stay for only a few nights. Located in the hills above Stanford University, Dolphin's home also serves as the setting for Jesus parties for as many as two hundred at a time. Conversions are recorded almost as

146

fast as the Christians circulating in the crowd can get around to talking to the guests. Dolphin, a scientist who has left his professional career to devote himself to meeting the needs of young people, also leads teams of laymen in forays into other localities to sensitize Christian adults to the needs of youth and to help those young people whom they meet. Lambert is quick to blame most of the problems of the children on parents. He is especially critical of homes in which there is either no father figure or a very weak one.

The PBC congregation has involved itself deeply with the revolution. Some of the church's laymen are members of the board of directors of a drug rehabilitation center operated by Ted Wise, one of the earliest Jesus People. This sort of union — the church with its stabilizing, but sometimes deadening, maturity, and the movement with its fresh, but sometimes misdirected, enthusiasm — demonstrates the best result of the revolution. It is around the movement's edges in churches like Hollywood Presbyterian and PBC who are willing to involve themselves with the revolution, that the benefits of the Jesus People are most pronounced.

Another ministry on the fringes of the Jesus Movement is Resurrection City, a Berkeley effort directed by twenty-two-year-old Mario Murillo, whose goal is to present the gospel to leaders in Berkeley's radical political scene — Black Panthers, Students for a Democratic Society, and others. Murillo places heavy emphasis on the charismatic gifts, and some of those in Berkeley who appreciate this emphasis are gravitating from the Christian World Liberation Front to Resurrection City.

David Wilkerson, founder of Teen Challenge and famous for his work with drug addicts, has taken his place as a helper on the fringes of the Jesus Revolution. His recently published *Jesus Person Maturity Manual* reflects a clear recognition of the need for spiritual growth among the new converts. The book offers sane, intelligent instruction in doctrinal areas and about such practical matters as occultism, homosexuality, venereal disease, and drugs — matters about which most Christians are silent but which converts from the counter-culture need to have discussed in a Christian perspective.

Yet another individual on the fringes of the movement proper who is having a beneficial impact is twenty-four-year-old evangelist Richard Hogue. Working mostly through Baptist churches in the Southwest and Midwest, he sets up crusades in schools and churches, replete with a Jesus rock group, Jesus cheers, and other external linkages with the Jesus Movement. His crusades are labeled Spiritual Revolution Now — SPIRENO.

The mingling of the movement with the institutional church is not confined to single scattered churches or to isolated individuals. Though that sort of relationship is by far the most common, there are several conglomerations of churches presently exchanging greetings with the movement. The most effective of these groups is Lutheran Youth Alive, sometimes heralded as the "Jesus People branch of the Lutheran Church." LYA cooperates actively with the Missouri Synod, American Lutheran Church (ALC), and Lutheran Church of America (LCA). The trappings of the revolution, at least most of them, decorate LYA adherents and their bumpers — from "Smile If You Love Jesus" and "Don't Be a Morsel for the Devil" to "Read the Bible; It'll Scare the Hell out of You." Though sometimes accepting the label "Lutheran Jesus People," LYA is somewhat more Lutheran than revolutionary. Its members deny affiliation with the movement, claiming that many who call the LYA Jesus People are misinterpreting their zeal as freakiness.

LYA began in 1969 under the leadership of David Anderson, a former youth director for Central Lutheran Church of Van Nuys, California, and a personal friend of Don Williams of Hollywood Presbyterian. Anderson generated the interest that sparked the organization and a ten-thousand-dollar donation from Lutheran Brotherhood Insurance through the publication of a five-thousand-copy newspaper featuring a convert's journey from drugs to Christ. The tabloid is still produced every two months, and circulation has jumped to 25,000. The ministry of LYA is for the most part restricted to Lutherans. Teams of mature LYA adherents, about ninety in all, spend their summers traveling and seeking to encourage Lutheran congregations throughout the country to revitalize and attune themselves to America's twentieth-century revival. Presentations, which generally include contemporary Christian music, are directed toward the establishment of permanent Bible study

148

and prayer groups. Although the focus of the organization is the institutional church, LYA is not blind to social issues. Under LYA impetus Renewal House, Inc., a drug rehabilitation center, started in the Los Angeles area in February 1971. Now financed by the Lutheran Social Service, the House was administered by LYA and supported through its donations for several months.

Anderson and most of LYA's population are described by those who know them as "quietly charismatic," but they do not make tongues a focal point of the organization. Nor are they excessively apocalyptic.

* * *

Unfortunately, many of the establishment's overtures to the revolution are neither sincere nor constructive. Content to hang on to the revolution's fame rather than help shore up the movement's deficiencies, many churches make well- or not-so-well-disguised attempts to ride the crest of the Jesus People's popularity. Churches throughout the country are increasingly realizing that there is much to be gained by inserting a few "Praise the Lords" and an occasional rhythmic "Hallelujah" to the routine. The most obvious (though perhaps least significant) witness to the self-induced Jesus People-ization of America's Christian bulwarks is the increasing appearance of movement slogans on bumpers and lapels.

Some traditional churches have exploited the possibilities of coffee houses. Patterned after the head-shop decor of the drug culture, replete with collage interiors, rickety furniture, and young people garbed in the finest of the Salvation Army thrift shop, little church-sponsored nooks, called anything from a Jesus night club to a rap session, are beginning to dot the edges of the action. The most blatant examples, predictably, are in Hollywood, and the most blatant in Hollywood is "Right On," the self-proclaimed pioneer of Hollywood's gospel night clubs. Ed Human, a former associate of Arthur Blessitt, is its director. Right On is supported by the nearby First Baptist Church of Beverly Hills and is a textbook example of contemporary Christian programming. Introducing a schedule of performing musical groups for summer 1971, Right On's management, in its best public relations voice, announced:

149

> The management of Right On proudly present the very best in Christian music for your enjoyment this summer. Our summer schedule offers a wide variety in music tastes. There is something for music lovers of all ages. From hard rock to gospel quartets, we have a great summer planned for you.

Right On is little more than the Saturday night social moved from the fellowship hall to the street or, more correctly, just off the street. Its appeal is more to church people who want to feel "with it" than to genuine street people or even Jesus People.

The club maintains all that characterizes the institutional church. The flyer continues:

> Reserved seat tickets are $2.00 per person, picked up upon arrival. Now reserved seats are $2.50 per person. All children under 12 are $1.00. With a group of 100 or more your church or club can reserve the entire club for an evening on Sunday through Wednesday nights. At your request we will furnish food and entertainment.

Apart from the language, which sounds like a diluted version of the *Hollywood Free Paper*, and sporadic visits by the movement's musical missionaries, the mentality displayed in Right On is not that of the revolution. Their message is the tried-and-true, church-focused gospel of organized religion; their medium, too, is establishment, though thinly disguised.

It is perhaps inaccurate to describe the church's night club ministry in terms of Right On, for it is better financed, better advertised, and far more commercial than most. More typical is the Mustard Seed, a small room sponsored by the First Baptist Church of Van Nuys in an effort to bring the church to the Van Nuys Boulevard strip. The symbols of the revolution are all there, but the spirit of the movement is missing. Charismatic experiences, judged divisive, have been barred from any of the studies or prayer sessions held at the Mustard Seed. There is little talk of the end, though mention of *The Late Great Planet Earth* will usually elicit a smiling "I think it's right on!" Evangelism at the Mustard Seed is conducted by leafleteers equipped with Campus Crusade's four spiritual laws, but the interior is populated by relaxing missionaries rather than weary travelers of this world.

Ministries of this type — efforts of Jesus People-ized churches

150

to grow their hair and to learn that Jesus is not the Rock of Ages but the Bridge over Troubled Waters — highlight the shallowness of some aspects of the movement and the short-lived glow of the national limelight. Just as the large folk ensemble and the folk mass were fads in the mid-sixties, the Jesus night club is "in" now. The mingling of the hip world and the straight church has become suddenly popular. The lasting impact of Right On, the Mustard Seed, and others — celebrated by both *Christianity Today* and *Eternity* as heralds of things to come — is doubtful. Many such efforts have already expired (as attested by the large number of unopened mail surveys returned to us from supposedly thriving outposts on the edges of the movement). It seems unlikely that the trend will reverse itself.

The fascination of some of America's mainstream evangelical stalwarts with the Jesus People (and its sometimes comical manifestations) is no match for the curiosity of some segments of established Pentecostalism. The sharing of ecstatic experience might suggest that the movement would be closer to organized Pentecostalism than to its uneasy friends in the noncharismatic establishment. But most Pentecostals are equally as confused about the rise of the Jesus People. The movement manifests the proper gifts, speaks the proper words (in English), and goes through all the motions of institutionalized Pentecostalism, but the environment is different. Gatherings are less structured, to the point of disorganization; styles are far removed from the average Assembly of God; and language, except when quoting Scripture, follows the tone of the street rather than the church. Pentecostal efforts to link up with the Jesus Movement are no less uncomfortable than that of, say, the management of Right On.

The shaky alliance of the youthful revolutionaries with classical Pentecostalists is typified by long-time evangelist Kathryn Kuhlman. In a series of telecasts made in late summer 1971, the Kuhlman ministry awkwardly but publicly joined hands with the saints of the movement. Standing among Chuck Smith ("Daddy Chuck," she called him), Lonnie Frisbee, and Duane Pederson, "Mama Kathryn" displayed an unconcealed eagerness to identify with the movement, despite an incredible ignorance of it. Her attachment to the popularity of the young movement was unmistakable — "I'm one of you, too; I'm part of the Jesus Movement, too" — and proud — "We're in it together; I'm so glad to be a part of it," if a bit confused. Not only did she label the *Hollywood Free Paper* a "great newspaper" and vaguely compare it to the Los Angeles *Times* before imploring Pederson to tell her what it was all about, but Mama Kathryn also unabashedly asked Chuck Smith to "Tell me about this Jesus People Movement of which I am a part."

* * *

Unfortunately, not all of the religious bandwagoning is as harmless as either that of Right On or Mama Kathryn. Zany sects known more for con games than conversions, which have long existed around the edges of the organized church, are enthusiastic in their welcome of the Jesus People as a new ally. The best known (thanks to coverage by *Life* and *Time*) is an old organization called "The Way" by its one and only prophet, Victor Paul Wierwille. The Way, centered in New Knoxville, Ohio, but with new outposts in Mill Valley, California, and Rye, New York, was virtually unknown until it began to appear in the publicity spotlight shining on and around the movement. Wierwille's association with the Jesus People can be traced to his successful procurement of two of the early Jesus Freaks, Steve Heefner and Jimmy Doop, to head up The Way East and The Way West, respectively. Wierwille knows a good thing when he sees it. The question is whether Heefner and Doop need him and his fifty-year-old's affectations of youthfulness — consisting mainly of a motorcycle plastered with Jesus signs. Friends of Heefner and Doop think that it is just a matter of time until they "see through" Wierwille.

The Way Biblical Research Center, the organization's full name, is an ultra-dispensationalist outfit that denies the Deity of Christ and indulges — somewhat incongruously for ultra-dispensationalists — in tongues speaking. At the family camps, which are the backbone of Wierwille's ministry, young children receive instruction in glossolalia: they are told to open their mouths and let out any sounds that come. The Way publishes a catalog consisting almost exclusively of books and pamphlets

152

by Wierwille. These claim to offer the true understanding of the Bible, lost since St. Paul's time but recovered now for the first time by Wierwille. The books purport to be the results of Wierwille's research in the original languages of the Bible.

The Way's reception into the revolution has been less than friendly. David Hoyt has distributed a mimeographed sheet warning the movement of the heresy fostered by Wierwille:

> Wierwille teaches that since salvation means forgiveness for past, present and future sins, one is free to partake of sinful desires. This idea has been particularly appealing to Christians coming out of the hip scene who still want to take dope and fornicate. This seems to us the major reason why people get into the Way, so that they can have a puny Jesus and their sin also. The message of repentance and obedience is not emphasized by the Way.

Hoyt's criticism is mirrored by Gordon Walker:

> I consider Victor Wierwille to be a false prophet. I think a lot of kids in The Way are real Christians. I think this thing that happened in Rye, New York, is of the Lord, but if Wierwille has his way he will completely subvert it. . . . I have no qualms in labeling much of it heresy.

Wierwille himself has few qualms about anything, especially his claim to be the only true preacher of the Bible since Paul. The Way, with the help of the undiscriminating media, is riding high on the crest of the revolutionary wave. While the ride has done Wierwille good, the movement has gained little but another hanger-on.

* * *

The interest of America's religious institutions, charismatic or otherwise, is only a segment of the popularity that the movement presently enjoys. The fascination of America with the new breed of spiritual revolutionary has outgrown the bounds of the religious establishment. While most of the church's adoption of the style and mood of the movement is a sincere but shallow attempt to transform the message of the establishment into the groovy gospel, the motives of other fringe elements are somewhat more calculated than evangelistic. The revolution itself is not free of commercialism, but most of it — sale of buttons, stickers, books (a few), record albums, and other paraphernalia

— is designed to support the movement's various operations. Some, however, is not so pure in heart, most notably a privately manufactured Jesus Medallion sold mail-order for $14.95 through the *Hollywood Free Paper*. Melodyland, of Anaheim, California, sells Jesus People watches and similar novelty items.

If the Jesus People themselves are tainted with crassness (as is almost inevitable in any movement with a sizable following), substantial numbers of hangers-on are consumed by the promise of gold at the top of Jacob's ladder. The two-disc album *Jesus Christ Superstar* has passed the million mark in sales, and the end is not in sight. Now appearing on Broadway, this rock opera enjoyed one of the largest advance sales in Broadway history. *Superstar's* appeal to Jesus People is small, but its appeal to straight Christians craving spiritual novelty is enormous. The music world is guilty of a great deal of capitalistic exploitation of the spiritual revolution, but all that is quasi-Christian is not insincere. The most lucrative exception is a true opera (as opposed to *Superstar's* rock qualities), *Godspell*. Among other unorthodoxies, it clothes Jesus in a Superman sweatshirt and the cast in clown costumes. From its humble beginnings as a potential master's thesis, *Godspell*, the story of Jesus from the Baptism to the Crucifixion, taken from Matthew and Luke as well as Anglican hymnals, has become a quick success. Its authors claim that the opera is not a bandwagon spin-off of the Jesus Movement but rather a serious attempt at religious — co-author Michael Schwartz terms it mythological — theater. Perhaps so, but whatever the case *Godspell* is not Christian opera. It may indeed be a sincere attempt at modern theater, but the absence of any understanding of the divinity of Christ precludes *Godspell's* classification, as some have asserted, as the avant-garde of a new Christian consciousness in contemporary musical drama. The same must be said of *Superstar*. It, too, treats Christ in humanistic terms and ends with Christ's death, not his resurrection.

Among the most grotesque examples of faddish commercialization of the recent wave of interest in Jesus are Jesus Christ jockey shorts and Jesus Christ bikinis. A new Jesus watch is advertised as follows: "Hi kids, it's me, Jesus. Look what I'm wearing on my wrist. It's a wristwatch with a five-color picture of me on the dial and hands attached to a crimson heart."

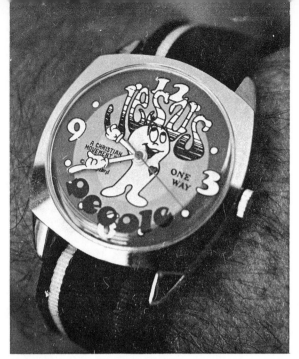

Hucksterism: a "Jesus watch"

The market for assorted Jesus products is varied and absorbs some of the movement as well as the turned-on establishment. The appeal of the Jesus music of popular radio stations (despite *Christianity Today's* claim that some of "Spirit in the Sky's" lyrics are "strikingly evangelistic") is not to the Jesus People themselves. Says Larry Norman of the pop Jesus music: "There is no real Jesus music out yet. No music that really sees Jesus as the Son of God who died for our personal salvation." Apparently the record-buying population of the institutional church (an essentially young one) is the source of such music's success. Indeed, most products appeal to the organizational Christian, but the movement itself is slowly being engulfed by hucksters. New clothing and new posters, each more stylish, each more clever than its antecedents, continue to appear, and being a right-on Christian, at least outwardly, is becoming more expensive all the time.

Spreading with nearly as much rapidity as new fashions for Jesus are numbers of just-about-anything groups for Jesus. Here the revolution has taken a page from the peace movement.

155

Instead of Surfers for Peace, Bikers for Peace, Karate for Peace, and Ham Radio for Peace, one now finds Surfers, Bikers, Karate, and Ham Radio for Jesus. Perhaps the most exotic of all such "for Jesus" collectives (though the suffix is not affixed) is a reportedly growing band of repentant Hell's Angels, now reverently known simply as the Angels. Surfers for Christ boasts such headliners as Margo Godfrey, one of the world's best women surfers, and Ric Griffin, cartoonist for *Surfer Magazine*. But for the most part the "for Jesus" groups rise with the movement's tide and fall quite quickly.

Groups riding the crest of the revolutionary popularity harbor the vast majority of the movement's soldiers of fortune. Blatant sensation-seeking comes from fading Hollywood stars. *Screen Stories,* a crypto-confession pulp magazine, recently ran a picture-studded exposé titled "Mia Joins but Liz Won't." It listed Johnny Cash, Terence Stamp, James Fox, Pat Boone, and Donovan as "stars who are rushing to get saved." This sort of sensationalism plagues the movement's edges, and since national magazine coverage came in *Time*, each of the nation's magazines seems bent upon producing its own provincial version of the Jesus story. *Screen Stories'* shoddy and incredibly obtuse caricaturization is not atypical. The movement has been butchered by Garner Ted Armstrong in *The Plain Truth*; and even the American Nazi Party's official organ, *White Power*, has put in its two marks' worth. The revolution is presently selling quite well, and where there is demand, there is supply. Jesus People, their artifacts, their story, and imitations of the real thing come in all shapes, sizes, and prices. The market is growing and will continue to do so until the fascination born of publicity begins to give way to the turning of the cameras to new manifestations of freakiness.

The edges are not totally engulfed with commercialism. There are the helpers, those seeking to educate and mature the zeal of the revolutionaries. Unfortunately, helpers are in shorter supply than their less sincere neighbors. It may be that the developments around the edges will tell the story of the future of the Jesus Movement. The atmosphere of Peninsula Bible Church, the efforts of Hollywood Presbyterian and the Salt Company, the handful of involved laymen like Lambert Dolphin — in cooperation with these the movement is indeed on the verge of deep and thoroughgoing revival. In these cases, the stability, the grounding of the revolution in the heritage of orthodox Christian thought offered by the institutional church (admittedly the number of churches with such concern is sadly small) is in counterbalance with the bubbling zeal of the movement. This amalgam is without doubt the best result of the spiritual revolution. Unfortunately, it occurs too infrequently. The Kuhlmans, the Wierwilles, and the *Screen Stories* rob the movement of its lasting impact. The future of the revolution is in the company of the church.

Without maturity, without education, without grounding in Christian thought, the Jesus People cannot avoid a commercialized end — what Larry Norman terms "pop Christianity."

Part Two

THE BELIEFS

eight

THE SIMPLE GOSPEL

If You're Saved and You Know It, Clap Your Hands

THERE ARE SOME CHRISTIANS WHO SAY, "ALL THAT MATTERS IS that a person is really born again." But if the issue of personal regeneration is the watershed issue, it does not follow that any theology — conscious or unconscious — held by a regenerate person is beyond criticism. That this is so is obvious from the stated and unstated conditions for fellowship in any congregation, even one of Christians who say that being born again is all that matters. We do not intend in these chapters to pass judgment on the testimonies of salvation given by individual Jesus People. We see no reason to doubt that the majority of them have experienced a genuine personal conversion to Christ. What we shall look at is the "theology" of the Jesus Movement, four major emphases that are common to nearly all of the groups we have discussed in chapters two to seven.

The single most important teaching of the Jesus People is the simple gospel. Jesus saves. But what does he save? The soul or the whole man? And what does the message of personal salvation imply? Is salvation merely a fire escape from hell, or does it entail a commitment to a life of service to God and to men in this world? If the latter, in what terms is this service to be seen? Is the service to be limited to evangelistic effort to win new converts and then teach them enough so that they can go out and win more? Or is the service to be seen in terms of

161

personal involvement within the social, political, and other structures of contemporary society? What is to be the relationship between the individual believer and the world order in which he finds himself living? Jesus People like to refer to themselves as the salt of the earth. But what does that really mean?

An editorial in *The Alternative* (which serves, incidentally, to distinguish it from the Jesus papers) states our concerns well:

> But what must we think of the Jesus Movement? Will it restrict itself to "religious" meetings, to an endless round of Bible studies, evangelistic concerts and Christian pep rallies? Or will it make meaningful contact with modern culture, relate candidly to daily living, and effect responsible social and moral renewal? Will the Jesus People only sit around holding each other's hands, singing songs and quoting precious verses, or will their faith grapple with the central issues of life, with the structures of society, with politics, economics, science, philosophy, business, labor, art, literature, education? Will it speak not only to the issue of death, but also the questions of life, to marriage, to social integration, to community life, to meaningful human values that work in the real world?
>
> To those "rolling" with the Jesus Movement, the question must be squarely faced: Is there in our relationship to Christ depth of Biblical understanding and breadth of social-cultural awareness — both of which go far beyond mere intellectual dogmatism on the one hand and ecstatic religious frenzy on the other — a rugged fiber of honest, seeking faith that can grapple with the whole of life, weather the hurricane of the world's cheap publicity?

To questions like these, the Jesus People give only superficial and deficient answers. With them, the simplistic mentality endemic to fundamentalism has surfaced once again, dramatically and emphatically. Whatever the problem, the simple plan of salvation is offered as the whole solution. The unbeliever is seen less as a man than as a potential convert. There is little concern for working from where the unbeliever is by showing specifically how the Bible relates to the particular questions he is raising.

It is not always a simple matter to read what the Bible says and do as it commands. What does it say? What does it command? Different readers come to different conclusions. Everyone is involved in interpretation. One may do only what he

162

High on Jesus

understands the Bible to have commanded, but his understanding will not be universally accepted. So all believers build their own individual theologies. The Jesus People do so too, though they would probably deny that, preferring to think they are simply following Scripture in whatever they do. And it is their heartfelt desire to follow Scripture down to the last jot and tittle. But however admirable that objective may be, it is a much more complicated goal than the Jesus People recognize.

The simple-minded and doctrinally unsophisticated approach that the Jesus People take toward the Bible has many ramifications. All these are a part of building their theologies. While they may want to limit their faith to the simple gospel, they in fact cannot avoid taking positions on such issues as the role of the human mind and its capacity for reasoning, the value of human cultural achievements in the arts and sciences, the worth of education, the role that political and social institutions play in human society, the meaning of the concept of time.

163

It is impossible to limit oneself to a belief in the simple gospel. Belief in the gospel affects one's views toward all matters. Believers differ in their attitudes about how the gospel relates to various areas of human life. While all would claim that they are seeking direction from Scripture, they all read Scripture differently. They interpret the Bible. And the Jesus People, whether they like the idea or not, are no exception.

It is our opinion that the ideas that attach themselves to the simple gospel the Jesus People propound are shallow and unsatisfactory. The common denominator of these inadequacies is a fragmentary and distorted view of the nature of man. Theologically, man is to be defined in terms of both the doctrine of creation and the doctrine of redemption. But the Jesus People minimize the doctrine of creation and emphasize to its virtual exclusion the doctrine of redemption. The effects of this are far-reaching. This chapter will elaborate on that issue.

* * *

The Jesus People are overwhelmingly — one could almost say exclusively — experience-oriented. It is important to recognize that they were so even before they became the Jesus People. The word "trip," as used by the counter-culture and now by the Jesus People, is a synonym for experience; a "high" is an experience. To be high on drugs means to have a drug-induced experience. To be high on Jesus means to have a certain religious experience. When those in the counter-culture talk about being turned on to Jesus, they are referring to an emotional experience that, for them, has striking similarity to the emotional experience induced by drugs.

Reason has always been highly prized in Western civilization, the tradition formed by the fusion of the classical and Christian cultures. It is not by accident that reason has throughout the centuries been seen as harmonious with Christian faith. But the carefully worked out relationships between faith and reason that loom so large in the works of Augustine and Thomas Aquinas are totally foreign to the Jesus People — and for a good reason. These new converts have come out of a background in the counter-culture with its emphasis upon drugs and other experiences. What the counter-culture is attempting to counter is the Western tradition, in which rationality plays so large a part. That is why so many counter-culture adherents have turned eagerly to Oriental mysticisms of one sort or another in order to find meaning in life. Timothy Leary in his prime argued that drugs were the way to discover authentic religious experiences. Religious yearnings are innate in all men, but the counter-culture has concluded that these yearnings must find satisfaction outside the Western tradition. And the component of the Western synthesis that is most adamantly opposed by the counter-culture is, precisely, reason.

One of the primary roles of reason in Christianity is apologetics, defense of the faith. Peter had this in mind when he exhorted his readers to "be ready always to give an answer to every man that asketh you a reason of the hope that is in you with meekness and fear" (I Peter 3:15). The lack of a carefully thought-out apologetic is one of the great weaknesses of the Jesus Movement in general, as the Children of God delight in pointing out about the other Jesus People. It is sad to stand on the sidewalk of Old Town in Chicago and listen to one of the Jesus People being soundly trounced in an argument by a well-read youthful unbeliever. In such a situation, the Jesus person is reduced to saying something like, "But I've had this experience, and I know it's true. I know I'm right." The Bible, however, exhorts its readers to test the spirits. Other persons have had other experiences, and for them these experiences have been most profound and earthshaking. According to what criterion can these competing experiences be judged? The criterion must lie outside the realm of experience itself. The following quotation from *Maranatha*, a Jesus Paper out of Vancouver, illustrates the dilemma of the Jesus People:

> How do we know it works? We know by the only method you can really trust . . . by experience. . . . After everything . . . ideology and the rest . . . has been stripped away, there's only the down-to-earth "Heavenly" experience as evidence that it really works. . . . I can accept other people with different beliefs . . . I doubt if there are any two people on this earth who believe exactly the same way . . . but I'm not talking about beliefs. My beliefs merely left me with a messed up head and nothing inside. . . . Experience is what really counts. . . . I'm not gonna try to say that Buddhism is wrong. . . . I haven't tried it and neither do I plan to. I have found where peace,

165

love, joy and the rest are available in abundance and, once I've found what I'd been crying out for inside for as long as I can remember, I'm not gonna walk away from it and try something else. . . .

That answer may be good enough for its author, but it won't do much to convince the Buddhist.

A similarly excessive reliance on feeling may be seen in the following words, which we heard from several Jesus People: "I haven't had a 'down' day since I found the Lord." What will happen to these converts when they finally do have a bad day? For surely the bad days will come. Scripture makes it quite clear that the servants of God are not exempt from "down days." Those who speak about being "high on the love of my Jesus" often add that that is a high that never stops.

In C. S. Lewis' *Screwtape Letters*, the devil Screwtape tells Wormwood about emotional troughs, which are a natural part of the psychological makeup of all men. There is a psychological principle of undulation. All men have their emotional ups and downs, and these are not always directly related to one's spiritual condition. Screwtape encourages Wormwood to capitalize on this situation by confusing the psychological with the spiritual.

> But there is an even better way of exploiting the Trough; I mean through the patient's own thoughts about it. As always, the first step is to keep knowledge out of his mind. Do not let him suspect the law of undulation. Let him assume that the first ardours of his conversion might have been expected to last, and ought to have lasted, forever, and that his present dryness is an equally permanent condition (p. 42).

Excessive reliance on feeling ("good vibes") is not a sturdy foundation on which to build an enduring spiritual life.

It is dismaying, though not surprising, to hear of Jesus People who have relapsed into drugs and illicit sex. We have heard of young people reading the Bible while high on drugs and unmarried couples first praying, then sleeping together. Entire ministries, communal and other, have fallen apart because of such relapses. It is particularly disastrous when leaders slip, for new converts find their faith severely shaken in these situations. But if there is no rational check upon the emotions, this kind of backsliding is predictable. The combination of devotion and libertinism is rooted in a dualistic view of man that separates value from the concrete times and places of human existence. If true salvation lies in the soul, one can be indifferent to the actions of the body.

The other side of experience-oriented Christianity is the anti-intellectualism of the Jesus People. They delight in quoting out of context such Bible passages as "Hath not God made foolish the wisdom of this world?" and "But God hath chosen the foolish things of the world to confound the wise," and "Beware lest any man spoil you through philosophy and vain deceit." In keeping with the all-or-nothing mentality that prevails in our times, they do not understand these passages to be saying that, whatever the intrinsic value of the wisdom of the world, it is foolishness in comparison to the revelation of God. God does not place a premium upon ignorance, though some of the Jesus People literally and emphatically do. Many are shocked to learn that Paul himself, the author of these statements, quoted from pagan poets right in Holy Writ at least three times.

Many of the Jesus People claim to read only the Bible, though some will allow that there are certain devotional guides that may be profitable, such as the books by Watchman Nee. Susan Alamo says that at the Christian Foundation the only person who reads anything other than the Bible is her husband, Tony, who reads the newspapers to see what prophecies, if any, have been fulfilled that day. The Jesus People feel no need to acquaint themselves with the issues of the day that should be met by an application of Scripture. A good witness must understand enough about his hearer's outlook to be able to apply the Scriptures to his particular needs. How can one who reads only the Bible ever know the specific issues to which its truth applies?

Although they read the Bible constantly, they tend to be proof-texters of the worst sort, taking verses out of context with abandon. (The Children of God even trot out a proof-text in favor of proof-texting — II Timothy 3:16.) This kind of Bible reading is designed to find some sort of scriptural support for previously decided positions. At the Peninsula Bible Church one of the most frequently heard phrases is,

"You have to read it in context," advice that is much needed in the movement proper.

As might be expected, the Jesus People see little value in education — at least in education beyond what is necessary to prepare one to read the Bible. At their Texas ranch, the Children of God did operate a Montessori school for their children, and they named the ranch the Texas Soul Clinic Bible College. What they object to is the study of philosophy, literature, political science, and the other academic disciplines. A Children of God elder reacted sharply to our question about education: "Education is all just shit." Linda Meissner refers, somewhat more mildly, to what is learned in college as "general blah. . . . For the hard-core Jesus People, we say it's a waste of time. It is man's wisdom." She sees only two reasons for Jesus People to go to college. God may call a disciple to attend a particular school in order to revolutionize that school. He would not go there to learn, but to witness. Or a Jesus person may need particular knowledge in order to minister in a particular place. For instance, since India will not allow a foreigner to enter simply as a minister of the gospel, if the Lord calls a disciple to go to India as a spiritual revolutionist, he may need some training to gain skills that will enable him to enter the country. In any case, the point of education is not to cultivate the intellect or to sharpen man's native abilities. It is only an adjunct to evangelizing.

* * *

Just as the Jesus People are anti-intellectual, so they are anti-cultural. In terms of H. Richard Niebuhr's four approaches to the relationship between Christianity and human culture (elaborated in his *Christ and Culture*), the Jesus People are casebook examples of the Christ-against-culture approach. This places them at odds with Augustine, Aquinas, Luther, Calvin, and a host of other great Christian thinkers. Rather than seeing the Bible as the criterion by which to judge all human attempts to discover truth, the Jesus People see the Bible as exhaustive truth. But the Bible does not provide an exhaustive exposition of all truth: it gives no description of the physical universe in all its complexity; and it is obviously a logical impossibility that the Scriptures, revealed during a certain time span in history,

168

could have an exhaustive account of history that followed the time of the writing of the Bible. Such examples could, of course, be multiplied almost endlessly, but the point is clear. The anti-intellectual, anti-cultural bias of the Jesus People can rest only on an obviously erroneous understanding of the Bible.

The root of the anti-cultural fundamentalism of the Jesus People is their inadequate understanding of the nature of man. On the basis of an extreme view of man's depravity, they see culture as something demonic, wholly bad, not as something human, therefore good and bad. Typical expression of this viewpoint is found in the books of Watchman Nee, one of the few extra-biblical sources that Jesus People are likely to read. In his book, *Love Not the World,* Nee asserts that "Christian civilization is the outcome of an attempt to reconcile the world and Christ" (p. 46). In his view,

> Politics, education, literature, science, art, law, commerce, music — such are the things that constitute the *kosmos,* and these are things we meet daily. Subtract them and the world as a coherent system ceases to be. . . . In the book of Genesis we find in Eden no hint of technology, no mention of mechanical instruments. After the Fall, however, we read that among the sons of Cain there was a forger of cutting instruments of brass and iron. . . . The same thing applies to music and the arts. For the pipe and the harp seem also to have originated with the family of Cain, and today in unconsecrated hands their God-defying nature becomes increasingly clear. . . . As for commerce, its connections are perhaps even more suspect. Satan was the first merchant, trading ideas with Eve for his own advantage. . . . But what of education? Surely, we protest, that must be harmless. Anyway, our children have to be taught. But education, no less than commerce or technology, is one of the things of the world. It has its roots in the tree of knowledge (pp. 14-15).

Obviously it is not a long step from Watchman Nee to the Children of God. Many Jesus People are susceptible to the radical teachings of the Children, for they share the common ground of being anti-cultural. Culture is not human, but Satanic:

> Do we acknowledge that Satan is today the prince of education and science and culture and the arts, and that they, with him, are doomed? . . . Test yourself. If you venture into one of these approved fields, and then someone exclaims to you: "You have touched the world there", will you be moved? Probably

169

not at all. It takes someone whom you really respect to say to you very straightly and earnestly: "Brother, you have become involved with Satan there!" before you will as much as hesitate. Is that not so? How would you feel if anyone said to you: "You have touched education there", or "You have touched medical science", or "You have touched commerce"? Would you react with the same degree of caution as you would if he had said, "You have touched the Devil there"? If we truly believed that whenever we touch any of these things that constitute the world we touch the prince of this world, then the awful seriousness of being in any wise involved in worldly things could not fail to strike home to us . . . (pp. 17-18).

Or suppose you are in engineering, or farming, or publishing. Take heed, for these too are things of the world, just as much as running a place of entertainment or a haunt of vice. Unless you tread softly you will be caught up somewhere in Satan's snares and will lose the liberty that is yours as a child of God (p. 24).

These anti-cultural assertions of Watchman Nee represent the kind of thinking that permeates the Jesus People. This outlook propounds a radical separation of Christianity from culture and blithely assumes that this is the only possible outlook that is genuinely scriptural. It is based upon the acceptance of the absolute worthlessness of the natural man. It is based, that is to say, on a view of man that is deficient and subscriptural. The Bible does say, "There is none that doeth good, no, not one." But the context of this passage refers to a man's inability to be justified by his own efforts. The emphasis is that man comes short of God's standard of perfection. The Bible also speaks of man's being created in the image of God, and one must be very careful about calling the pinnacle of God's creation bad. Francis Schaeffer reminds us that the Bible does not allow us to call man "junk." It is true that man fell and that the fall *marred* the image of God bestowed on man at creation, but that image was not *erased*. Even fallen men are still in the image of God. They have such characteristics of God as rationality, aesthetic sensibility, personality, ability to communicate, ability to have personal relationships.

Total depravity does not mean that every time man has a choice, he makes the very worst possible one. Common sense and observation are enough to show that some unregenerate men are on occasion good neighbors and capable of performing good deeds. But God's standard for a personal relationship with him is perfection, and no man is capable of this. Total depravity means that man's sinfulness cuts across every area of his life — spiritual, emotional, physical, moral, and others.

The doctrine of creation balances the doctrine of man's sinfulness. Created in the image of God, man — even though fallen — is to subdue the earth and have dominion over it. This is what makes cultural enterprises — education, art, science, human government, technology, and the like — legitimate. On the other side the doctrine of sin shows that man will never be able to operate in these spheres with perfection and that he must not therefore hope for a solution to the human condition in human achievements.

Christian literature demonstrates over and over again that man is both great and miserable, but he is never viewed as worthless, as a piece of junk. It is only since the Christian synthesis of the Middle Ages and the Renaissance has broken down and man has come to consider himself as a god that the view of man has taken a turn for the worse. In general, modern literature does not show man as great; it shows him only as miserable. It has flattened out the richness and diversity of human nature. It has reduced man's status to that of the animal or the machine. If a Christian thinks that secular society views man as good and not in need of help from an outside source, he is only showing his ignorance of the society in which he lives. Inadvertently, he demonstrates the need for education that will give him the knowledge of the culture in which he lives, even if for no other reason than to be an effective witness in it. The pacesetters of our culture today see man not as great but as miserable. It is the greatness which has been lost and which the Christian must be at pains to assert in order to recall the biblical image of man.

The anti-church sentiments of the Jesus People may be seen, in part at least, as an extension of this anti-cultural bias. The church is a human institution, and all human institutions are corrupt. It is possible to criticize the abuses of an institution without denying its right to exist. But the radically individualistic stance that the Jesus People take to religion lacks a feeling for the tradition of the church — good and bad. Their all-or-nothing mentality leads them to automatic condemnation of and contempt for the church as an institution.

* * *

Part and parcel of the anti-cultural stance of the Jesus People is their anti-social attitude. Since the heyday of the Social Gospel there has been tension in Christendom between preaching the gospel as a call for alleviating social woes and as a call to personal salvation. It has taken decades for evangelicals to see that there is no contradiction between the two. The Jesus People do not see this. They emphasize individual conversion to the almost total neglect of the social dimension of the gospel. One of Larry Norman's songs, "Right Here in America," says in part:

> Let's stop marching for peace and start marching for Jesus,
> And peace will take care of itself.

Getting Jesus' peace into one's heart may be the best single contribution which an individual can make toward world peace, but it is not sufficient by itself. Even if everyone in the world became a Christian, it is doubtful that peace would "take care of itself." Church history offers little reason for such high hopes. Squabbling between and within denominations has historically been one of the sorriest blights on the church. Even a small congregation is likely to fall prey to conflicts between individuals. Though these lyrics of Norman do not show him at his best, they unfortunately do represent the thinking of the vast majority of Jesus People.

In his book *A Plea for Evangelical Demonstration,* Carl Henry points out that "the Biblical view declares both individual conversion and social justice to be alike indispensable. The Bible calls for personal holiness and for sweeping societal changes; it refuses to substitute private religion for social responsibility or social engagement for personal commitment to God" (p. 107). Henry argues that evangelicals must emphasize social involvement today, because they have minimized it in recent years.

> The Christian not only has liberty to protest flagrant social injustices publicly, but he has in fact a double basis, his humanity and his religious vision, for applying fearless moral pres-

sure against unjust power pockets. . . . The time is overdue for a dedicated vanguard to move evangelical witness to frontier involvement in the social crisis, an involvement to be followed, pray God, by universal engagement of the evangelical churches in social witness and betterment (pp. 19, 22).

The underground newspapers of the Jesus People do occasionally demonstrate some awareness that the world about them is racked by great social issues. But they use these issues as a clever jumping-off point for a call to individual conversion. The issue itself is avoided. As we mentioned in chapter three, the *Hollywood Free Paper* is skilled in capitalizing on, but actually avoiding, social issues. Under the headline "How Moral Is War?" one ought not to expect a thoughtful Christian analysis:

> Nobody digs war. Pain and suffering are not cool, that's for sure. But the really weird thing is that everyone is responsible for war. Nope. We're not talking about Vietnam, we're talking about personal warfare inside of the individual. Dig?
>
> Most people are right in the middle of a super-heavy battle right now. That's right! But it's happening inside of them. Sure, they might shoot off their mouths about how immoral the "war" is and few will deny that fact. But, they've really got no platform to gripe. Not until they get their own personal war worked out inside their heads. Get the point?

We do, of course, but we had wished for something more substantial. Another headline blares, "Release the Prisoners." It deals neither with the conditions in American prisons nor with the POW issue:

> It's really a bummer when you flash on to the fact that we're all really born prisoners. Whether we dig it or not, we're all slaves to our ego-trips. Yea, that's right! We're born behind bars and the freaky thing is that most of us prisoners end up building bigger prison walls every time we try to escape.

Ecology?

> There's a lot of talk flying around about pollution — air pollution, water pollution, etc. Whether you're hip or straight, "ecology" seems to be what's happening in the news, and for obvious reasons. Nobody seems to dig pollution, no matter what side of the "credibility gap" they're on.
>
> Now God's "ecology" is unique. Man has raped the earth and polluted it because he lost his dominion. This is the reason

173

for the very worst kind of pollution — soul pollution. We've all got it. It's caused by what we call sin — ego-tripping.

God knows that pollution in nature won't be solved until man gets his dominion back. Therefore, the first thing to take care of is the soul pollution problem. That's step number one. God wants us to have dominion, and Jesus makes it possible for us to have it once again.

When we accept Jesus as liberator from sin (soul pollution), our dominion is individually and personally restored to us. He purchased the right for us to get back when he died on the Cross. Isn't that heavy? That's part of the inheritance we get as a free gift when we become a Christian.

A light veneer of counter-culture jargon smeared over a soul-winner's tract is *HFP*'s substitute for dealing with social issues:

Maybe it's time we get off our stupid soap box and quit waving our little flag. Maybe it's about time we stop bitching at the establishment for screwing up when we haven't offered a better solution yet. Better yet, why don't we just shut up for two seconds and let God tell us His solution.

It's strange, but dig this. A couple mills ago God sent his son into a similar situation as the one we're in. It was similar in that the Roman establishment was trying to manufacture plastic people. A lot of our brothers back then tried to smash the system by violence and it was a real bummer.

Right in the middle of all that, Jesus came to do God's thing. But it was weird. No guns, no bombings, no griping at the power freaks. Jesus just loved people that's all, and it got the attention of the whole world. As a matter of fact, He still does. Heavy, isn't it?

* * *

The Jesus People are also anti-historical. This is something they share with the counter-culture out of which many of them have come. It is no accident that the Jesus Movement began in California and is still strongest there. Southern California is the epitome of the rootlessness that plagues greater and greater segments of Western society today. It is the birthplace of innumerable zany sects and cults, and the characteristic that almost all of these share is an anti-historical stance that goes along with alienation from Western civilization.

The whole period during which Christian values shaped human culture is now seen by the Jesus People as one Dark

174

Age. Time is collapsed between the period of the Book of Acts and the present day. Almost all Jesus People see themselves as the church of the Book of Acts reincarnate, not as Christians standing in a line of thinkers and workers of the generations between the time of Pentecost and today. In their minds, historical continuity is broken. (One cannot help observing the irony in the fact that many of them read the King James Version of the Bible as *the* inspired text. The KJV was the literary creation of men steeped in Christian culture. But, then, consistency and clarity of thought are not prominent among the Jesus People.)

Given this anti-historical dimension, it is not surprising that there are tendencies toward exclusivism within the movement. People who call themselves Christians but do not identify directly with the Jesus People are suspect. A letter to the editor in the *Hollywood Free Paper* illustrates the point:

> . . . I'm positive that the "Jesus People" are bringing back New Testament Christianity and are living like Jesus really wants. This part of the country is called the "Bible belt," which is really a laugh because about the only time the Word is preached is Sunday morning (the same time when the people meet together to tell each other that they are Christians). Just a few of us are waking up to the Jesus scene all over America and we need your help.

Duane Pederson says, "If you don't dig the Jesus People, you can bet your eternal life that you don't know Jesus."

Various elements within the Jesus Movement view other elements as nonelect — sometimes even as demonic. The Children of God see themselves as the only ones; some other Jesus People see the Children of God as a Satanic imitation of the genuine article. The Alamos' followers declare that *they* are Joel's Army — and they do not mean that they are a part of it. They *are* it. Even individual communes imagine that they are the only ones true to God. To the extent to which the tendency toward exclusivism becomes developed and full-blown, the Jesus People contribute to the divisiveness among Christians. Fortunately, there are tendencies within the movement that pull in the opposite direction. It is not clear at this time which pull will eventually be stronger.

* * *

The general simple-mindedness of the Jesus People has wide-spread effects. It is directly responsible for the faddishness of much of the movement, for example, the "bumper-sticker" mentality. Bumper stickers and posters by their very nature can contain only very short statements. They are good for sloganeering, but not for much else. They do little to enhance precision of thought. Jesus bumper stickers are occasionally clever ("Read the Bible, It'll Scare the Hell out of You"), but usually they are not ("Honk If You Love Jesus"). In any case they seem to represent a mentality that does not penetrate beneath the surface of issues. This superficial thinking also characterizes their identification with the counter-culture: the use of hip lingo is seldom more than a point of contact.

We found most Jesus People singularly difficult to interview. Whatever the question, the first word of their response is "I." This is not because of egotism, but because they are experience-oriented. Thus, all of their answers are narrative. This is frustrating if the question calls for a descriptive or analytic response. Jesus People generally perceive life as a series of consecutive experiences like pearls on a string. They cannot usually step back and view life as a totality set against the background of the tapestry of history. They are radically existential.

Another manifestation of the simple-mindedness of the Jesus People can be seen in their response to psychological and even physiological disorders. They place a great emphasis on faith healing and immediate cures through conversion for personal problems like homosexuality and drug addiction. We do not doubt for a moment that divine power can bring miraculous cures for any human ills. But one must also recognize that God has created a moral order in which actions have consequences. Faith in Christ does not erase that moral order, and actions committed before conversion can have physiological, psychological, and moral consequences after conversion.

A typical discussion of homosexuality is found in Arthur Blessitt's *Turned On to Jesus:*

> I've prayed with dozens of homosexuals who've told God that they'd give up unclean sex. I've led several to the Lord, notably a twenty-three-year-old gay named Carlos who ran the largest ring of male prostitutes in Hollywood. He had a large pad, a big car, and bank accounts and had been on dope since he

first tried opium while serving in Vietnam. I worked with Carlos for several days, and God granted him conviction, giving him a totally natural desire for women. He came to the Lord with his whole heart and soul, making a total commitment, finding the strength to overcome his deviation. He dates only girls now, and is as joyful a Christian as there is on this earth. He plans to marry and have a family (p. 124).

A letter to the *Hollywood Free Paper* says, "I was a homosexual and Jesus set me free! It happened with a prayer and a baptism that now I can look to my own sex and desire only that he find Jesus too!"

Great care is necessary when discussing immediate cures for drug addiction, which happen often upon conversion according to Jesus People. We have spoken with members of other religious groups who are not Jesus People and in some cases not even Christians, and have heard of the same kind of success in curing drug addiction. The Black Muslims make the same claim. If Jesus is just an emotional experience, a new high to replace the drug high, why isn't a different experience that accomplishes the same end just as valid? David Wilkerson makes it clear in his recent book, *The Untapped Generation,* that many converts must struggle long and hard with the process of withdrawal. The new birth does not exempt them from this difficult and painful process. Nevertheless, we have heard too many convincing testimonies of this phenomenon of an immediate cure from drug addiction to discount them altogether.

Dr. Hardin B. Jones, professor of physiology and medical physics at the University of California, has done extensive research in the area of drug abuse. He has interviewed many Jesus Freaks who have told essentially the same story. They say that they have reached the end of their rope and are fearful that a continued use of drugs will soon cause them to die. In their extremity they pray, and when a great sense of relief comes, they commit themselves to Jesus. Thereupon, the stories run, they go to sleep and usually sleep for about twenty-four hours. When they awake, they have lost their dependency upon drugs. He can give no adequate scientific explanation for this phenomenon and calls it the closest thing he as a scientist has seen to a miracle. He points out that there are other cures for drug addiction that avoid the process of withdrawal. A traumatic shock can sometimes do the job, as can a conversion to

177

Buddhism or an entering into one or another form of Oriental meditation. However, his experience has been that the Jesus Freaks have had a full and immediate restoration of physical and sensual powers, which has not accompanied the other avenues to an immediate cure of drug dependence.

There seems then to be substantial evidence that the testimonies of Jesus Freaks about being cured from drug addiction without going through the process of withdrawal are based on fact. For persons to give testimony to that experience is proper and unobjectionable. What is objectionable is the accompanying inference that God must and will always perform this same miracle in the life of any drug addict who accepts him. There is equally abundant evidence to support this side of the equation: many Jesus Freaks face a long, hard struggle to overcome their drug habit after conversion.

In this discussion of the simple gospel and its effects, we have not intended to suggest in any way that a person must have sophistication or a refined intellect to become a genuine Christian. There is a simplicity in Christ that some of the Jesus People have successfully recovered. Furthermore, not all of the Jesus People are as simple-minded as the more extreme of those instances cited in this chapter. But there is a strong tendency throughout the movement toward simple-mindedness, and this tendency is unhealthy. For it leads to the proclamation of only half of the truth. It would be equally fragmentary to proclaim the intellectual, cultural, social, historical, and other ramifications of the gospel without first paying attention to the matter of individual regeneration. But the situation need not be one of either/or; it should be one of both/and. When it is not, a person is guilty of not declaring the whole counsel of God.

nine

THE LAST DAYS

Here Comes the Son

NEXT TO THE SIMPLE GOSPEL, PERHAPS THE MOST PROMINENT IDEA of the Jesus People is that we are living in the last days. Without exception, the Jesus People with whom we talked believe that these are the last days and that Christ will return in their lifetimes. They cannot imagine themselves growing old and dying a natural death. Many believe that they will not die at all. Others believe that they will die as martyrs for Christ.

Everything in the Jesus Movement is colored by this apocalyptic mentality. Bumper stickers flaunt it; songs repeat it; witnessing returns to it over and over again; sermons and personal conversations are obsessed by it. Typical is Larry Norman's song, "I Wish We'd All Been Ready," which envisions a married couple being separated by the rapture, since one member is saved and one is not. The standard handbill passed out on Hollywood Boulevard by the Christian Foundation teams reads, "Repent now. Jesus is coming soon." Chuck Smith, Pastor of Calvary Chapel, says,

> The last days are upon us, and the Spirit of God is being poured out upon us. And it's just God's plan. It's just coming to completion. The Bible is full of prophetic utterances which described the last times, and we can see that the world's really living in a whole lot of chaotic, bad ways. You want to call it sin. That's what the Bible would call it. It's prophesied in

179

the Bible that the Lord will pour the Spirit down upon all men, and I believe that is happening. And I believe that it won't be long until we see the Second Coming of the Lord.

David Hoyt has written,

> We look forward to the end harvest and the coming of our Lord. He is coming soon for a living bride, full of Grace and Truth and eagerly waiting his return. Our wonderful Lord deserves much more than a barren old maid of stale religion based on carnal division and the doctrines of men.

Linda Meissner concurs:

> As the final stages of fulfillment are upon us of Jesus' immortal words 'Go ye into all the world, and preach the gospel to every creature,' God is raising up a great last day army. It is becoming a reality through the method of reproducing reproducers.

To our question about whether we are living in the last days, she replied:

> Absolutely. We believe this is the last generation. And what are the signs? They're all over the place. . . . I believe the return of Christ is very, very close. We also believe that . . . there's a heavy storm coming. . . . No one can say the day and the hour. If you would ask the people in the Jesus People Movement, they would say three to twenty years. That's not very long, when you think that it's our job to fulfil the Great Commission in this generation. And it's storm conditions in which we're going to have to do it.

Similar sentiments abound in the Jesus underground papers.

* * *

While some of the Jesus People say that Christ could come at any moment, others say that there are still a few signs that need to be fulfilled before that great event. Tony Alamo says that the Temple of Jerusalem must be rebuilt first.

> But that could be done so fast with modern day architecture. . . . It could be very fast. But it says it will be rebuilt, and just recently they found it. It didn't say they'd build a new Temple. It says the Temple in Jerusalem will be rebuilt and there it is. . . . They unearthed it, and what would they have to do to rebuild it?

He suggests the modern architectural technique of erecting

180

prefabricated buildings as a possible solution for an extremely quick rebuilding of the Temple.

The belief that these are the last days is intimately bound up with the anti-cultural stance of the Jesus People. There is no time left for the luxury of going to college, no time for the long, slow process of infiltrating into the social institutions and bearing a Christian witness through involvement in them. There is only time for the preaching of the gospel of repentance, for saving souls from the coming wreckage. And there is barely enough time for that.

The end times will manifest consummate evil, and this means that true believers will suffer persecution at the hands of a godless society. A recent issue of *Truth* includes an account of Jesus People being beaten up by unbelievers. It concludes:

> We have included this account, not to impress anyone with our exploits, but because we have done nothing besides that which God commands. We simply want the people everywhere to wake up to the fact that Christians are being persecuted right here in our town with increasing frequency. The above incident is not the first. Jesus People have suffered numerous attacks. Several weeks ago a brother's face was slashed with a knife because he said Praise the Lord around the wrong people. His picture would have been too unpleasant to print. It is time that people realized that Jesus People are deadly serious about serving Christ. We are not a bunch of hippy kids playing games. We are preaching the gospel at the expense of physical abuse. The Bible states quite explicitly that this will happen. "Yea, and ALL that will live Godly in Christ Jesus SHALL suffer persecution." II Tim. 3:12. But anyone who is waiting for persecution to come through closed church doors is going to be disappointed. Persecution only comes when you live your faith and spread the gospel to the world.

The Alamos also tell of being persecuted by the police. Arthur Blessitt sees police efforts to clean up Sunset Strip directed in part against his ministry to hippies. Los Angeles-area Jesus People frequently explain that while beer busts and pot parties in private homes are not illegal in their county, prayer meetings and Bible studies are. A member of the House of Ebenezer in San Francisco, one of the Harvest House communes, told us that there were posters all over Haight Street urging the killing of all Christians. He also explained that a few days earlier the newspapers had carried a story of the Black Panthers declaring war against the Christians in the Bay Area. We went to the specific area where he said such signs abounded, but there was no evidence of them.

The apocalyptic mentality is very strong today in American society at large. The invention of the atomic bomb began the current apocalyptic mood, and one of several more recent manifestations of it is the powerful concern with pollution of the environment. Another is the radical view of the political situation in America: that American government is beyond reforming and must be destroyed totally in order for something new and better to take its place. While the apocalyptic mood cuts across a wide swath of American society, it is perhaps strongest in the counter-culture. Many of the Jesus People are converts out of the counter-culture, and they still share its radical and apocalyptic views of our times.

Jesus People like to point out that even non-Christians are well aware of impending doom. There are, they say, plenty of secular arguments supporting the notion that the world cannot go on much longer. When asked for evidence to support his assertion that we are in the last days, Duane Pederson replied:

> Well, the people who are involved with the ecology trip — they say that we're done. They say that we're all wiped up as a world. We can't last. That's what they say. This isn't any religious freaks that are saying that. Professors from all major colleges — they say that we're wiped out. Are we going to believe them? If we read the Bible, it says about the same thing. Are we going to believe the Bible? Or we can put them both together and believe them both and we're still wiped out.

Linda Meissner says,

> We believe that the Son's coming, and it's interesting that most of the subculture believes the storm's coming. You talk to straight society and they'll tell you, "Oh, the money's going to hold together and the times are going to be good, and everything's just going to be fine." But if you talk to the subculture people, they'll tell you there's a storm brewing. There's something going to happen. Non-Christians did a survey in the Bay Area, and they asked the kids why they were into drugs. . . . The top three answers were the end of the world is coming, Jesus is coming back to us again, and a third world war. Kids on the streets know there's something going to happen. They know that this is the last generation. You can feel that there's a storm in the air. . . . We believe that we're going to have a

short period in which we can preach the gospel in freedom. We believe that we'll have a little bit longer time to break the storm and to preach it.

Jesus People see in current events abundant signs confirming scriptural prophecy about the end of time. Meissner goes on:

There have been more earthquakes per time period now than ever in history. That bears it out. I've heard varying figures. Some say every hundred years, four major earthquakes. Someone said now that we've had twenty-six or twenty-four, but it's a fantastic figure. It says in the last times that there will be pestilences. Well, right now there are terrible plagues that are coming in different countries all over the earth, and the scientists are scared. We read that in the newspapers. Famines — the scientists tell you that. Pollution — the Book of Revelation says a third of the life in the seas are going to die and a third of the green trees, and a third of the sun is going to be hid. And that's just pollution. The moon's going to become red as blood. It doesn't say it is going to be blood. It's from the pollution in the air. When you're in Los Angeles, in the morning or in the evening, you can't see the sun because of pollution. Unrest, unthankfulness, all of them are there. . . . Our country and the world is in the greatest crisis it's ever been in any time of history. . . .

She adds, "Like the Bible says, in the last days the whole world would be on dope. It is."

Another sign is the emergence of the false church. This is, of course, the institutional church, particularly in its ecumenical manifestations, "the Great Whore of Babylon," as the Children of God are fond of saying.

The many conversions to Christianity occurring in Indonesia are seen to be signs of the last times. Jesus People recite accounts of the raising of the dead by young Christians there. Related to this is the phenomenon of a large number of Jews now coming to Christ. Tony and Susan Alamo both claim to be Jews by birth, and their followers proudly point to their elders as Hebrew Christians. David Berg, founder of the Children of God, says that he is Jewish. Many of the Jesus groups boast about their Jewish converts. Some of the Jesus People participate in a ministry called "Jews for Jesus." The dances of the Children of God are called the dances of Judah, and the Children follow as much as possible the life style of an Israeli kibbutz, with children being raised communally, not by parents.

183

The Children of God also take on Jewish Old Testament names and attempt as much as possible to follow the organizational pattern of ancient Israel, using the names of tribes and, wherever possible, imitating things Jewish.

Perhaps the most important signs of all are those relating to the nation of Israel. Linda Meissner says,

> Israel is a fantastic timepiece. It speaks of the Battle of Armageddon, and everything's going to happen over there, and it's lining up for that right now. We're all looking toward Vietnam, but we really know that the big one's going to come around Israel and Arab [sic].

When Israel allegedly regained its previously lost territory in the 1967 war, God supposedly set in motion the prophecy of Joel that young people would spearhead the great evangelistic effort of the last days. The Jesus People see themselves as the fulfilment of that prophecy. The Christian Foundation sees itself as Joel's Army. Most other Jesus People see themselves in terms of that same prophecy. The prophecy, which is one of the most important passages in the Jesus People canon, is found in Joel 2:28-32.

In his sermon on the day of Pentecost, Peter quoted that prophecy and prefaced it with the remark: "But this is that which was spoken by the prophet Joel" (Acts 2:16). But since the Jesus People collapse all history between the Book of Acts and the present moment, they see themselves as the continuing fulfilment of Joel's words. As the church in the Book of Acts represented "the former rain" that brought the first fruits, the Jesus People adhere to the standard Pentecostalist view that they are "the latter rain" referred to by the prophets and that they will bring in the last fruits of the great harvest which will immediately precede the second coming. Even now, say some Jesus People spokesmen, the Antichrist is alive and walking the face of the earth. It is not clear who it is, but that will become clear very soon.

* * *

Most of the Jesus People are appropriately hazy about the exact details of the apocalypse. They emphasize that "no man knoweth the day nor the hour," but they have no doubt whatsoever that these are the last times. Naturally, detailed explanations of this have been worked out.

Perhaps the most bizarre is that of R. D. Cronquist, a carpenter-turned-preacher who pastors the Grace Chapel of Imperial Beach, California. He explains, "The Bible says no man knows the day or the hour. But he did not say that no man can know the year or the month or even possibly the week." He adds, "I know that I will be a martyr for Christ." According to him, the Bible contains exactly thirty-seven prophecies concerning Christ's first coming, all of which were fulfilled. "There's almost three times more prophecies concerning the second coming. . . . In fact, there's one hundred twelve." The first was fulfilled in 1948 when Israel became a nation. "Since that time, one hundred six of those prophecies have been fulfilled. Up to five years ago that was so. Up to the June war in 1967."

Jesus ministered three-and-one-half years on this earth, but since seven is the number of perfection, "Jesus has got three and a half years yet to fulfil." In this second three-and-a-half years, Jesus will come in corporate form, not as an individual. His message will be that of the seventh angel of the Book of Revelation. Since a biblical generation is, according to him, forty years long, this means that the second coming must occur before 1988, which would be forty years after 1948. He claims that spiritual Israel was also reborn in 1948, as well as physical Israel: "In 1948 God poured out his Spirit upon Azusa Street in Los Angeles, California, and then came the gifts of the Spirit in operation again for the first time since the beginning of the church age." This final "prophet generation" will have the task of "restoring the earth back to its Edenic state. And then shall Jesus return." Cronquist continues:

> A few years ago I thought that 1970 would bring the end. And then I received more light, and I thought that 1973 or 74 would bring the end. Then I received more light, and I thought 1977 or 78 would bring the end. Then I received more light, and I feel that it could possibly go to 1980 or 81 or possibly 82 or somewhere in there.

Cronquist says that we are either in the beginning of the Great Tribulation or in the time of sorrows. He considers the pre-tribulation rapture "one of the most damnable heresies of the

185

church." He adds, "Every believer that does not have the Baptism, the infilling of the Holy Spirit with the evidence of talking of tongues, will not be in the rapture."

Tony Alamo also hints darkly of the possibility that we may already be in the period of Great Tribulation, although, for a welcome change, he is not dogmatic. But he is sure of this much: "I know we're going to go through some of the heavy tribulation."

There are three different premillennial views of the rapture of the saints by Christ: post-tribulation, mid-tribulation, and pre-tribulation. Some believe that Christians will endure all seven years of the Great Tribulation, others that they will endure the first three-and-a-half years of the Great Tribulation, still others that they will be taken out of the world at the beginning of the Great Tribulation and not endure any of it. All three views are present among the Jesus People.

The Children of God are the most notable proponents of the post-tribulation view. Thus they see communal living as the only acceptable pattern for Christians. According to their schema, all persons living during the Great Tribulation will have to have the Mark of the Beast, 666, inscribed upon their foreheads in order to buy and sell. Those Christians who participate in the world system will be unable to endure to the end without accepting the Mark of the Beast, and that mark will doom them to hell. Only the Children of God will survive this greatest of all persecutions. They will perhaps be broken up and will have to flee to the hills in order to survive, but they will have been prepared for survival apart from the system. Each one will have to be strong enough to stand on his own, which is why there is a need for the intensive study of the Bible which they are presently engaging in. Like Cronquist, they see the pre-tribulation view as a delusive heresy and its proponents as dreamers who are attempting to avoid the harsh discipline necessary to prepare for the tribulation. David Hoyt explains:

> Many of you today have been led astray in thinking that the world shall continue on as it is, or that one sunny Sunday morning while you're leaving church that Jesus will come and take you home to glory. Today's "leaders" speak of how Jesus can come at any moment while they take up a collection for a

Expectation of the rapture

10-year building program. This all stems from a lack of knowledge about Bible prophecy which many of us have had. The Lord, however, is not coming before the tribulation, He is coming after the tribulation. . . . The big emphasis on "the rapture" is a trick of the Enemy and an excuse to mislead us so that we would never have the rigid preparation, training, and discipline that will be necessary for the bride of Christ during the Great Tribulation. This tribulation is rapidly approaching whether the world believes it or not.

The Harvest House ministries of San Francisco also reject the pre-tribulation view, though they do not make a clear distinction between mid- and post-tribulation views. Tony Alamo leans toward the mid-tribulationist view: "Just like the Bible says, the born-again Christian will be raptured out of the real bad stuff."

A recent best-seller that spells out a typical pre-tribulationist view is Hal Lindsey's *The Late Great Planet Earth*. This book has had a widespread appeal among the Jesus People — at least among those who read books other than the Bible (and the pre-tribulationists are more likely to read books, it seems, than are the post-tribulationists). Lindsey's book is a popular rehash of the pre-tribulational premillennialism that has been propounded widely during the past century. Its novelty lies in the fact that new historical events are further grist to the mill of the interpreters of Bible prophecy.

Lindsey sees the state of Israel as the most important element in the reading of the signs of the times.

To be specific about Israel's great significance as a sign of the time, there are three things that were to happen. First, the Jewish nation would be reborn in the land of Palestine. Secondly, the Jews would repossess old Jerusalem and the sacred sites. Thirdly, they would rebuild their ancient temple of worship upon its historic site (pp. 50-51).

187

Two of these three have been fulfilled, and the remaining one is the building of the Temple.

> There is only one place that this Temple can be built, according to the Law of Moses. This is upon Mount Moriah. . . . There is one major problem barring the construction of a third Temple. That obstacle is the second holiest place of the Moslem faith, the Dome of the Rock. This is believed to be built squarely in the middle of the old temple site. Obstacle or no obstacle, it is certain that the Temple will be rebuilt. Prophecy demands it (pp. 55-56).

He cites an interview with the Israeli historian Israel Eldad, who says, "From the time that King David first conquered Jerusalem until Solomon built the Temple, just one generation passed. So will it be with us." When Israel Eldad was asked about the obstacle of the Dome of the Rock, he replied, "It is, of course, an open question. Who knows, maybe there will be an earthquake" (p. 57).

Lindsey's explanations expand to cover the whole globe. Africa, he says, will become Communist. The Asian hordes will wipe out a third of the earth's population (Rev. 9:18). The form prophesied for this destruction of life is "an accurate first-century description of a twentieth-century thermonuclear war" (p. 82). China will be the spearhead of this great power called "the kings of the east." The Common Market and the trend toward European unification are the beginnings of the ten-nation confederacy predicted by Daniel and the Book of Revelation. This prediction entails that the United States will cease to be the leader of the Western world and will be a tangent to the European sphere of power. The leader of Europe will have his seat of government in Rome, and this "Future Fuehrer" will be the Antichrist. The Antichrist will be a person who seems to have come back from the dead after having suffered a critical wound.

> This is something which will cause tremendous amazement throughout the world.

> We could draw a comparison to the tragic death of John F. Kennedy. Imagine what would have happened if the President of the United States, after being shot and declared dead, had come back to life! The impact of an event like that would shake the world.

> It is not difficult to imagine what will happen when this

coming world leader makes his miraculous recovery. This man, the Antichrist, will probably not be known as a great leader until the time of his revival from the fatal wound. After that, the whole world will follow him.

He will have a magnetic personality, be personally attractive, and a powerful speaker. He will be able to mesmerize an audience with his oratory (p. 108).

The joining of churches in the present ecumenical movement is seen to be a preparation for the establishment of a great religious system that will be in cahoots with the Antichrist. The Great Tribulation will commence when a pact is signed between the Israeli leader and the Antichrist. The battle of Armageddon will pit "the combined forces of Western civilization united under the leadership of the Roman Dictator" against "the vast hordes of the Orient, probably united under the Red Chinese war machine" (p. 162).

Lindsey's belief in the impending holocaust leads him to make certain predictions.

I believe that open persecution will soon break out upon the "real Christians," and it will come from the powerful hierarchy of unbelieving leaders within the denominations. . . . Because of the persecution of the believers, there will grow a true underground church of a believing remnant of people (pp. 183-84).

Internal political chaos caused by student rebellions and Communist subversion will begin to erode the economy of our nation. Lack of moral principle by citizens and leaders will so weaken law and order that a state of anarchy will finally result. The military capability of the United States, though it is at present the most powerful in the world, has already been neutralized because no one has the courage to use it decisively. When the economy collapses so will the military (p. 184).

Look for drug addiction to further permeate the U.S. and other free-world countries. Drug addicts will run for high political offices and win through support of the young adults. Look for drugs and forms of religion to be merged together. There will be a great general increase of belief in extrasensory phenomena, which will not be related to the true God, but to Satan (p. 185).

We believe that in spite of all these things God is going to raise up a believing remnant of true Christians and give one last great offer of the free gift of forgiveness and acceptance in Jesus Christ before snatching them out of the world as it plunges toward judgment (p. 186).

The Jesus People, of course, see themselves as the fulfilment of this last prediction.

Lindsey's approach probably finds favor with a greater number of Jesus People than any of the other approaches. Although he avoids asserting that ours are definitely the last days, his matching up of prophecies and current events makes that conclusion overwhelmingly probable. His Jesus People readers, ignoring his slight caution, consider it a certainty.

Although there are differences in detail among the various Jesus People, it is important for purposes of understanding the Jesus Movement to see the similarities between the competing viewpoints. All of the Jesus People fervently believe that we are in the last days and that they are God's chosen instrument to give the world one last chance to repent. The differences in detail will doubtless be enough to cause serious divisions within the movement and to aggravate those already present, but there is an observable unity running through the whole movement that is more important than the differences.

* * *

An apocalyptic mood is not new in the history of Christianity. Throughout church history men have believed that they were living in the last times. Inevitably, they have pointed to the world around them and asked how it could possibly get any worse. Yet somehow the world managed to go on and perhaps even to get worse. The times that seemed to be the worst of all possible times seem now in retrospect often to have been not so bad.

The pre-tribulationist reading of the last times is of more recent vintage, dating back a century to John N. Darby, the founder of the Plymouth Brethren. Like Victor Wierwille and many others, Darby imagined that he was recovering a long-lost truth, hidden from Bible readers for almost 1900 years. Like the apocalypticists of our time, Darby believed that the church had not merely become corrupted but was in utter ruins. Its apostasy was a sign that the end was near. He, too, applied a rigid literalism to biblical prophecy and urged believers to forsake and repudiate the government and human culture in general.

One hundred years have gone by since Darby's prediction

that the end was near. Is it at all possible that one hundred years more could go by following the predictions of the Jesus People that the end is at hand?

While the emphasis on the impending apocalypse is not new to Christianity, the mixture of the charismatic experiences traditionally associated with Pentecostalism with the eschatology traditionally associated with dispensationalism is new. There was a small and short-lived similar combination in Great Britain during the nineteenth century known as Irvingism. The Irvingites were followers of Edward Irving, who saw the gift of tongues as being one of the signs of the last days. But this movement had no appreciable historical impact, and until the twentieth century the mixing of Pentecostalism and dispensationalism was unknown in church history. Perhaps the closest parallel is the Montanism of the second century.

The interpretation of biblical prophecy is very difficult, as is obvious from the multiplicity of readings that have been offered throughout church history. It is particularly difficult to interpret prophecies with a satisfactory degree of certainty before they are fulfilled. Prophecies are inevitably the most opaque passages of Scripture. After a prophecy is fulfilled, it is easier to see how the event that occurred was predicted long before in the Bible. Fulfilment of prophecy legitimately serves as a verification of the authenticity and reliability of Scripture. But prophecies are sometimes fulfilled in parts. Joel 2 was partly fulfilled at the day of Pentecost, according to Peter. In his first epistle Peter explains that the Old Testament prophets foresaw both the sufferings of Christ and the glory that should follow, but they were unable to see the huge gap of time that was to transpire between the sufferings and the glory. This mystery was clarified only after the passage of a great amount of time.

Many Bible scholars claim that one reason for the opacity of prophecies before they are fulfilled is the natural desire of believers in the prophecies to make them come true. This is certainly the case with the Jesus People, who try to make the prophecies about the last times come true by playing roles that they see as assigned to them. Though these efforts are understandable, they constitute an improper response to the prophetic passages. It is not for nothing that Jesus warned that no

191

man could know beforehand the precise time when prophecies about the last days would be fulfilled. Though the Jesus People know the verse, they do not take its implications with full seriousness. They believe that they, in fact, do know the general time of the end, and only a very literal reading of "day and hour" will suffice to forestall any objection to their confident certainty that they are the last generation of youth to walk the face of the earth.

What if they are not the last generation? What if the end is not now? What if today's youth grow old and die a natural death? What will happen to a movement that views itself as a direct fulfilment of an explicit biblical prophecy if that prophecy turns out not to be fulfilled in them? Is not such a confident and monolithic reading of obscure and difficult prophetic passages then a built-in source of future disillusionment? While the Jesus People scoff at such shilly-shallying questions now, will they still be scoffing thirty years from now? Psychologically, it seems inevitable that if the prophecies are not fulfilled in the precise way they expect them to be fulfilled, disastrous effects will follow. If fulfilled prophecies can serve as an index to the reliability of the Bible, unfulfilled prophecies can serve as an index to the unreliability of the Bible. And if the Bible seems to them to have been proved unreliable at this point, there is no reason for them to accept its veracity at all other points.

The early church, too, anticipated the imminent return of Christ. Surely, part of the staying power of the church depended on its ability, in the face of disappointment, to work out credible theological schemes by which the delay could be understood and accepted. So far the Jesus People face that "disappointment" without the powers of reflection that alone saved the early church from utter despair.

Since the whole ministry of the Jesus People is geared to the confident expectation that Jesus Christ will return in the very near future, the movement is inherently transient. Jesus People ministries come and go with alarming rapidity. Jesus People give no thought to the establishing of long-term ministries, because Christ will return soon and all of the work must be done in the immediate future. It is logical to surmise that if he does not return soon, this revival will lack some of the
192

staying power that has resulted from other revivals. The impact of the movement is more like a match that flares brightly but briefly than a steady candle flame of lower intensity but greater duration. To observe the intensity of many of the ministries, which sometimes involve an almost around-the-clock work load for certain leaders, is to wonder how long these energies can be sustained. If this is not the last generation, someone will have a lot of pieces to pick up — and that someone will have to have a Christian faith not so thoroughly linked to the fiercely apocalyptic mood of the Jesus People.

It is possible that the Jesus People themselves will mellow and mature. Perhaps the apocalyptic mood will wane. After all, almost all of them are very young. They may be able to develop some staying power that will see them through whatever disillusionments come if their eschatology turns out to be inaccurate. Of course, all of these worries will be unfounded if their views turn out to be correct. But how much of the future of the Christian church will we want to wager on that?

ten

POWER TO THE PEOPLE

Getting It On with the Holy Spirit

As a large-scale religious movement, Pentecostalism dates back to the beginning of the twentieth century. Until recently, it has been associated largely with a few denominational groups (such as the Assemblies of God) and a multiplicity of smaller groups and sects ranging from storefront missions to the snake handlers of Appalachia. Pentecostalists have traditionally been associated with the lower social and economic segments of our society. The title of a chapter in Vance Packard's popular book *The Status Seekers* indicates the nature of the popular image of many Pentecostals: "The Long Road from Pentecostal to Episcopal."

During the mid-1950s and especially during the 1960s, this long road was shortened considerably. To the dismay of some social theorists and to the amazement of many churchmen, the charismatic phenomenon began to invade denominations thought to be the furthest removed from Pentecostalism. Episcopalians, Lutherans, and Presbyterians began to be involved with charismatic phenomena. The new movement has come to be known as Neo-Pentecostalism. Old-line or "classical" Pentecostals have been very warm and generally accepting toward these newly arrived charismatics. Reflecting their traditional and often highly liturgical backgrounds, Neo-Pentecostals tend to be more subdued and less demonstrative in exercising their faith. The most recent manifestation of the spreading Neo-Pentecostal revival has been the emergence of the Catholic Pentecostal movement, sometimes known as the Charismatic Renewal of the Church.

Whatever label is attached to any of these subgroups within the larger Pentecostal movement, they share a basic orientation and certain characteristics. The Pentecostal is concerned above all with what he sees as a new dimension of spiritual life centering on the person and work of the Holy Spirit. The focal doctrine is Baptism in the Holy Spirit, which represents a new fulness, "an experience in which the Christian knows that the Holy Spirit not only dwells in him, but that he dwells in the Spirit" (Kilian McDonnell, "Holy Spirit and Pentecostalism," *Commonweal,* Nov. 1968, p. 198). In this chapter we shall discuss some of the experiences and manifestations unique to Pentecostal believers.

One of the most distinctive hallmarks of the Jesus Movement is its involvement in the Pentecostal scene. A number of Jesus People disavow any association with the label "Pentecostal," however. Some of the Jesus People are quite aware of the excesses that have characterized much of classical Pentecostalism, and they are attempting to avoid a repetition of these. Breck Stevens, assistant pastor of Bethel Tabernacle in Redondo Beach, California, states: "We've completely dropped the label 'Pentecostal' because of so much ungodliness going on under the name 'Pentecostal.' " Others dislike the emotionalism and fanaticism traditionally linked with some Pentecostal groups. Tony Alamo disclaims any association with the Pentecostal churches because, he states, "We don't believe in wild-eyed fanaticism. We're not holy rollers. We don't toss babies up in the air or handle snakes." Carl Parks of Spokane feels that the Pentecostal church at one time was a work of the Holy Spirit but that it has departed from its original purity and is now just another victim of tradition. A minister in one of the hip churches discussed in chapter four specifically requested that his church not be referred to as a "tongues" church, although charismatic phenomena were commonly experienced by members of his congregation.

Catholic theologian Kilian McDonnell describes Pentecostals as "People of the Bible" whose amazing growth is related to

195

their "spiritual vitality," "devotional ardor," the "clarity and immediacy of the sacred Word in their lives," and their "rich, even exaggerated view of the supernatural" (p. 199). These traits certainly characterize the Jesus People. They bring to mind the observations of Henry Van Dusen, former President of Union Theological Seminary. Writing about what he termed the new "third force" in American Protestantism, Dr. Van Dusen comments:

> There are several sources of strength which have made the third force the most extraordinary religious phenomenon of our time. Its groups preach a direct Biblical message readily understood. They commonly promise an immediate life-transforming experience of the living-God-in-Christ which is far more significant to many individuals than the version of it found in conventional churches.
>
> They directly approach people — in their homes, or on the streets, anywhere — and do not wait for them to come to church. They have great spiritual ardor, which is sometimes but by no means always excessively emotional. They shepherd their converts in an intimate, sustaining group-fellowship: a feature of every vital Christian renewal since the Holy Spirit descended on the disciples at the first Pentecost. They place strong emphasis on the Holy Spirit — so neglected by many traditional Christians — as the immediate, potent presence of God both in each human soul and in Christian fellowship. Above all they expect their followers to practice an active, untiring, seven-day-a-week Christianity (*Life*, June 6, 1958).

Obviously this description is as applicable to the Jesus People as it is to the "third force" Pentecostals whom Van Dusen was discussing. One is immediately reminded of the zeal of the Jesus People in their witnessing — on the beaches, on the street corners, at the rock festivals — and of the frequency of their gathering for Bible raps, fellowship sessions, or worship services.

* * *

Pentecostalism, both inside and outside the Jesus Movement, is popularly identified with speaking in tongues or glossolalia. Both secular and religious writers have given perhaps undue emphasis to this one dimension of the movement, giving the impression that Pentecostals do little more than speak in unknown tongues. Understandably, many Jesus People and tradi-

196

tional Pentecostalists resent this lopsided image. Nevertheless, the tongues issue remains a continuing source of discussion among Jesus People. Our purpose here is neither to present an historical analysis of the entire Pentecostal movement, nor to extend the existing theological debate, pro or con. But it is a matter of fact and observation that the majority of what we are calling Jesus People recognize speaking in tongues as a valid spiritual and devotional experience.

Ted Wise, a pioneer in the Jesus Movement, notes three groupings within the movement with regard to the question of tongues. First are what he terms "standard, hard-lined" Pentecostalists, who stress a kind of uncontrolled speaking in tongues and ecstatic utterances. According to Wise, these extremist elements do not conform to prescribed biblical patterns for the use of the gift of tongues. A second, more moderate group follows the biblical injunction that the gift of tongues should not be exercised unless there is present someone who possesses the gift of interpretation. These Jesus People feel that the private use of tongues is to be preferred over public demonstration. Third, there are those Jesus People who have been involved with the tongues movement and who have been, in his words, "burned by it." These individuals have rejected the tongues phenomenon and harbor varying degrees of disaffection for those who are participants in the charismatic movement. From our research, these would seem to be few.

Many charismatic Jesus People fear the abuse of tongues by individuals who allow pride and "the flesh" to predominate in their spiritual lives. Carl Parks, who was brought up in the Assemblies of God, states that ninety percent of the tongues speaking heard prior to joining the Jesus Movement were not of the Holy Spirit but "of the flesh," nothing more than another kind of ritual. Pentecostalists refer to "tongues of flesh" when describing people who are not moving in the Spirit as they should, but allowing their own human desires to prevail. These people want to make a demonstration before other people, and in this way they attempt to "use" the Holy Spirit. Breck Stevens claims that he and the pastor, along with a dozen others in Bethel Tabernacle, have the gift of discernment and therefore can determine whether a given instance of tongues speaking is of God or not. "We can spot it right away — even if they

197

come in here saying 'Praise God,' we can tell." According to the people at Bethel Tabernacle, "The devil has counterfeits for everything God has."

Parks is strongly opposed to teaching people how to speak in tongues. "When the Holy Spirit wants to speak in tongues, He can — He doesn't need our help." Victor Wierwille of The Way does not share this sentiment. He believes that one can learn to speak in tongues through practice: just open your mouth and try. Wierwille's followers have been known to interrupt conversations that they find distasteful by speaking in tongues. If young people in their group experience problems or make mistakes, a common response is "You weren't speaking in tongues enough." But Wierwille's radical tongues theology is not typical of the Jesus People. Most follow the classical Pentecostalists in teaching that the Baptism in the Holy Spirit is subsequent to salvation and is always accompanied by speaking in tongues. But this experience is differentiated from the gift of tongues, given only to some according to God's sovereign will. For some Jesus People, as with many Pentecostals, there is a "seeking" of tongues, a "tarrying" for the Spirit Baptism. Some converts claim a baptism experience almost concurrent with their salvation. Others point to a passage of time, usually no more than a few days or weeks, between their conversion and the infilling of the Spirit. Jesus People have been known to be converted, "delivered" from drugs, and baptized with the Holy Spirit all in the same evening. Still other young converts claimed no knowledge of a tongues experience until after having received teaching on the matter and often after receiving the "laying on of hands."

It is not at all unusual to encounter Jesus groups that claim that all of their members have spoken in tongues. Pentecostal proselyting is not unknown among the Jesus People; however, there is considerable acceptance of those who have not spoken in tongues. Sometimes Jesus People will point with pride to the fact that all nine gifts of the Spirit (the word of wisdom, the word of knowledge, faith, healing, miracles, prophecy, discerning of spirits, diverse kinds of tongues, and the interpretation of tongues) are in operation within the given fellowship. Frequently they single out classical Pentecostalists

198

as having only the gifts of tongues and interpretation of tongues in operation.

As we pointed out earlier, Jesus People use the gift of tongues both in private and in public. Unknown tongues, or, as they are sometimes referred to, the "tongues of angels," are often employed in private prayer. Public demonstration of tongues occasionally involves the use of a recognizable language. The avid beach evangelists at Bethel Tabernacle claim to have witnessed to people in both Spanish and Italian using the supernatural gift of tongues. John Sherrill's *They Speak with Other Tongues* relates instances of tongues speaking in Hebrew and Arabic, languages totally unknown to the speakers. Sherrill goes on to point out, however, that unrecognizable languages are still the kind most frequently encountered in Pentecostal circles (p. 91).

Tongues are by no means the focal point of Jesus People theology. "Outsiders are much mystified by the phenomenon of tongues, and their fascination with it makes them attribute an importance to it that it does not have in the life of the Pentecostal community. Pentecostals do not gather for the precise purpose of speaking in tongues" (McDonnell, p. 199). In fact, Jesus People are the first to acknowledge that glossolalia is the lowest of the spiritual gifts.

* * *

The experiential knowledge of God's presence in the lives of the Jesus People is also revealed in their attitude toward divine healing. Examples of healing phenomena are cited again and again by Jesus People everywhere. Almost unbelievable accounts of healing are related in matter-of-fact terms and with a casualness that sometimes appears unreal. Ted Wise tells the story of the dramatic healing of the wife of Pat Matrisciana, one of the founders of the Christian World Liberation Front. She wore a brace on her neck due to a serious injury sustained in an automobile accident. During a prayer session one day prior to a special meeting to be held at the university campus in Berkeley, she was in great pain. As Ted relates it,

> We walked over and prayed for her and she was healed. . . .
> Nobody put their hands on her and talked weird or believed

199

hard or anything. Nothing like that at all; it was just ordinary. It was just God's will and she was healed.

A young man in the San Francisco Bay Area stated that he had been totally deaf, but after prayer and the laying on of hands, his hearing was completely restored within five minutes. Rev. Anderson of the Sierra Madre Congregational Church tells of Jesus People going into canyon areas and praying for hippies who were remarkably healed on the spot. In his own congregation Rev. Anderson tells of a little girl scheduled to have open heart surgery who was prayed for and healed. Doctors acknowledged that a miracle had occurred.

Miracles and healing manifest the overpowering sense of God's presence that seems to characterize most of the Jesus People. It is easy for an outsider to be somewhat skeptical at some accounts of miraculous healing. But Kilian McDonnell reminds us that,

> Unless one is willing to admit the act of God not only in Christ but in the lives of Christians then one has to abdicate all pretensions to a Biblical spirituality. It is appropriate to be somewhat skeptical about the miracles, prophecies and numerous divine interventions claimed in Pentecostal circles, but it would impoverish the Gospel to rule out, *a priori*, the numinous and the wondrous from the lives of ordinary Christians (p. 199).

The Jesus People's preoccupation with the supernatural can be seen in their frequent reference to visions and visitations. Tony Alamo claims that the Lord visited him in person and spoke to him one day in an office in Beverly Hills. "My ears shut off, and I felt this warm feeling come over me, and it was just like an accordion all over. I could hear all over, in my legs, in my arms, in my feet, everything." Alamo was afraid that his friends would think he was crazy, but "the Lord told me to stand up and tell the people in the room that the Lord was coming back to earth, or I'd die." He now hears God speaking to him in an audible voice regularly.

A young man associated with Harvest House Ministries in San Francisco explained to us that he spends three or four weeks "studying out" each vision he receives from God. He told us: "Since the Billy Graham Crusade [in Oakland] the Lord has really begun to minister to me. It's so heavy that I'm behind on visions now." One of the visions he described for us involved a dramatic sunrise followed by a great flash of light. Another was described as actually "a series of dreams showing things that would take place" in the future. Others included an exhortation to "get on with love, to pursue love," and one in which "God showed me where the Christian walk was at." We asked whether his friends saw visions also:

> I don't think so. A lot of them don't. I put my total life upon the leading and ministry of the Holy Spirit. When I get into a problem, I lay down and let the Spirit minister unto me. And the Lord does come and minister to me. He tells me what he wants and how things are and why they are that way, and a lot of people don't understand that. But Christ actually does come to me, actually does minister to me. The vision I had last night was — like two and two is four. But until you put two and two together, you don't come up with four. I prayed about that all night long, and the only thing I could come up with was ourselves and Christ, and until you put these two together and make it into one with Christ, you're wasting your time.

More rational accounts of dreams and visions originate in Jesus communes and hip churches. In one of the churches discussed in chapter four, the pastor related how one of his parishioners had a vision of the current revival in the church three-and-a-half years prior to its outbreak. Another woman in the same church was reported to be having visions foretelling problems in her marriage. At a summer retreat sponsored by Calvary Chapel of Costa Mesa, it was reported that several young women were awakened in the middle of the night by strange sights and sounds. All of the girls experienced a distortion in their visual perception. The very walls of their cabin took on new dimensions, and the shapes of familiar objects seemed strangely changed.

Such phenomena, along with the constant reference to miracles, healings, and other charismatic activity, point to the quest for spiritual stimulation, the great desire for direct perception and experience of the supernatural that characterizes the Jesus People. As Linda Meissner put it, "These kids want to see miracles." This same need to experience the supernatural can be said to motivate participation in Eastern mystical religions and the world of drugs, two areas familiar to most of the flower children of the 1960s. It is more than coincidental that many successful drug rehabilitation programs were founded and are staffed by Pentecostals, who have strong affinities with miracle-oriented youth.

Jesus People also exhibit a strong sense of the presence of evil and the role of the demonic. Many of them were involved in astrology, witchcraft, and demon worship prior to their conversion, and this in part explains their sensitivity toward the Satanic. The exorcising of demons occurs with some regularity at Jesus People gatherings.

"Singing in the Spirit" is a Pentecostal phenomenon displayed by some Jesus People. John Sherrill gives the following description of this enigmatic experience.

> As the music continued, several people at the tables began to sing "in the Spirit." Soon the whole room was singing a complicated harmony-without-score, created spontaneously. It was eerie but extraordinarily beautiful. The song leader was no longer trying to direct the music, but let the melodies create themselves: without prompting, one quarter of the room would suddenly start to sing very loudly while the other subsided. Harmonies and counterharmonies wove in and out of each other (p. 118).

The people at Harvest House note that the Holy Spirit provides a new song at each of their meetings. "There have been meetings when thirty people will be singing, and the Spirit will come upon them, and all thirty will be singing the same words." It is very common for Jesus People to state that the Holy Spirit gives them a song in English, individually or in groups, to enrich their worship and witnessing.

* * *

During the fall of 1966 and the spring of 1967, when the Jesus Movement was in its formative stages, Pentecostalism emerged as a movement within the Roman Catholic Church. Charismatic renewal within Catholicism can be traced to the campus of Duquesne University, where a group of faculty members gathered to discuss and share the quality of their lives in Christ. A series of events led them to David Wilkerson's *The Cross and the Switchblade* and to contact with Protestant Neo-Pentecostals. The movement quickly spread to the

University of Notre Dame and Ann Arbor, Michigan, now the two main centers in the United States of the Catholic charismatic renewal. Many of the leaders in the movement are young people, many of them recent college graduates. For the most part, these young Catholic charismatics are not long-hairs, hippies, or ex-drug-users; in fact, nearly all were strong Catholics before their involvement with the charismatic gifts.

Catholic Pentecostals and Jesus People do share many common interests and experiences. Catholic charismatics express a new interest in prayer and Bible study; they also spend hours witnessing to friends and strangers about their new-found Christian life. The movement's main leaders are laymen who urge members to remain within the church and to avoid the emotionalism associated with many Protestant Pentecostal groups. A young Catholic charismatic theologian, Kevin Ranaghan, sees the movement as an outgrowth of a period of public housecleaning that has characterized the Roman Catholic Church during the last ten years and a direct answer to the prayers of Catholics everywhere during the Second Vatican Council, when the faithful were urged by Pope John to pray for renewal within the Church.

Catholics who have experienced charismatic renewal are estimated to number more than fifty thousand in the United States alone. Why are Catholics in increasing numbers joining the Pentecostal ranks? The answers bear a striking similarity to the reasons advanced to explain the success of the Jesus Movement. First of all, the movement is viewed as the sovereign moving of God's Holy Spirit in our day. More specifically, the Catholics see it as an answer to Pope John's prayer for a renewal of the wonders of Pentecost. Second, Catholics are attracted to the Pentecostal movement because Pentecostals offer not a doctrine but an experience of God. "For persons brought up within the tradition of an arid intellect-and-will, catechism-Catholicism and within the ambience of a raging objectivism (in liturgy, piety, prayer, law), an experience with God in the Pentecostal sense can be the discovery of a new dimension in life" (McDonnell, p. 204). Just as Protestants in the Jesus Movement have sought to go beyond the structures of organized religion, young Catholics are seeking to reach behind the formalities and rituals of a church embedded in time and tradition in order to recapture a sense of reality and immediacy in their religious experience. In this context the Jesus People, the Catholic charismatics, and the other Neo-Pentecostals are all a manifestation of the contemporary quest for transcendence, a quest with both religious and secular dimensions.

Unlike many in the Jesus Movement, young Catholic charismatics evidence a strong loyalty to their church. Catholics who leave the Church are thought to be "disobedient to the Spirit and cause the charismatic renewal great damage" (*Christianity Today,* July 16, 1971, p. 32). The charismatic renewal is seen as a solution for the crises in faith and leadership facing the church today.

Catholic charismatics claim a new appreciation for sacraments as a result of their spiritual renewal. Also, a new sense of community prevails in charismatic circles. In fact, Catholics use the term "community" or "prayer community" to refer to their various local groups, i.e., the "Saint Charles Community." Young people in the movement share a strong sense of belonging to one another. One observer noted: "The Pentecostal movement in the Catholic Church means nothing unless it's related to community."

At the fifth annual Conference on the Charismatic Renewal in the Catholic Church held at Notre Dame in June 1971, five thousand delegates rose to their feet to shout "Jesus Christ is Lord!" This exclamation preceded a ten-minute standing ovation for the Lord reminiscent of some Protestant Jesus festivals. Although Catholic charismatics are said to be more reserved and restrained than their Protestant counterparts, it is not uncommon to encounter a big smile and a "Praise the Lord!"

* * *

How can we account for the charismatic phenomenon that prevails within the Jesus Movement, and what is its significance for Jesus People? First of all, it cannot be passed off simply as a manifestation of hysterical behavior or psychic malfunction. Unstable personalities are to be found in the Jesus Movement, to be sure. But to explain charismatic involvement largely in terms of a kind of hyper-emotionalism would be unjust. If it is true that the Jesus Movement attracts some neurotic types, it is just as true that most religious movements do.

> Many Christians look down on the glossolalist as a neurotic, insecure person who can express himself only in unseemly emotional ways. But some psychological tests have indicated that the opposite may be true. Glossolalists do not suffer from a higher incidence of abnormal personality than other people, and in many cases the gift as a religious experience seems to contribute to mental health (Clark H. Pinnock and Grant R. Osborne, "A Truce Proposal for the Tongues Controversy," *Christianity Today*, Oct. 8, 1971, p. 7).

The Jesus Movement will undoubtedly continue to alienate those in traditional evangelical churches who maintain a position relegating the charismatic gifts to apostolic times. Don Williams of the Hollywood Presbyterian Church sees a greater openness toward tongues and other charismata developing among segments of the established church. As a result of contacts with Jesus People, some churches no longer look on charismatic gifts as posing a threat. In the article previously referred to, Pinnock and Osborne go so far as to say: "Instead of condemning and ostracizing, let us put glossolalists to the test: welcome them into worship, fellowship and service. That is the only Christian way" (p. 7).

Some have explained the practice of tongues as an expression of social and cultural conflict. (We shall discuss this further in chapter twelve.) Charismatic movements, they feel, are a source for resolving conflicts between people and a means of relating to a disjointed social order. But whatever theory of explanation is advanced, the Jesus People are sure to conclude that spiritual matters can only be understood spiritually and that the very nature of the charismatic gifts precludes rational inquiry and explanation. They would certainly agree with Robert Munger:

> It baffles the systematic schemes of many staid theologians, but there are manifestations of the Spirit's power among these young people that were thought to have died out with the apostles: dramatic healings, speaking in tongues, and a quality of love and joy that gets through even to hardened news reporters ("God's Spirit is Breaking Through," *Eternity*, Aug. 1971, p. 14).

The Jesus People are convinced that this is the promised out-pouring of the Spirit upon "all flesh" mentioned in the Book of Joel. Regardless of what others may think, the Jesus People believe that they represent fulfilment of this predicted spiritual baptism that will rock the world before Jesus returns.

eleven

CHRISTIAN COMMUNES

The Abundant Life Family-Style

OF THE CONTRIBUTIONS THAT THE JESUS PEOPLE HAVE MADE to American Christianity, the most interesting and most misunderstood is the Christian commune. Experiments in group living, whether religious or secular, are not new to America: New York had its Oneida; Indiana its New Harmony; North Dakota its Hutterites. But the commune has never fared well in a public opinion shaped in the mold of rugged individualism and has been particularly battered by the evangelical establishment. Pooh-poohed as the idle dream of mystic visionaries and condemned as a standing invitation to sexual orgies, the commune as a viable life style has been unhesitatingly dismissed by the church, despite the affirmations of religiosity by commune members. Yet the proliferation of Christian communes in recent years is forcing institutionalized Christianity to reevaluate its attitude.

There are several factors that contribute to the commune's slowly rising stock among America's evangelicals. First, the sincerity of belief of residents of the movement's communal houses, or at least most of them, is increasingly clear. Deciding to join a commune is a much deeper commitment than pinning on a One Way button. Communes lack the faddishness of much of the revolution. Second, the communes of Jesus People do not manifest the sexual aberrations often thought to be synonymous with group living, nor are they just Christian substitutes for the drug culture. With the exception of Leon's nomadic excursions into promiscuity (see chapter two), the communal aspect of the movement is free of both harlots and hashish. Finally, the establishment itself is beginning to involve itself in communal living to a certain degree. Church-sponsored crash pads — in reality nothing more than contemporary extensions of skid-row rescue missions — are appearing in cities throughout the United States. Though not communal in any real sense of the word, the effort has at least demonstrated that the younger generation, long hair and all, is not as licentious as had long been proclaimed. There are also some more genuine communal situations in institutional Christianity. David Wilkerson's Teen Challenge is operating a number of what can be called communal houses in its program of drug rehabilitation. While church-run houses may lack certain characteristics of full-fledged Jesus communes, the church's timid experiments in group living have stirred the realization that Christianity and the commune are not necessarily antithetical.

* * *

The movement's growing fascination with the commune is much deeper than the church's, and the revolution's experiments have produced results unheard of, and generally undesired, in more organized Christianity. The most obviously revolutionary communes are the flourishing communities established and maintained by the Children of God and Tony and Susan Alamo. Their group living is unmistakably related to their religious idiosyncrasies, which fence them off markedly from the church and, to a lesser extent, the rest of the movement. The Saugus community and the widely dispersed colonies of the Children differ from each other in some details about the holiness practices necessary to Christian living — an obvious example: the strict sexual segregation of the Alamos' Foundation, which is far more rigid than the more relaxed, though not unrestricted, relations existing in the Children's colonies. But the two are united in purpose. Unlike establishment efforts, these communities do not view themselves as temporary groupings designed to promote spiritual growth or as Christian hotels to travelers of this world. Rather, the Children and the Foundation see the commune as a new and permanent life style for America's true believers.

"New" is a bit inaccurate when applied to the communal doctrine of the Children of God. The Children themselves deny that the commune is new to Christian experience; rather, for them the terms are synonymous. Since the time of Pentecost those few Christians untainted by the demonic influence of the corrupt church have lived communally. Like the rest of the Children's dogma, the proof of the commune is in the proof-texting. Acts 2:44-45 provides the foundation, and the sincerity of the Children's efforts to abide by the supposed command is obvious. The colonies are truly communal; possessions, including even such things as clothes, are group property, and activity is seldom oriented toward the individual. Money, except in the hands of an elder, is unheard of. The colony provides all, just as it asks all. For the Children the colonies are foolproof insurance against being absorbed by the worldly system that turned the Bride of Christ into the Whore of Babylon.

The efforts of the Children to sever Christianity's long-standing ties with secular culture are certainly not half-hearted. They are striving, with slowly increasing success, to achieve complete self-sufficiency, a goal rooted in the expectation that the Antichrist and his reign of terror will not be long in coming. The future of the colonies is not often discussed, but when it is, the vision seldom stops at a network of relatively small communes spread throughout the nation. In the words of an elder, Abraham, the Children dream of "whole cities of Christians" totally apart from the society of Antichrist. The apocalypse and its accompanying disasters, coupled with the Children's post-tribulationism, make self-sufficiency imperative if they are to avoid compromising with a world order under the Mark of the Beast. Josiah, chief elder of the Children's eastern Kentucky farm, says: "We feel we've got to become self-sufficient, you see, because things are going to get worse in this country. All the things that are prophesied in the Bible are coming to pass — wars and rumors of war, nation rising against nation, all this trouble with insects and pollution."

Besides insulating disciples from the contaminating world, an equally crucial function of the colony is social control. The

Unpacking furniture for communal living

lack of privacy, the hierarchical power structure, the strict, no-questions-asked regime — all the oddities listed in chapter two make the colonial structure quite stable. The attrition rate is low, and most of those who do desert are persuaded by relatives, distraught pastors, and indignant friends, not by their own inclination. Colonial authority resides, totally and without question, in the local elder. Assumed to be imbued with the authority of God himself, the elder's word is law, and the disciple's submission to it is total.

The differences between the Children and the Christian Foundation clearly stem from the presence of Tony and Susan Alamo. Their justification for the communal situation existing in Saugus does not include the Acts proof-text, nor does one hear from them the clarion call to forsake all, though Foundation residents have given up most. The Alamos, rather, root their commune totally in the expected horrors of the impending Tribulation. Alamo fully expects the Foundation to retreat from the edge of the city to the mountains and eventually envisions a martyrdom for himself and his disciples under the bullets of the Antichrist, though the wounds will hurt "no more than cigarette burns."

Another parting of the ways — a theoretical one to be sure — is the Alamos' avowed intention to produce a new clergy to win the world before the end. Tony Alamo speaks of the

210

Foundation in this sense as a temporary training ground. On the other hand, he admits that no one has yet left Saugus for the world and that he expects the apocalypse to be ready before his disciples are. Alamo claims that the Foundation is a training center, but his actions prove it to be a full-time, permanent house. Separation from the world is less rigorous at the Foundation, the main breach in security being the good-sized influx of regular visitors for Susan Alamo's services. Her husband was quite willing to lead us on a grand tour of the main meeting hall, but he flatly refused to show off the Foundation's living quarters.

The Alamos are unquestioned and generally unavailable; still, their word, conceived by Susan and repeated by Tony, is revered law. The Foundation should survive the slings and arrows of the future, at least as long as the Alamos do. But unlike the Children, who continually cultivate elders in spite of their expectation of the end, the Foundation has no such insurance scheme. The colonies of the Children could probably survive even a deferment of the apocalypse. It is unlikely that the Foundation could outlive its patron saints.

* * *

The authoritarian communal structure of the Children and the Foundation is duplicated in other scattered communities throughout the movement, but it would be incorrect to assume that only the more fanatical, totalitarian, cultic manifestations of the revolution delve seriously into the world of communal living. Significant efforts at establishing Christian communes are sprinkled throughout the movement. These communities are, for the most part, designed as training schools where believers can mature and gain firm grounding in Scripture and Christian living before returning to the secular city. The practical value of the commune as perceived by the Jesus People is enunciated by the elder of the House of Emmaus in Toronto:

> People's experience has become impersonal, too abstract, and thus impractical. Communal living creates situations which keep your experience on a level of reality. That is, you may get into situations where you are confronted with the fact that you need more love, patience, humility, forgiveness towards a brother and you have to go to God continually for help in changing yourself. You must, so you do.

The communal idealism, while not realized in every instance, is not an exercise in spiritual wishful thinking. A good example of the merits of the movement's communes can be found in a collection of thriving houses in and around Pasadena, California. "Our Father's Family," as the members of the old, rambling house in a residential section of Pasadena call themselves, began through the efforts of two young converts, Paul Danchik and Don Pauly. (Pauly has since moved to Florida, leaving Danchik to manage the Pasadena House.) The house and its members are much more open and cordial than either the Children of God or the Alamos and their disciples. The property has several smaller dwellings in addition to the main house and includes vegetable gardens. The smaller buildings are occupied by Danchik and his wife Nina, along with the family of another elder, and are furnished quite starkly. The simplicity of the elders' quarters matches that of the large house, which accommodates the co-ed population of about thirty. House regulations govern the times for rising and breakfast and require residents to inform the elder of their whereabouts, to participate in communal activities, and to contribute to the house's treasury.

The Pasadena House screens prospective residents to keep out those unwilling or unready to accept the life style. Most of the Family come from permissive and unstructured backgrounds, and many have dabbled in drugs, though heavy experimentation seems to have been rare. New residents give up neither their possessions nor their jobs. Indeed, each of the male residents is employed — some in structured situations, others as free-lance gardeners — and contributes a share (sometimes more than ninety percent) of his income to maintaining the commune. The women are responsible for upkeep of the house and meals, and occasionally take baby-sitting jobs. Few if any of the Family attend college, simply because, in Danchik's words, "They just aren't the kind of people who are interested in that sort of thing."

Theologically the Family has, almost by trial and error, managed a charismatic but well-balanced structure. Danchik readily admits to both doctrinal and practical mistakes in the commune's development. There were stages of fixation during which the House's fascination with various aspects of the Chris-

212

tian life, especially the charismatic gifts and the power of exorcism, excluded other, less spectacular issues. At each stage, diligent Bible study has served as a corrective, and a balanced theology has replaced the narrow fascination by a broader appreciation. The process has been worked out by maturing believers. Danchik, converted just three years ago, is now collected, personable, and disarmingly sincere.

The House has had remarkably little aid from either established churches or other Jesus People and continues to remain a quite isolated group. Residents do occasionally attend institutionalized worship services, usually in small groups. Danchik knows of the Jesus Movement only through the media. The House shares many of the movement's dogmas — the charismatic experience and the nearness of the apocalypse are common to both — but lacks the preachy, buttonholing quality of many spiritual revolutionaries. Danchik himself thinks that the term Jesus People profanes the name of Jesus. Instead, he regards the Family as "children of God" (in the nonrevolutionary sense of the term). The communal operation in Pasadena surely deserves that title.

Another highly successful communal chain, numerically at least, known as the Shiloh Houses, includes thirty-seven settlements from Oregon (where it started) to the Eastern seaboard. The first Shiloh House was established in the countryside near Eugene by John Higgins, an associate of Lonnie Frisbee in the movement's early days. Since then the commune has grown steadily, and the original Shiloh community now has a school and farm. Its doctrinal position is somewhere between the balanced theology of Our Father's Family and the more exotic dogmas of full-fledged revolutionaries. Like many communal groups, Shiloh disavows the Jesus People label, saying that the movement is too shallow to survive. Shiloh's leaders laud the commune's commitment and claim that this attribute will make their ministry a lasting one. Again, these communes share the typical characteristics of the charismatic gifts, the apocalyptic mentality, and strains of anti-intellectualism.

The three Shiloh Houses in Denver are typical of the association's communal style. Under the direction of Pastor George and his assistant, Deacon Lyle, one house is occupied by males, one by females, and another by married couples and the over-

213

flow from the male house. Life is somewhat regimented; curfew is at 11:00 p.m. Bible studies are held nightly with the exception of Sunday. The houses are open to crashers, and most residents are willing to venture into the outside world for occasional employment, but only at positions where small groups of Shiloh's members can labor together. The commune's emphasis is on personal evangelism, a concern spurred by the conviction that the apocalypse is just around the corner.

Both the hyper-evangelism and intense apocalypticism of Shiloh prevent it from cultivating the maturity shown in Pasadena. Still, Shiloh is quite removed from the cultishness of the Alamos and the Children. The middling ground occupied by Shiloh is attractive (witness the chain's thirty-seven outposts) and apparently the communes are sufficiently stable to prevent any of the branches from withering on the vine. Newsletters and training teams from the Oregon headquarters knit the communities together in a union far more professional — a trained bookkeeper is listed among the headquarters' residents — than most of the movement's fledgling associations. The Shiloh Houses continue to grow both in number and in stability. The chain is evidence that the movement's experimentation with communes is more than a wide-eyed fascination with the storied counter-culture. Rather, it is a growing attempt to establish a life style that is uniquely Christian.

Most of the movement's efforts at communal living have met with neither the success of Shiloh nor the maturity of the Pasadena House. More typical is the Koinonia Community of Santa Cruz, California, founded by Mrs. Margaret Rovick, a fundamentalistic Methodist turned revolutionary. Mrs. Rovick is generally unavailable for interviews. The community began in 1967 as a simple coffee house ministry and went communal in November 1968. It has since added a restaurant, boutique, and bookstore (of sorts). The group now has two communal houses.

Some of Koinonia's twenty or so members resent any insinuation that Mrs. Rovick is the leader of the group. They claim that all members are equal and that Mrs. Rovick is just another member, though they admit that chronologically she was the first. Nevertheless, the commune residents are described by outsiders in the Santa Cruz area as "automatons" who function at Mrs. Rovick's beck and call. A decided majority of the members are female. Most residents are "reformed" street people. Koinonia also provides a home for several youthful probationers assigned to Margaret Rovick by nearby counties.

Koinonia has no regularly scheduled worship services or Bible studies. Occasionally, the group puts on a folk mass, one of the few elements from established churches that they deem worthy of imitation. Koinonia's revulsion from institutional churches is marked: "Emphatically we are not a church, and therefore refuse to get involved in doctrinal hassles." The lack of structured spiritual exercises seems strangely inconsistent with the regimentation found necessary for operating the community. The favorite exercise of devotion is fasting.

Like many elements of the movement, Koinonia is uncomfortable with the Jesus People label. This probably stems from their exclusivist temper: they consider themselves special in the eyes of God, and to link them with other groups would dilute their elect status. Still the Koinonia Community shares major traits of the Jesus Movement. It explores the charismatic gifts. It is violently anti-institutional. Its exclusivism is pronounced: visitors from nearby Mount Hermon Christian Conference Center have been barred from the community as representatives of Satan on the basis of a vision revealed to Mrs. Rovick.

While most of the Jesus Movement focuses on Christian love and joy, Koinonians are fascinated with the reality of Satan and the fear of God's retribution. The most interesting manifestation of their enthralment with the power of evil is their belief that Satan controls a section of Highway 17 on the way to San Jose which is frequently marred by accidents. The demonic control is thought to result from a number of "Satanist-hippie" colonies purported to be in the area. As members tell it, Koinonia has insured its own travel through the area by prayer and fasting and has yet to come under the demonic, accident-producing influence.

Koinonia Community takes itself very seriously. It is not a relaxed place. Visitors are welcome only if they "sincerely want to ask questions about the Christian concept of God." To underline the no-nonsense approach, one of their flyers rather pugnaciously declares, "Because we work long hours to support ourselves and because we give of all our free time to serving our fellow men, we will not encourage lazy people to hang around us in the hopes of somehow 'getting religion.' "

Mrs. Rovick and her band do not defend their life style by quoting scriptural injunctions to communal living, as do the Children of God. Nor do they view their commune as a refuge from the rapidly approaching Tribulation. The community exists in the name of expedience. Through it Margaret Rovick hopes to realize a viable pattern for Christian living. All she wants from the outside world is to be left alone.

* * *

Sadly, Koinonia and many of the movement's other experimental clusters have not been as fortunate as Our Father's Family of Pasadena. The balance of maturity and enthusiasm at the Pasadena House is the infrequent exception, not the rule. Most communes of the movement depend almost solely on themselves for leisure activities as well as interpersonal relations. They rely on the teachings of a single elder and have little meaningful contact with fellow believers. This social and theological isolation quite often produces an inbred ethnocentrism. Koinonia's brittle exclusivism, which characterizes itself as God's only outpost among the heretics of Santa Cruz County, is more extreme than most, but it is a direct result of the intellectual and spiritual walls erected at edges of the commune.

Such narrow vision is certainly not unknown in past religious movements. Much the same development happened in the pre-Christian Essene community, which preserved the Dead Sea Scrolls. Of the Essenes, Geza Vermes says, ". . . they were convinced that their beliefs and way of life conformed fully to the will of God and qualified them to claim the honor of being the only true Israel" (*The Dead Sea Scrolls in English,* p. 17). Though they were "a company of poor humble men constantly attentive to the word of God and grateful for His favors" (p. 51), Vermes acknowledges the probability "that their convictions gave rise to rigidity, bigotry, and hatred" (p. 52).

Though the name "commune" suggests an equality among the members, the fact is that most Jesus communes foster an unhealthy dependence on the local elder. The Alamos, Margaret
216

Rovick, and the elders of the Children of God thrive on that sort of blind loyalty far more than other commune leaders, but even less rigidly structured communities create a hierarchy topped by someone whose pronouncements are not to be questioned. The isolation characteristic of the colony mitigates against the development of critical, evaluative thinking, another phenomenon discussed by Vermes:

> God had chosen to reveal knowledge and understanding of His purpose and will to their [the Essenes'] Teacher of Righteousness and to those of the Teacher's followers who trod the path laid down by him, the Way of Holiness. Only the Teacher was able to decipher the mysteries concealed in the Scriptures; consequently only those who accepted his interpretation of the written word of God could be sure of living in conformity with His desire (p. 35).

Working out one's salvation with fear and trembling is widely accepted in theory, but it is seldom practiced in the commune.

Despite the many misguided efforts, the revolution has been steadied by the commitment required in group living situations. Life at the commune is sobering. It is here that the revolution must put up or shut up. Communal living is at times exceedingly difficult both physically and psychologically. The Children of God were often hungry before manna from the hand of Fred Jordan descended; the Alamos' disciples still lead a Spartan existence; even the Pasadena House is minus the usual luxuries — including privacy — that grace the typical Christian home. Whatever the aberrations might be, the dedication of most of the movement's communal dwellers is impressive. Like the Essene community, Jesus communes are well-intentioned, sincere attempts to work out viable alternatives to establishmentarian religion. Ironically, it is precisely the unswerving, unquestioning, naive dedication of young revolutionaries that creates rigidity and its frequent handmaidens, bigotry and hatred.

Perhaps it is unjust to judge the Jesus Movement's efforts at communal living so hastily. Most are of recent origin. Many, like the Koinonia Community, have evolved from coffee houses and related sorts of undertakings and are still developing and adjusting. The Pasadena House, beginning its third year in operation, has had more time to mature than even the Alamos'

Foundation. Much of the revolution's communal effort seems to have progressed toward a maturity but has, for a variety of reasons, become mired down in narrow, often cultish beliefs.

The Harvest House Ministries, Inc., of San Francisco plainly shows this retarded maturity in ways that are typical of the revolution as a whole. The corporation began as a Jesus commune named Harvest House in Haight-Ashbury. Its residents are apocalyptically and charismatically oriented; visions and dreams are commonplace. Organizationally Harvest House differs little from other of the movement's efforts. Oliver Heath, a student at Golden Gate Baptist Seminary, supervises the operation because, according to a resident, "The Lord has given him a position of Pastor and he's the head of all these houses."

The maturity produced by the communal situation at Harvest House is best expressed in the community's production of a well-written, sometimes cogent newspaper, *The Oracle*. Once it was one of the raciest of the hip underground papers. Then its editor David Abraham was converted through Chris D'Allessandro, a Harvest House member. He promptly turned the paper over to Harvest House, and D'Allessandro is now one of the co-editors.

Replete with psychedelic drawings designed to appeal to "the San Francisco-type people," *The Oracle* expresses theological understandings far more developed than those expressed in the *Hollywood Free Paper* and its imitators:

> Has it ever struck you how extraordinary it is that the children of God can hear so much and *express* so little? . . . The reason for this lies in the *unrenewed mind*. They may have truly received the Holy Spirit but, speaking reverently, he is "locked up" in the spirit, and cannot get through the blocked channel of the mind. One reason is that many children of God do not soak themselves, so to speak, in God's thoughts. . . . You must never let the mind become "slack", or careless in its thinking, or it will soon fall prey to the watching enemy. The "mind" should never be idle, or without "grist for the mill." It must be active if it is in a normal condition.

The appreciation for the intellect bred at Harvest House is in short supply at other Jesus People strongholds and is indeed a step toward a balanced conception of the Christian life.

Harvest House has expanded to include other programs and is now incorporated as Harvest House Ministries, Inc. One of its new operations is a restaurant serving health foods, known as Vege-Hut. These efforts at outreach are far more complicated than the typical Jesus People fixation with face-to-face evangelism. The commune conducts the business of both *The Oracle* and the Vege-Hut for evangelistic rather than capitalistic reasons and sees merit in such indirect evangelism.

Still, there remains an extreme fascination with both the supernatural and the apocalypse, which lifts many of the houses' residents into an almost mystic world where even the smallest occurrences take on a cosmic explanation. Says one of Harvest House's family: "Like the last days are really here, and I believe it so strong that every second I look for Christ. Every time I see a lightning flash or street car thing out here flashing, I think it's Christ." Some in the houses seem to have developed what amounts to a martyr complex — not a willingness to suffer but a desire to do so. Harvest House's living situation is responsible for the cultivation of attitudes like these, which are hardly conducive to the well-rounded Christian world view.

Our impression is that Harvest House harbors young people who were more deeply involved in the counter-culture than most segments of the Jesus Movement. The houses have accepted many young mothers with illegitimate children. Sexual problems have not yet all been overcome. One young man we spoke to was rocking a baby whom he admitted was his. The unwed mother lives in the same house. The father reluctantly admitted that his sexual activity was wrong, but added that he was not the only one who had trouble in this area. The situation, he said, was now fully under control. The leadership of Harvest House, especially Heath, seem reasonably mature; and there is good reason to hope that Harvest House will achieve a pattern of growth paralleling that of Our Father's Family.

The communal style of life adopted by a substantial portion of the Jesus People may last for a long time, whatever the attitude of church people may be. It has many potential advantages: the sense of spiritual belonging, a substitution for fatherless or otherwise deficient family units, economy in meeting material needs. But it also isolates a small group of believers from the larger household of faith, and so far this disadvantage has outweighed the potential advantages more often than not. Here, as elsewhere, the Jesus People need communication

219

with other Christians. Brotherly acceptance of Jesus communes by outside Christians may not (and should not) lead to the demise of the houses, but it will minimize the dangerous tendency toward cultic isolationism. On the other hand, condemnation of the Jesus communes by straight Christians as Satanic, un-American, or otherwise disreputable will only build a higher wall of separation between the Jesus People and the rest of the Body of Christ. Once again, the fate of the Jesus People is not entirely in their own hands. Church Christians are going to have a lot to say about the outcome of the Jesus Revolution.

Part Three

RETROSPECT

twelve

THE JESUS PEOPLE AS A SOCIAL MOVEMENT

A Great Awakening or a Gentle Stir?

ANY SOCIAL MOVEMENT — RELIGIOUS, POLITICAL, ECONOMIC — must be understood in the context of its social and cultural setting. To comprehend fully how the movement arises and develops and where it ends up, we must first describe the "spirit of the age" within which it functions. In his book, *Modern Social Movements,* William Bruce Cameron notes: "The purposes of a social movement cannot be evaluated, nor the actions of members understood, unless we clearly perceive the background of the society against which they play their part. Social movements . . . are made of the stuff that is at hand" (p. 21).

The "stuff" of the sixties and seventies has been delineated, categorized, and analyzed by sociologists, journalists, philosophers, psychologists, and assorted other "people-watchers." One of the more provocative endeavors at this is Rollo May's *Love and Will.* Another is *The Making of a Counter Culture* by Theodore Roszak. We shall draw on the works of these and other commentators on the American scene in order to place the Jesus Movement in a context appropriate for analysis.

* * *

We live in an impersonal, computerized, assembly-line, shopping-center society where all the old anchorages have been lost or weakened and where alienation has become the common malaise. Thomas Cottle, in his perceptive volume, *Time's Children*, speaks of "our televised and instant replay society" where few secrets are allowed and "we become frustrated when we cannot discover the exact frame on which is recorded a President's death" (pp. 86-87). It is a society in which young people especially have been subjected to a tremendous over-stimulation — by the various media, by the myriad of confusing alternatives of vocation, religion, and morals, and by the mechanisms of an economic system that provides unparalleled affluence and a seemingly endless stream of material goods for consumption.

At the same time that modern technological man has felt that he has the tools to control the universe and the material possessions to make life worthwhile, he has experienced a spiritual emptiness and personal disorganization perhaps unequaled in human history. Our technical sophistication has not brought about any culmination of human happiness, as Barbara Hargrove explains in her book, *Reformation of the Holy*.

> There is a growing awareness in modern society that the basic assumptions of technical progress and scientific knowledge may be leading, not to Utopia, but to a loss of humanity if not total destruction. Not only is this so, but that awareness is compounded by the feeling that the technological machine cannot be stopped, that we are caught in an ever-descending spiral of our own making from which there is no escape (p. 281).

The introductory chapter of May's *Love and Will* is entitled "Our Schizoid World." "Schizoid" means "out of touch; avoiding close relationships; the inability to feel" (p. 16). He sees this schizoid orientation as a general condition of our culture and the people who comprise our society. He describes our world as one

> where numbers inexorably take over as our means of identification, like flowing lava threatening to suffocate and fossilize all breathing life in its path . . . where "normality" is defined as keeping your cool; where sex is so available that the only way to preserve any inner center is to learn to have intercourse without committing yourself . . . (p. 32).

Young people experience this schizoid world more directly than their elders, according to May, because "they have not had time to build up the defenses which dull the senses of their elders" (p. 32). Without the old values and symbols that served as a touchstone of orientation for past generations, today's generation is increasingly forced inward, pushed toward apathy, toward a state of affectlessness. This results in a society characterized by estrangement, indifference, anomie, and depersonalization. Ultimately, asserts May, such a process eventuates in violence. "When inward life dries up, when feeling decreases and apathy increases, when one cannot affect or even genuinely *touch* another person, violence flares up as a daimonic necessity for contact, a mad drive forcing touch in the most direct way possible" (pp. 30-31).

The contemporary age has been characterized as one of "new freedoms" and a new morality. Our highly vaunted permissiveness in the area of male-female relations has revealed the fact that "sex for many people has become more meaningless as it is more available . . ." (May, p. 14). May continues: "What we did not see in our short-sighted liberalism in sex was that throwing the individual into an unbounded and empty sea of free choice does not in itself give freedom, but is more apt to increase inner conflicts" (p. 42).

If this is the age of liberated man and anonymous man, it is certainly the age of technocratic man. "Technocracy's Children" are the offspring of a social and economic system, writes Theodore Roszak, "which is so organized that it is inextricably beholden to expertise" (*The Making of a Counter Culture,* p. 19). They have come of age in a society of experts and scientism where efficiency and successful management are the order of the day. They have learned that performance counts, and the pressures to compete and succeed are often overwhelming. "One must be good in school, good at home, good at sports, good at pot and good in bed" (Cottle, p. 87).

It was in this complex social and cultural milieu that the Jesus Movement emerged. The 1960s saw armies of young people attempting to get "involved" with society's ills, trying to effect changes in the system. Barbara Hargrove relates the sequence of events that led to what she calls the "apocalyptic mood" of the present:

225

> Failure of civil rights and poverty programs, and of anti-war activity increased the feeling that the present system could not be changed or redirected. By the mid-sixties the quest had begun to turn inward. The disastrous political campaign of 1968, with its assassinations, its hopes, and its riots, added to the disenchantment with political solutions. The widespread politicization of the campuses after the Cambodia-Kent State-Jackson State debacle in 1970 has apparently ended in the spread of disillusion and alienation from political processes (p. 282).

The decade of the sixties was a period of radical cultural disjuncture in America. It was a decade of transition, which gave birth to the counter-culture and witnessed the emergence of the hippie as a new social type. The hippie subculture represented a protest against the sterile technocratic society of the middle-class establishment. "What makes the youthful disaffiliation of our time a cultural phenomenon, rather than merely a political movement, is the fact that it strikes beyond ideology to the level of consciousness, seeking to transform our deepest sense of the self, the other, the environment" (Roszak, p. 49). Roszak describes the contemporary youth culture as being obsessed with feeling and passion as opposed to intellect and reason. There is a searching after visionary experience and an unprecedented penchant for occult and magical phenomena (pp. 124-25). Perhaps most significant of all is the counterculture's preoccupation with drugs, particularly the hallucinogenic drugs. In their frantic search for new experience and meaning, the flower children of the sixties sought to modify their consciousness through psychedelics and to connect with a new form of reality through pharmacological linkages. Hargrove observes that the so-called "mind-expanding" drugs represent "symbols of membership in a new society with different cultural values" and have been used "as a means of establishing new patterns of perception upon which that society could be based" (p. 283).

With the demise of the Haight-Ashbury scene in San Francisco came the realization that "personal salvation and the social revolution [cannot] be packed in a capsule" (Roszak, p. 177). As the use of drugs (especially the so-called "hard" drugs like heroin) leveled off and even declined, interest in mystical and Eastern religions increased. As Hargrove notes:

226

More and more the young are rejecting the drug-induced experience as part of the unnatural "plastic" world they seek to escape, and they turn instead to the consciousness-manipulation of Eastern religions. The greater apparent willingness of Eastern religions to treat man as a part of nature rather than as its master has much appeal in a time of awareness of Western environmental bungling (p. 283).

* * *

While some hip youth looked to Eastern mysticism, American Indian religious lore, or meditation for some kind of transcendental experience, others discovered Jesus — not in the institutional church, for organized religion held little appeal, but in the simple message of the gospel and the teachings of Christ. It is significant that these experience-oriented members of the counter-culture found meaning not only in conversion and the dramatic transformation that it entails, but also in those practices of primitive Christianity that had been all but forgotten by the historic Christian churches — healing, tongues, and other gifts of the Holy Spirit. In addition to meeting very real and deeply felt spiritual needs, the charismatic gifts experienced by many Jesus People may be thought of as ways to resolve more general inner conflicts. The teeny-boppers and flower children of the technocratic society are, more often than not, the victims of multiple inner conflicts. These tensions arise from several sources: from relations with parents and other authority figures in the establishment, from the demands for performance and achievement that haunt young people at every turn, from the desperate search for identity and the means to cope with the problems of our society.

The notion that charismatic phenomena fulfil a need in the lives of individuals who are experiencing conflict is discussed convincingly by Marvin Mayers in the September 1971 *Journal of the American Scientific Affiliation*. Although Mayers primarily is concerned with the attraction that charismatic groups have for some members of traditional churches, his explanation is also valid for new converts from the hip subculture:

> The established church seems to be traditional in its ways, impersonal in its approach to outsiders and even towards its own members. It appears to be like a machine that is interested more in keeping moving and keeping its gears oiled

than in developing spiritual insight and experience in the lives of its members. Especially young people want to be thought of not as a part of a machine, but as unique persons. They thus become disgruntled with the church and its practices. At this point they seek out more personal organizations, leaders who relate to them more individually and personally, who treat them as valid persons, and who communicate personalness to them. . . . Too often, in the impersonal established church the individual feels unwanted, rejected, alienated. Holy Spirit movements reverse this process. The key is involvement, participation, the bringing of the individual into the total experience (p. 92).

This no doubt explains why an increasing number of young people attend a church like Calvary Chapel (chapter four) on weeknights and perhaps Sunday nights while attending the church of their parents on Sunday morning — and why some traditional church people seek out small charismatic prayer and fellowship groups while retaining ties to the home church.

Mayers does not suggest that the individual who resolves his conflicts through encounter with charismatic groups is necessarily emotionally disturbed. He recognizes, however, that "there are varying stages of conflict that may or may not result in emotional disturbance. But more, these people are ready for a new experience; one that promises them vitality, involvement, and participation. They are ready to flee from some bad experience or some bad situation" (p. 92).

Many of the converts in the Jesus Movement were indeed fleeing from bad experiences and deteriorating life situations. Large numbers of them were heavy drug users. They had withdrawn from society. Their encounter with Jesus Christ made them once again participating members of the human race. Frequently, but not always, they were encouraged to get jobs, return to school, and make amends with parents and the law. The Jesus Movement provided the opportunity to restore some sort of order, stability, and meaning to their lives. It put them in touch with the supernatural and made involvement in the form of witnessing a new and vital dimension to their lives.

The teen-aged runaway is one of the sad by-products of our schizoid culture. This social phenomenon represents, as Roszak points out, much more a flight *from* than a flight *toward*. "Certainly for a youngster of seventeen, clearing out of the

Witnessing to a Hari Krishna follower

comfortable bosom of the middle-class family to become a beggar is a formidable gesture of dissent. One makes light of it at the expense of ignoring a significant measure of our social health" (p. 34). The tragic dimensions of this youthful exodus can only be fully understood when one talks in person to the parties involved, as we did in the course of research for this book. Thomas Cottle eloquently discusses the failure of the parental generation in his volume, *Time's Children:*

> No one as yet has studied the notes written by parents to their runaway children in New York's East Village or San Francisco's Haight Ashbury district. . . . These pitiful missives document so well the lack of generational space and the confession of failure in parenthood and adulthood. They could almost be the letters of children who, wishing to come home, promise never again to misbehave. . . . The "Come back home — all is forgiven" notes stand as a testament to what must be seen by the young as a crumbling structure or a tragic reversal of intentionality and interpersonal competence (p. 89).

229

Whatever their reason for leaving home, hundreds of teen-agers have been converted to Christ at places like Bethel Tabernacle in Redondo Beach, California, and have been reunited with their parents. Older teen-agers and young adults have found a strong sense of family in Christian communes and with groups like the Children of God. "Their rigid discipline and strong fellowship provide a solid base for anomic young people who have found no place for themselves in the technological culture of the society" (Hargrove, p. 284).

The need for fellowship and close interaction felt by the Jesus People reflects the quest for community that characterizes the youth culture in general. Hargrove relates this quest to a more general search for religious meaning on the part of young people today.

> Young people are especially affected by the loss of strong kinship and community support, particularly since social patterns relegate them to a category somewhat separate from the rest of society. They attempt to overcome feelings of isolation by banding together in groups which can offer personal and social support. . . . One reaction to this is withdrawal into intimate groups in which a real effort is made to reveal and support the identities of members. Much of this kind of activity falls within broad definitions of religion, and often it is specifically labeled religious. . . . Religion is more than ever an appropriate topic for "rap sessions," but many of these groups go beyond verbalizing and intellectualizing their religious quest. They meditate or pray together, often holding hands or putting their arms around one another; they develop other ritualistic expressions of their common quest, sharing food or drugs or personal insights. The criterion on which they judge these and other experiences is the recognition of a sense of "real love." They may investigate meetings or communes; they evaluate them as to whether or not they are "loving." The word "love" may mean anything from a warm glow to full sexual activity, but it is important, and its main importance lies in its affirmation of the individual as a person. Whatever else the religious quest may involve in the modern world, it nearly always carries this dimension of social support for personal identity (pp. 284-285).

The ideas of community, of sharing, of respect for the uniqueness of the individual are all central to the visionary book by Charles Reich, *The Greening of America*. Reich predicts the advent of a new and liberated man in a new and more human community. This is to transpire through what he terms "a change of consciousness," the creating of a whole new life style. The beginnings of this new ethos based on individuality and a new sense of "togetherness" can be seen, according to Reich, in the searchings of the present new generation. "What the new generation has already achieved is a way of being with other people that is closer, warmer, more open, more sensitive, more capable of sharing, than prior generations have known" (p. 252).

The hang-loose generation of the sixties and seventies has articulated what May calls "a new morality, not of appearance and forms, but of authenticity in relationship" (p. 306). New significance has been attached to terms like acceptance, tolerance, feeling, concern, spontaneity, sharing, and, above all, love. As May and other observers have noted, the so-called "love generation" advocated a love based on the immediacy, spontaneity, and emotional honesty of the temporary moment, of the "now." But love also requires enduringness. What was needed was a love with staying power.

Some of the positive traits of the hip generation that May identifies have been transferred to the Jesus subculture, where they take on new meaning:

> They seek an honesty, openness, a genuineness of personal relationship; they are out to find a genuine feeling, a touch, a look in the eyes, a sharing of fantasy. The criterion becomes the *intrinsic meaning* and is to be judged by one's authenticity, doing one's own thing, and giving in the sense of making one's self available for the other (p. 306).

The difficulty with this ethic, May observes, is the lack of content and authoritative basis for these values. "The content *seems* present," he writes, "but it turns out to be based to some extent on whim and temporary emotion. Where is the permanence? Where is the dependability and lastingness?" (p. 306).

The Jesus People would answer these questions in the context of their newly found faith in Jesus. He has become the bridge over troubled waters; he is the dependable friend, the ultimate high; the love of Jesus has staying power; real people are those who are part of God's forever family. And it is this kind of certitude, this hint of durability, which makes the

231

Jesus People a phenomenon of more than passing interest to students of social movements.

* * *

A social movement can be defined as a large-scale, widespread, informal effort by a fairly large number of people to modify or in some way influence the existing social order. Social movements usually arise spontaneously and assume various forms. Some comprise an indefinite, shifting, unstructured membership, with the members rarely if ever meeting face to face. Other movements are more highly organized, tightly knit, intimate groups who collectively promote some program of change. The Jesus Movement is an unorganized social movement in the sense that it is composed of widely scattered subgroups that, although sharing common interests and certain basic concerns, are not united under a single leadership structure or a clearly articulated set of goals and objectives. The various subgroups are, however, internally often highly structured and influenced by very strong leaders. While they sometimes acknowledge a vague linkage with a larger movement that is not well defined — to them at least — these groups are often fiercely independent and ethnocentric. If we keep this kind of grass-roots diversity clearly in focus, it is valuable to consider the Jesus People as constituting a social movement.

Characteristically, social movements attempt to modify the social order by extensive proselyting — by incorporating more people within the movement and imposing certain behavioral demands upon them. According to Turner and Killian in their book, *Collective Behavior,* "To the degree to which collectivities proselytize as a means toward changing society, they become true social movements" (p. 309). In his classic, *The True Believer,* Eric Hoffer also attaches special significance to the activity of proselyting. He sees it as "a search for a final and irrefutable demonstration that our absolute truth is indeed the one and only truth" (p. 102). The true believer strengthens and reinforces his own faith by converting others.

We have looked at considerable evidence of the extraordinary missionary zeal that the Jesus People display. The intensity and conviction of the evangelism of groups like the Children of God matches any of the soul-winning ventures of America's

232

revivalistic past. They are passionately primed to bestow on the listening world The Truth, for as every true believer knows, there is only One Way.

Whatever unity the Jesus Movement may appear to have, it is probably explained by this shared sense of mission — a compelling desire to bring people to Jesus, and, of course, to enlist them in the local band of true believers. Since the diverse units of the movement are really in no way coordinated at a national or even regional level, the success of the Jesus People must be attributed in large measure to the skill of the many local leaders. (We grant the Jesus People's conviction that in an ultimate sense the "success" of the over-all movement cannot be explained apart from God, but for purposes of analysis at the sociological level, it is realistically impossible to overlook the role played by very human leaders.)

Most Jesus People are preoccupied with the concept of authority. Hans Toch points out in *The Social Psychology of Social Movements* that an authority can be anything which serves as a source of beliefs. "It can be a book or a pamphlet, a person or a group of persons. Whatever its nature, it derives its authoritative quality from the fact that people use it to help them decide what they should believe" (p. 135). It goes without saying that for all Jesus People, the Bible is the ultimate source of authority. (With some groups, the King James Version of the Bible is the *only* acceptable form of Scripture, as we have pointed out.) But the interpretation of Scripture and the relating of biblical teaching to everyday life are crucially dependent on available leaders and teachers. In the case of the Christian Foundation, for example, all facets of life and spiritual questions are referred to Tony or Susan Alamo for resolution. This submission to "pastors and elders in the Lord" is typical of the entire movement. The leader serves as an example for his followers, to be sure; but more importantly, he functions as a decision-maker. And, as the Langs point out in their book, *Collective Dynamics,* the leader's "*directives* are accepted as solutions because of the faith, trust, and authority he enjoys" (p. 518).

Marvin Mayers has noted that many leaders in Pentecostal movements tend to be highly authoritarian. Our research involving the Jesus People confirms his analysis.

The Holy Spirit movements tend to be dogmatic and authoritarian. Our society has moved away from authoritarianism and dogmatic pronouncements toward a certain permissiveness. It has moved from assured self-confidence to uncertainty regarding what to do in certain situations and with certain problems. In these areas of concern, the Holy Spirit movement comes with a fresh air of authority. Many of its leaders are "dictators." Even though they claim to rely on the Holy Spirit, much of the development within the group is through their own whim (p. 92).

As we have noted, many of the leaders in the Jesus Movement are much older and more at home in straight society than their followers. They seem to have been thrust into positions of leadership (or, in some cases, to have suddenly found themselves at the helm as a result of unanticipated events) from backgrounds that provided little direct preparation for their roles in the spiritual revolution now occurring among hip youth. This pattern is not unusual in the annals of social movements. As Turner and Killian point out,

The characteristics . . . that distinguish the leaders of movements may not be altogether apparent in the individual before he assumes leadership, but may exist largely in the capacity to respond to his role and his public image in an effective way. . . . To the degree to which the leader is an individual who is precipitated into a leadership position by a unique historical conjuncture and whose effective retention of leadership depends upon supporting the image which his followers create and upon making decisions in keeping with trends in the movement, it may appear that the leader is merely a puppet (p. 478).

Leaders like Carl Parks, Duane Pederson, and Jack Sparks came from the straightest of backgrounds, but they were able to respond appropriately and effectively to new situations that soon developed into leadership roles. The same can be said of the pastors of hip churches, whose backgrounds were largely traditional. The movement has unquestionably thrust some names into the spotlight (with a big assist from the media), and this has led to their self-enhancement, although in all fairness it should be said that, to date, the Jesus Movement has made no one within it rich. Cameron has noted that leaders often come to see social movements as the extension of their own personalities. This, too, can be seen among Jesus People. "Some leaders become so ego-involved in their work that what

234

they are doing becomes less important to them than the fact that they are doing it" (p. 169).

Many of the converts in the Jesus Movement are highly dependent upon others for support and have difficulty making decisions and asserting their will. This essentially passive state is not necessarily a result of their participation in the Jesus Movement, but it expresses the larger social and cultural context from which they come. It indicates, as Rollo May emphasizes, the psychological upheaval of the transitional age in which we live. The "basis of our capacity for will and decision has been irrevocably destroyed" (p. 182). Whether the situation is as bleak as May indicates is debatable. His conclusion that many contemporary young people are adopting a passive role squares with the impressions gained through research, however. As he states, "Not only in the medium of advertising, but in matters of education, health, and drugs, things are done *to* and *for* us by the new inventions; our role, however subtly put, is to submit, accept the blessing, and be thankful" (p. 186).

May pursues his thesis by pointing out that the phrase used in the hip subculture for exploring new levels of consciousness through psychedelic drugs or other "happenings" is to "turn on."

> The phrase "to be turned on" points toward the spontaneity of letting ourselves be stimulated, be grasped, be opened. But it is no accident that it is also the phrase we use when we "turn on" our electricity, our motor cars, our TV's. . . . Does not the essence of the act of taking a drug have within it the same element as the using of the machine in that it too renders us passive? (p. 187).

The experiences of the Baptism of the Holy Spirit and speaking in tongues as described by the Jesus People and other Pentecostalists involve a surrender of the will and an apparent loss of control of the physical powers. Could it be that one reason that the Jesus People so readily seek and accept this charismatic infilling is that their prior experiences and conditioning in the drug world have made them more "open" to things "done *to* and *for*" them? In this respect they may indeed be more receptive and less fearful of such experiences than their elders or more straight peers.

Members of social movements are usually highly committed to "the cause." This commitment may become so fervent that, in effect, the person relinquishes an autonomous individual existence. The following comments by Eric Hoffer are directly applicable to a group like the Children of God:

> An individual existence, even when purposeful, seems to him futile and sinful. To live without an ardent dedication is to be adrift and abandoned. He sees in tolerance a sign of weakness, frivolity, and ignorance. He hungers for the deep assurance which comes with total surrender — with the whole-hearted clinging to a creed and a cause. . . . He is even ready to join in a holy crusade against his former holy cause, but it must be a genuine crusade — uncompromising, intolerant, proclaiming the one and only truth (*The True Believer*, p. 82).

Virtually every act of membership, Toch reminds us, "involves a sacrifice of privacy and autonomy, at least in the sense that the member must accomplish some of his objectives as part of a group, rather than as an individual" (p. 133). Some students of mass movements feel that this sacrifice, in and of itself, appeals to certain kinds of people. "Although there unquestionably are *some* persons in *some* social movements whose main concern is to lose themselves in a collective enterprise, most members view their group commitments — including their sacrifice of individuality — as necessary attributes of their brand of life, rather than as ends in themselves" (p. 133).

Compared to their "unsaved" counterparts in the youth culture, most Jesus Freaks lead sober, disciplined lives. They readily submit to the restrictive rules and regimented existence of the many Christian houses and communes. For many outsiders the word *commune* conjures up images of unbridled freedom and permissiveness. As we have seen, this is not true in the Jesus communes. The converts recognize their need for structure and a new sense of order in their lives. Their reaction is against what Will Herberg calls "the moral laxity and putrid permissiveness that have gone so far in corrupting American middle-class, especially suburban middle-class, society" (*New Guard*, Nov. 1971, p. 15). For Herberg the Jesus People represent a movement seeking "to exorcise the demons and heal the putridities of [the] counter-culture, and to reintegrate it into the continuing American consensus" (p. 16).

The Jesus People come from a society characterized not

only by permissiveness, but one saturated with boredom. The children of technocracy are restless, dissatisfied, and bored. And as Hoffer has stated, "There is perhaps no more reliable indicator of a society's ripeness for a mass movement than the prevalence of unrelieved boredom" (p. 53). In the Jesus groups the old boredom has been replaced by a new and purposeful activism — the frantic round of witnessing excursions, the invigorating devotional exercises of speaking in tongues, group singing, and quoting memorized Scripture passages, and the satisfaction of intimate sharing.

A tightly knit group can easily lead to a tightly closed mind. We have referred again and again in the preceding chapters to the dogmatism of many Jesus groups. Social psychologists have devoted considerable attention to the phenomenon of "closed-mindedness" in their research of social movements. The implications for the Jesus Movement of Hans Toch's observations are obvious:

> The social movement that presents its inductee with authorita-tively reinforced beliefs responsive to his problems unwittingly initiates a chain of events which may culminate in the confined, self-contained world of the veteran member. . . . As the believer becomes more intensely dedicated to the repair and buttressing of his current constructs, these come to assume greater personal significance for him. Moreover, supporting efforts tend to systematize beliefs. As a result, it becomes of greater import that new data conform and extreme pains are soon taken to this end.
>
> At a given point in this process, the believer has walled himself in. Every event he encounters must be processed in terms of his beliefs. Every opportunity must be used to cement his system. At this stage, only authority can produce innova-tion (pp. 155-56).

Every social movement has its peculiar jargon and symbols that act as unifying factors binding the participants together. The Jesus Movement has its One Way sign, its Jesus cheers, and its favorite expressions like "Praise the Lord," "Jesus Loves You," and "Right On!" Just as the Ku Klux Klan has its elaborate regalia and secret rituals, the Jesus Movement has its own cultic uniforms and unusual activities, such as the silent vigils of the Children of God. The garb, the vigils, the beach baptisms, the bumper stickers, the huge Bibles, the music — these all provide some of the "color" of the movement, and they also serve as a means of positive identification with the movement and as a way of engendering a certain pride in belonging.

* * *

In this chapter we have outlined the major characteristics of the Jesus People as a social movement. Although other social movements demonstrate the same traits in different configurations, in the case of the Jesus Movement it must be remembered that its members find divine sanction for practices that ordinarily would be explained at the socio-psychological level only. For example, students of social behavior would seek to explain the authoritarian leader and his submissive following in terms of the human dynamics of the relationship. But the Jesus People themselves would insist that their obedience to the elder is merely a response to the clear-cut teaching of the Bible. And at every other point in a sociological analysis of the movement, its participants would quote the Bible as justification of their actions and attitudes.

Part of the systematic analysis of social movements is an exploration of variables like social class, sex, age, economic status, geographic location, educational level, and racial or ethnic background. Since we conducted no formal surveys of these factors in our research on the Jesus People, we have had to limit ourselves to the impressionistic information that is presented throughout this book. For purposes of summary here, suffice it to say that the Jesus People are a highly diverse group of individuals found throughout the nation, but predominating in California and the Pacific Northwest, coming from virtually all social and economic levels, but including very few Blacks or other minority group members. The fact that few black young people are in the movement is no doubt significant and deserves additional research.

In the final analysis, the Jesus Movement is really an example of what sociologists of religion call "revitalization movements." Such movements involve more than reform or renewal; they can best be understood as revolutionary. Movements of revitalization include a reaching out into the unknown for new patterns, rather than simply a return to the more familiar. As

Barbara Hargrove points out, "Revitalization is distinguished by its potential to recombine those familiar elements into creative new patterns" (p. 277).

A number of observers have compared the Jesus Revolution with the Great Awakening of mid-eighteenth-century America. Herberg, for example, feels that the Jesus People, because of their revivalistic pietism, have "placed themselves squarely in the line of 200 years of American revivalism." He continues: "Note how thoroughly traditional their pietistic religion is, even in their anti-establishment posture" (*New Guard,* Nov. 1971, p. 16).

While to some commentators the Jesus People may appear to be "thoroughly traditional" and represent a return to a familiar, earlier fundamentalism, upon closer analysis one must conclude that the Jesus Movement demonstrates a new kind of response to the continuing search for ultimate meaning and a transcendent God. It retains elements of the familiar, to be sure. But its distinctions are far more striking and significant. It is for that reason that this chapter has set the Jesus Movement against the background of the culture, for the cultural crisis of our times has left its distinct imprint upon the youth who now make up the Jesus Movement. Thus, though this revival has many similarities in common with earlier religious awakenings in America, the distinguishing features of our times cause close analogies between this and the previous revivals to be inadequate because oversimplification is inevitable.

Is the Jesus Movement a Great Awakening, or is it merely a "Gentle Stir"? Perhaps the answer to that question is found in a statement of Dr. David L. McKenna appearing in the Fall 1971 issue of *United Evangelical Action* magazine:

> At the present time, it is an eddy outside the mainstream of American life. If it is a genuinely spiritual awakening, it will also change the direction or the quality of the stream. That is the long-range test of spiritual awakenings that only time can answer (p. 14).

In short, we must wait until more of the evidence is in.

thirteen

CONCLUSION

One Way — or Another?

WHATEVER ONE'S FINAL OPINION OF THE JESUS PEOPLE IS, THEIR existence is a searing indictment of a desiccated, hidebound institutional church. Until the Jesus People phenomenon occurred, the church as a whole had almost completely ignored the young people of the counter-culture, except for occasional denunciation of them as typical examples of the decadence of our times. It was only after there was a stirring of interest in Christianity generated from within the counter-culture that church leaders began to pay some serious attention to these young people as a potentially fruitful mission field. Even now, many church-attending Christians have their minds closed to the possibility that any genuine moving of the Holy Spirit may be occurring among these youthful rebels.

To the counter-culture, the established church appeared as a comfortable middle-class ghetto of mutual admirers who damned the rest of the world, complacently approved the status quo, and felt no need for a radical critique of the materialism and decadence of American society. Their coming to Christ has not changed their opinion of the established church. Many — perhaps most — of them do not attend a local church, even after becoming converted. They recognize the need for fellowship and growth, but seek alternative forms to those provided

240

by church services. And it is difficult to fault them too much for this alienation.

The question remains: what will become of this movement? Is it a fad? Or is it of the Holy Spirit? The answer seems to be some of both. It is impossible for us to deny that the Spirit is moving among American young people today in a new and powerful way. It is equally impossible to deny that many faddish elements remain in the Jesus Movement: the One Way signs (one finger pointed in the air), the Jesus cheers (give me a J, "J," give me an E, "E" —), the hip lingo, the hippie clothing, beads, medallions, long hair, beards, and the like, and the rock music. These things will pass, but the people who are now in the movement will live on. What will happen to them?

The Jesus People have their answer: Christ will return soon, and the movement will continue until the rapture. The whole question is thus irrelevant, because there is not much future left to project into. Talking with some of them, we felt that Christ had better come soon, because they could not long sustain the emotional high and the intensity of life that they were presently enjoying. Indeed, all Christians should look forward eagerly to the day of Christ's return, as the Jesus People in fact do. But what if he does not come back soon? Other true believers in other times thought that his return was imminent, and they were incorrect. What if Christ's return is not in the next ten or twenty years? What if this is not the last generation to live on the face of the earth? What if the Jesus People are not the fulfilment of Joel's prophecy? The only way to judge whether they are is, finally, after the fact. Before the fact, one can do no more than speculate about it.

* * *

All social movements that emphasize spontaneity tend either toward institutionalization or dissipation. Institutionalization may be seen in such diverse groups as Calvary Chapel, the Children of God, and the Alamos' Christian Foundation. Dissipation may be seen in Arthur Blessitt's ministry, probably in Duane Pederson's ministry, and in the many unattached, anti-established-church individual Jesus People. As time goes by, we will see more and more polarization between various

241

elements of the movement, as they move toward institutional-izing or dissipating. This in no way discounts the working of the Holy Spirit. It is simply a fact of human social movements. (And even in dissipation, a social movement may have a profound impact — witness the hippies.)

Three paradigms present themselves to us as likely directions that individuals within the movement will follow. The first is that of David Hoyt. Hoyt came out of the counter-culture and into the general flow of the Jesus Movement. But Hoyt is a man who hungers and thirsts after righteousness, and he was keenly aware of the imperfections of those in the movement. His desire for perfect purity and holiness has led him away from the spontaneity and hang-loose approach to life that characterizes many in the movement and toward the rigidity and legalism most thoroughly seen in the Children of God. He has seen much of his following fade away and has decided that tighter discipline is the only corrective. We have seen too much evidence of the greater sticking power of the Children of God as compared to many other elements in the Jesus Movement to take lightly the possibility that a significant num-ber of Jesus persons will follow his example. Linda Meissner and Russ Griggs and some of their followers already have. The faddish elements of the Jesus People and the excessive emotionalism and inadequate spirituality of many of them may well result in a covy of isolated and bizarre mini-establish-ments with their own rigidities and inflexibilities. For it is virtually certain that the Children of God are not the end of the line. Splits will inevitably occur.

The second paradigm is that of Ted Wise. Here is a man who was in on the very beginnings of the Jesus Movement. According to his own testimony, there is nothing that the more extreme elements of the Jesus People now say and think that he at one time did not say and think. But there has been a tremendous evolution in his life since he has become a Chris-tian. He would be the last one to deny that he has not arrived and that he is still growing, but the changes are monumental and of far-reaching importance. He worships in an established, if not a typical, church — Peninsula Bible Church. He operates a drug center with churchmen on its board. And though his critique of established Christendom is sharp, he has chosen to
242

try working inside the structure to bring about reform and purification. He has been fortunate to find a church and church people willing to accept him as he is. He has left behind notions of exclusivism and bizarre doctrinal eccentricities. If large numbers of Jesus People follow his model, it will augur well for both the Jesus People and the churches. In that case, the current revival among young people will have a far-reaching and long-lasting impact on the direction of contemporary Christianity.

The third paradigm is that of the burnt-out cases. A substantial number of these are already to be found, and doubtless many more have dropped from sight. They are young people who have seen in the Jesus Movement their last chance for finding meaning in life. But for them the Jesus trip has proven futile and unsatisfying as the drug trip and other trips they tried in the past. Jesus has been, for them, no more than a temporary emotional high that passed with time. David Wilkerson, in his *Jesus Person Maturity Manual,* records the comments of a former Jesus Freak:

> I'm back on acid. I used to be tripped out on Jesus. I was really zapped by the Spirit. I was really up on Christ. But it was a bummer. Nobody told me about forsaking the crowd — nothing about temptations, about the devil trying to bring me down. Somebody wasn't honest with me. Be sure you always tell kids to quit tripping with their heads and start learning how to die.

Arthur Blessitt's ten thousand Sunset Strip converts have melted away — only God knows where. Linda Meissner's ministry in Seattle recorded over seven hundred converts, but only sixty to eighty were with her when she joined the Children of God, and only ten or fifteen made the move with her.

Mario Murillo, the twenty-two-year-old Pentecostalist minister in charge of Resurrection City in Berkeley, expressed a keen awareness of the terrifying possibilities in this direction. In his opinion, the end of the Jesus Movement could be ten times worse than its beginning. Unless the new converts are established in the faith and in organized fellowships, he fears that great numbers of them will eventually fall away and will become ruined beyond recall and that their influence will be

243

Prayer in the woods

devastating for any future endeavors at evangelism. In that case, Gary North's gloomy prediction will come true:

> What will happen, as has happened after every other anti-nomian revival in history, is that thousands of people will be permanently scarred religiously. Finney himself gave the name to the phenomenon, "the burned over districts." A community will be brought to a peak of religious enthusiasm, only to be left spiritually dead a year later, a completely unworkable field for future evangelists. An imitation faith will have led these people of the "burned over district" into destruction. It was almost Christianity (*Christian News*, June 4, 1971, p. 10).

Just as there is no anti-Communist like an ex-Communist, so there is no anti-Christian like an ex-Jesus person. Such is the way with true believers (in Eric Hoffer's use of the term) who have lost the faith.

* * *

We see, then, the need for the Jesus People to come together with church Christians. What is needed is a linking of the intense personal experience of the Jesus People with the mature reflection of adults, of the enthusiastic zeal of the new with the stability of the old, of youth with age, of hip with straight. Too much of the anti-established-church bias of the Jesus People is really an anti-adult bias. The Jesus People

244

must relinquish their generation-gap pride in themselves as youth, a pride that modern advertising and American society, with its fear of growing old and dying, has done too much to foster. On the other hand, older persons must convey a sense of genuine acceptance of the young with all of their adolescent idiosyncrasies. This acceptance must not be based on the sentimental ooze that kids will be kids and that they'll eventually grow up and that everything will turn out okay. It must move beyond the indulgent insipidity of a some-of-my-best-friends-are-kids mentality. It must be based on first-hand personal acquaintance with young people. Straights must be as willing to have long-hairs in their homes as they are to have fellow-straights, even if it means the end of the perennial round of clubby coffee klatches following the Sunday evening service. This in no way suggests an uncritical approval of the young. Precisely because they are young and relatively inexperienced, they need guidance from wiser, more mature brothers in the faith. But the long-hairs must be seen as genuine brothers. Straight and hip must be able to discuss things openly as equals before the Lord.

We are not suggesting that older Christians attempt to run out in front of the Jesus People and tame the movement or even derail it. Cooperation is the name of the game, not co-optation. Larry Norman has put it well:

> Is there no burden within the established church for the movement of . . . the Jesus People . . . ? Where are the workers and elders that are needed to help the new flock grow strong and scripturally sound? Will we like children lead each other as the blind lead the blind while they criticize our immaturity and find faults with our doctrine? Neophytes need support and guidance. And while the Jesus People may need the stability and biblical background of the church, the church itself could certainly use the energy and joy of the children.

There are already positive signs that this kind of fusion is beginning. Ted Wise is not the only example of an extreme Jesus Freak who has moderated. Larry Norman himself is an example of the moderation which is to be desired. Another is Ron Salisbury, leader of the hard-rock group, "Ron Salisbury and the J.C. Power Outlet." Calvary Chapel is an example of a whole congregation in which straights and hip mix comfort-

245

ably and congenially. This desired mixing is precisely why some of the healthiest manifestations of the Jesus Movement are those on the fringes of the movement, where established churches welcome the new converts.

But these positive developments are not the only things that are happening to the movement. The radical separation from church Christians seen in the Children of God and the Christian Foundation is in no way being moderated; if anything, it is hardening. And while it is virtually inconceivable that the Christian Foundation can outlast for long the presence of Tony and Susan Alamo, the Children of God and whatever splinter groups they spawn could go on for a long time. Other more moderate groups could harden into cults along the same line. Also, some have already lost the faith; and, given the right (or wrong) circumstances, many more could follow their lead. There is nothing sadder than to meet one of these Jesus People dropouts.

Which way will the Jesus People go? They had better go the way of Ted Wise. Down any other route lies permanent and irreconcilable alienation from the church, which for all its faults is still the main bearer of the tradition of the historic Christian faith that links not only believing men in various parts of the world but believing men in various ages of history, forming the substance of the Body of Christ. Simply because the Holy Spirit may be considered to be present within the movement does not guarantee that only good results can possibly come. In other revivals the work of Christ in the world has been befouled by the tragic errors of the corrupt human instruments, and there is no guarantee that it will not happen again. It may be the case, once again, that the devout believers who have not lost their grasp on doctrine nor severed their ties with culture will be left to pick up the pieces and carry on. The net result of the Jesus Movement could be a situation worse than before the movement ever appeared. We do not think that such will be the case, and we devoutly pray that it will not be so.

INDEX